Sixty People
Who Shaped
the Church

SIXTY PEOPLE WHO SHAPED THE CHURCH

LEARNING FROM SINNERS, SAINTS, ROGUES, AND HEROES

ALTON GANSKY

BakerBooks

a division of Baker Publishing Group
Grand Rapids, Michigan

© 2014 by Alton Gansky

Published by Baker Books
a division of Baker Publishing Group
P.O. Box 6287, Grand Rapids, MI 49516-6287
www.bakerbooks.com

Printed in the United States of America

Library of Congress Cataloging-in-Publication Data is on file at the Library of Congress, Washington, DC.

ISBN 978-0-8010-1539-7

Unless otherwise indicated, Scripture quotations are from the New American Standard Bible®, copyright © 1960, 1962, 1963, 1968, 1971, 1972, 1973, 1975, 1977, 1995 by The Lockman Foundation. Used by permission.

Scripture quotations labeled HCSB are from the Holman Christian Standard Bible, copyright 1999, 2000, 2002, 2003 by Holman Bible Publishers. Used by permission.

Scripture quotations labeled KJV are from the King James Version of the Bible.

The author is represented by MacGregor Literary, Inc.

14 15 16 17 18 19 20   7 6 5 4 3 2 1

To Dr. George Hare and Dr. Gary Coombs,
chancellor and president
of Southern California Seminary, respectively,
for showing me the joys of theology.

CONTENTS

CONTENTS

ACKNOWLEDGMENTS

I wish to thank the scholars of history who have made a difficult subject understandable. These often unheralded researchers have provided a great service to everyone who understands that history is the light that illuminates the future.

I also wish to thank my agent, Dr. Jerry "Chip" MacGregor, for conceiving the concept for this book and for his constant support. Happy is the writer who has a good agent; blessed is the writer who has an agent who is also a friend.

For every book there is a team of editors, people who believe in the dream enough to invest time and talent. The good people at Baker Books are great teammates, and their talent and experience are boundless. Special thanks goes to Jon Wilcox, my editor, for his patience and editorial prodding.

Heartfelt thanks goes to longtime friend and fellow writer Jack Cavanaugh, who made his training as a historian and his massive library available to me, and who also endured scores of questions.

I would be remiss if I did not thank my wife, Becky, for her undying encouragement and patience during the writing of this book (and all the others).

INTRODUCTION

For about a decade, I made my living in architecture, drawing plans ranging from small room additions to mid-rise, steel-frame office buildings. Every building starts with the foundation, then comes the framing, plumbing, electrical, and interior and exterior coverings. Christianity has a lot in common with buildings. The church, as we see it today, did not spring forth fully formed. Doctrines that we take for granted were debated, researched, and fought over before they were accepted. Even then, not all denominations agree. We, as a church, are still in the process of becoming.

In school, I learned there were two ways to teach history. There are those who teach it as a string of events from the days of the ancients to the present. That's fine, but I better enjoyed those classes that taught me about the people behind the events. I found it far more interesting to know about how Ben Franklin lived than about what he achieved as ambassador to France. Most people I know are the same. History intimidates us; historical characters intrigue us.

One of my favorite television programs is *History Detectives* on PBS. In the show, a team with wide-ranging backgrounds track down the history of arcane objects and the people who owned them. The objects can be anything from a flag used at a women's suffrage campaign to a business card used by a gambler with ties to the mob. People, not historical dates, remain the center of the program.

I have undertaken a similar approach in what you're about to read. I wanted to focus on the people who shaped the church. Of course, by doing so, we will see the events that molded the contemporary church, but we will study the flesh-and-blood folk.

Is this important? I think so. Church historian Bruce L. Shelley said, "Many Christians today suffer from historical amnesia."[1] He goes on to note that the time immediately after the apostles up to the present day is a blank in the modern Christian mind. This is a shame. The churches we attend today exist and have been shaped by remarkable and fascinating people. Some sacrificed dearly, like the Anabaptist minister who was executed for baptizing his children, and the misunderstood scientists who not only changed science but changed the way we look at ourselves. And some of these people who shaped the church weren't even Christians.

This book is a collection of sixty people who shaped the church: sinners, saints, rogues, and heroes. I began with a much longer list and agonized over each personality I crossed off. I felt as if I should apologize to each one. Still, a book must have parameters.

In these pages you'll discover the intriguing lives of people you may or may not have heard of, and in each case see how their lives changed the way we live our Christianity in the twenty-first century. This book is not a dusty tome of historical facts but rather a book about ordinary Christians who made extraordinary contributions to the church—*your* church.

So sit back, and let me introduce you to some remarkable people.

Alton Gansky, Litt.D.

1

PETER

Blue-Collar Businessman

(c. 1 BC–64 AD)

> You are the Christ, the Son of the living God.
> Simon Peter (Matt. 16:16)

Visit a dozen churches, each preaching a sermon about the disciple Peter, and you're likely to leave with a dozen different views of the man. Was Peter the big, verbally clumsy man so often depicted? Was he a boastful man needing attention who ultimately folded under pressure from an unrelenting servant girl? Or is he the foundation stone for the church and the first pope? Peter has a bit of an image problem. No one doubts his importance to the early church and no one questions his role as a disciple; many, however, focus on just one or two aspects of the man and so miss the giant of faith who forever changed the church.

Peter was part of Jesus' ministry from the beginning. He was brash and exuberant, so much so that he often made statements he would have to backpedal from moments later. He was a blue-collar businessman, a man who worked long and hard.

A Workingman

Jesus came as a commoner, and he chose commoners to lead his church. Every Christmas season we celebrate the incarnation of Jesus—the coming of God in the flesh. We set up manger scenes to show the humble, harsh environment that served as the backdrop of Jesus' entrance. Preachers remind us that Jesus wasn't born in a palace or a mansion; his parents were people of humble means living their lives under Roman oppression and the religious scrutiny that marked the day. Jesus never departed from these humble roots. He even informed an eager follower that he had no place to rest his head (Luke 9:57–58), meaning he claimed no home of his own. Jesus depended on the support of others. It seems natural that he would pull his disciples from the ranks of those with calloused hands or who were social outcasts such as Matthew the tax collector.

Peter was one of the former. He was a fisherman, part of a family business. His days were spent mending and casting nets along with directing his brothers and probably other workers. The best we can tell, the business was a good one based in Capernaum (Mark 1:21, 29), a town situated on the north shore of the Sea of Galilee. Commercial fishing was difficult work, but it was practical, oftentimes profitable, and the kind of occupation a man could invest his life in, support his family with, and leave to his sons when the time came.

Then Jesus came on the scene with an offer to make Peter and his brother Andrew "fishers of men."

Peter's calling came in stages, the first while he and others were plying their trade (Mark 1:16–20). Jesus must have been known to the people of Capernaum, for Peter, Andrew, James, and John all seemed to respond to Jesus without hesitation. They simply stopped their work and followed Jesus, leaving behind their nets. This is significant; few laborers would leave the tools of their trade behind. Perhaps Peter had employees or other family with whom he left the business. Either way, Peter appeared decisive in his acceptance of Jesus' offer.

Why choose Peter? Why the other fishermen? What did Jesus see in them that he didn't see in others? The answers to these questions aren't fully revealed until three years later. Peter's light would not shine until the darkness was impossibly thick.

Peter has given us an important but often overlooked gift: he was flawed. He spoke out of turn, he challenged Jesus, and he was often slow to understand his Master's teaching. In other words, we can relate to him. Movies and books often offer plastic heroes, those who are free of faults and mistakes. The Bible shows its heroes in a realistic fashion. Peter is one of the most important people in New Testament times, yet is shown with warts and all. We see his courage and cowardice; we see him in moments of great insight despite his sluggish grasp of Jesus' message; we see him hiding, fearful of facing the same people who crucified Jesus, and yet later hear his bold proclamation of faith.

Peter. Cephas. Simon. Simeon. It was not unusual for someone like Peter to be known by several names. His home of Galilee, the northern part of the Holy Land, was a cosmopolitan area and most Jews went by three names based on language: Aramaic, spoken by first-century Jews; Latin, the language of the Roman occupiers; and Greek, still widely used in Peter's day (the New Testament was written in Greek). It was common for people in Peter's day to have a working knowledge of all of these languages.

The man we call Peter was named Simeon bar-Jonah (Matt. 16:17). Simeon is the Hebrew name that becomes Simon in Greek (hence, "Simon Bar-Jonah" in the Matthew account). His Aramaic name was Cephas, which means "rock," hence Petros in Greek, which becomes Peter in English. Four versions of his name, but one person. It is none other than Jesus who first calls Peter "Cephas."

"You are Simon the son of John; you shall be called Cephas" (John 1:42).

Chairman of the Board—Peter as Leader

Jesus had many followers. At the beginning of the church, about 120 of them met for prayer (Acts 1:15). There was a closer circle of disciples referred to as "the Seventy" who went out in pairs with the message of Jesus. The most familiar circle, however, was "the Twelve," the hand-selected disciples who accompanied Jesus throughout his ministry. This is the group we normally think of when we hear the term "the disciples." There was also one smaller ring of men around Jesus. Of the twelve disciples, there was an inner circle comprised of three: Peter, James, and John. These three saw and experienced things the others did not. They saw the resurrection of the synagogue official's daughter (Mark 5:35–43), the Transfiguration (Luke 9:28–45), and were with Jesus in the Garden of Gethsemane (Matt. 26:36–46).

In ancient texts like those of the New Testament, prominent individuals were listed first. In every mention of this inner circle, Peter's name comes first. Every time. This is also true for each list of disciples (Matt. 10:2). When representatives from the temple came to collect the temple tax (all Jews paid a tax to meet the needs of the temple in Jerusalem), they came to Peter. At the greatest event in history, the resurrection, angels told the women who had come to the tomb to take the news to Peter and the disciples.

He was also the spokesman for the group, speaking to Jesus on their behalf. He was, by nature, a leader of men and the others deferred to him. Still, he was far from perfect.

Flubs and All

There's a tendency to portray Peter as a big, slow-thinking lug. This is a mistake. It wasn't ignorance that tripped up Peter but rather enthusiasm. Even his greatest fault, denying Christ on that crucial night, didn't arise from ignorance or even self-preservation but rather confusion. Several events show his unbridled enthusiasm.

Peter Walks on Water

The Gospel of Matthew records a strange event (14:22–36). The disciples were taking a boat across the Sea of Galilee while Jesus stayed ashore for a time of private prayer. As sometimes happens with large inland seas, a storm arose quickly, battering the boat and the disciples in it. Although Peter and some of the others were seasoned sailors, the storm was proving too much for them. Through the darkness they saw the dim figure of Jesus walking on the water, untroubled by the gale. At first they assumed the figure to be a ghost.

What could make things worse? Darkness *and* ghosts. Then Jesus called to them, telling them not to fear.

Peter makes a strange request: "Lord, if it is You, command me to come to You on the water!"

Jesus simply said, "Come."

For a brief time, Peter did what only Jesus has done: walk on water in a storm. Then he took his eyes from Jesus, focusing on the stinging winds and threatening waves. As Peter began to sink into the storm-tossed sea, Jesus reached out and rescued him. Although it wasn't a perfect example of faith, it was nonetheless bold and showed great courage. Peter, if for only a moment, displayed a belief that Jesus could enable him to do the impossible.

Jesus Washes Peter's Feet

During Jesus' most difficult day, those hours before his betrayal, arrest, torture, and execution, he gathered with his disciples in the upper room where he instituted the Lord's Supper. He also did something that stunned the disciples, especially Peter: Jesus washed their feet (see John 13:5–11). To the twenty-first-century mind, this may not seem like much, but washing someone else's feet was considered demeaning in Jesus' day. While it was customary to provide water so guests could clean the dust from their feet, it could not be required that the host do the job for his guests. Not even Jewish slaves could be required to wash the feet of another. Yet Jesus chose to do this humbling task.

It was too much for Peter. Seeing Jesus on his knees, water bowl nearby and towel in hand, unsettled him. "Never shall You wash my feet!" he exclaimed. Jesus' response was pointed: "If I do not wash you, you have no part with Me."

That brought an immediate change. "Lord, then wash not only my feet, but also my hands and my head."

The List Is Longer

Matthew 16:21–23 records Jesus' harshest correction of Peter. Jesus had been once again teaching the disciples about his pending suffering and death in Jerusalem and the resurrection that would

19

follow. Peter, focused only on Jesus' words about his death, proclaimed, "God forbid it, Lord! This shall never happen to You." It was beyond imagination that his Lord would go through such affliction. Peter's words come across as a reprimand and Jesus returns it with intensity. "Get behind Me, Satan! You are a stumbling block to Me; for you are not setting your mind on God's interests, but man's." What makes this interesting is Jesus had, moments before, called Peter and his confession of faith the rock upon which the church would be founded. Again, Peter's unrestrained enthusiasm brought him grief.

Peter would do other things that he would regret, but none more devastating than making a promise he couldn't keep. In the same upper room where Jesus had washed his feet, there unfolded a brief dialogue that haunted Peter the rest of his life.

> Jesus: "You will all fall away because of me this night, for it is written, 'I will strike down the shepherd, and the sheep of the flock shall be scattered.' But after I have been raised, I will go ahead of you to Galilee."
>
> Peter: "Even though all may fall away because of you, I will not."
>
> Jesus: "Truly I say to you that this very night, before a rooster crows, you will deny me three times."
>
> Peter: "Even if I have to die with you, I will not deny you." (see Matt. 26:31–35)

It is difficult to understand the depth of sorrow percolating in Jesus. Before him were the eleven remaining disciples, Judas having already left to become history's most famous traitor, each staring back at him and attempting a courage they surely felt but couldn't maintain.

They left the upper room and walked from the city, across the Kidron valley to the Garden of Gethsemane, where Jesus would begin an inward suffering that few can imagine. Peter, James, and John slept nearby while he agonized.

Then came the hour of arrest. A mob consisting of Roman soldiers, temple guards, religious leaders, and their servants, perhaps numbering in the hundreds, came for Jesus. At the front of the pack was Judas.

Peter, in defense of Jesus, courageously attacked with his sword, cutting off the ear of a servant. We can be certain Peter wasn't aiming for the man's ear. Peter was ready to die to protect Jesus—just as he said.

Before further violence occurred, Jesus stopped Peter, told him to put the sword away, and healed the wounded servant. Jesus left with the mob willingly, leaving Peter and the others to follow at a distance.

After enduring much persecution, Jesus was led to the home of the high priest Caiaphas. Peter and others waited in the courtyard of the house.

A servant girl approached Peter, and said, "You too were with Jesus the Galilean."

Peter responded, "I do not know what you are talking about." He let the lie hang in the air and moved to the gate.

Another servant girl spoke up. "This man was with Jesus of Nazareth."

Peter denied the accusation, adding an oath most likely calling God's judgment on himself if he were lying. "I do not know the man." He had come a long way from confessing Jesus as the Christ, the Son of the Living God. Now he just referred to Jesus as "the man."

Then someone made the third accusation. "Surely you too are one of them; for even the way you talk gives you away." The last comment may have been a reference to Peter's Galilean accent.

Peter swore. Peter cursed. "I do not know the man!"

And then the rooster crowed. Peter fled in tears, a wreck (see Matt. 26:69–75).

Was this cowardice? Maybe, but he had been willing to take on a large crowd single-handedly, so something else must also have been at work. His world was collapsing. He had failed to protect Jesus in the garden; his Lord was bound and enduring abuse. In the maelstrom of emotion and confusion, Peter folded. It is doubtful anyone would have done better.

The memory would never leave him. It dogged his steps and haunted the halls of his mind. It also forged him into the greatest leader the church has seen. And all of this was just the first act.

From Darkness to Light

The New Testament records twelve resurrection appearances of Christ. He appeared to key women such as Mary Magdalene, to the disciples in the upper room, and to as many as five hundred on a hillside in Galilee.

In Paul's letter to the Corinthians, he records "He appeared to Cephas" (1 Cor. 15:5). *Cephas*, Peter's Aramaic name and the one Jesus gave him. We have no details of that meeting, just a reference to its occurrence. It was a private meeting between the denied and the denier. We have no idea what Jesus said, but whatever words passed restored Peter's faith and enlivened his mission.

A month later came Pentecost, the outpouring of the Holy Spirit upon the disciples and other followers of Jesus. Scholars believe this to be the birth of the church. Prior to this event in Jerusalem, the church was nothing more than a huddle of frightened disciples and about 120 followers who feared they would suffer as Jesus had.

Preaching a message that still echoes through time, Peter, once the man backed down by a servant girl, called thousands of eyewitnesses at Pentecost to turn to God through faith in Jesus Christ (Acts 2). Not only was the message of Christ's resurrection made clear, so was Peter's leadership role. Where once was a boastful man who descended into a nervous breakdown, there now stood a champion, fearless and outspoken. It was a finger-wagging sermon, one that not only exalted Jesus but laid the responsibility of a crucified Christ at the feet of religious leaders, political leaders, Romans, and all of those in the crowd who had chanted, "Crucify him!"

No one could back Peter down that day, or any day thereafter. A group numbering around 120 followers had, by day's end, grown to over three thousand.

On the Job Adjustments—Learning to Love the Gentiles

Peter led the church in Jerusalem and its outreach for years after. He had to make several adjustments to his own thinking. Jews of the day had little respect for Gentiles. It would take a vision from

God for Peter to accept the idea that Gentiles could be Christians too (Acts 10:1–33). Peter had become teachable.

After years of leading the church in Jerusalem, Peter was called to leave Jerusalem and begin a mission to the Gentiles. Many think Paul was the first to take the message of Jesus to the Gentiles, but it was Peter who first charted that course. When it became Paul's primary mission, Peter had already been preaching to Gentiles for some time.

Pope?

Peter remained faithful throughout his life. Unlike Paul, he did very little writing. The New Testament has only two of his books, 1 and 2 Peter. In them, we can sense his dedication to and love for the church. Peter was the first pastor/bishop and, along with the other disciples, one of the first missionaries. He was a transitional man who took a fledgling church and guided it into something great.

Jesus made two predictions about Peter. The first, Matthew 16:13–19, is the most debated:

> Now when Jesus came into the district of Caesarea Philippi, He was asking His disciples, "Who do people say that the Son of Man is?" And they said, "Some say John the Baptist; and others, Elijah; but still others, Jeremiah, or one of the prophets." He said to them, "But who do you say that I am?" Simon Peter answered, "You are the Christ, the Son of the living God." And Jesus said to him, "Blessed are you, Simon Barjona, because flesh and blood did not reveal this to you, but My Father who is in heaven. I also say to you that you are Peter, and upon this rock I will build My church; and the gates of Hades will not overpower it. I will give you the keys of the kingdom of heaven; and whatever you bind on earth shall have been bound in heaven, and whatever you loose on earth shall have been loosed in heaven."

The debate centers on the supremacy of Peter over the other disciples. Roman Catholics and others see this as the setting apart of Peter to be the first pope. Protestants believe Jesus is talking about the confession of faith Peter makes but not about Peter himself. Certainly, Jesus bestowed a great deal of authority and responsibility on Peter, more than any other disciple. No matter what view we take on the controversy, we can agree that Peter, from the day he was called by Jesus, was the leader of the disciples, and eventually was leader of the first church. Others would follow and do marvelous things, but there must always be a first—and Peter was it.

The Upside-Down Cross

Peter was also one of the first to suffer under persecution, landing in jail several times for preaching about the resurrected Jesus. Persecution would spread throughout Jerusalem to the rest of the world. The New Testament doesn't reveal how Peter died, but tradition tells us that he was martyred in Rome and, at his request, crucified upside down.[1] There is also a tradition, an account also not found in the New Testament, that Peter's wife was also martyred, something he was forced to witness.[2]

Peter's life continues to inspire the church through the honest portrayal of his courage and his faults. He is the apostle behind the Gospel of Mark, most likely the first Gospel written. With the aid of John Mark, he became the first to spread the story of Jesus in written form. Through that Gospel and his two letters, he continues to guide the church that was born on Pentecost, the same day Peter was transformed into an unstoppable force.

An entire book would not be enough to analyze this great shaper of the church. One chapter scarcely does the job. Still, we see a complicated man who lost then regained his courage, a man who became the catalyst in the rise of Christianity. His contribution to the early church is matched only by one other man . . . Paul.

2

PAUL

The Unstoppable Apostle

(5–67 AD)

For I am the least of the apostles, and not fit to be called an apostle, because I persecuted the church of God.

Paul (1 Cor. 15:9)

"No one did more for the faith, but no one seemed less likely," Bruce L. Shelley says of Paul in his *Church History in Plain Language*.[1]

Only those with the hardest of hearts could have looked on the scene without emotion. Several men carried the lifeless body of a man out of the city of Lystra. It was the last act of a mob stirred to action by the man's enemies. His body showed the torture he had endured.[2]

He was a victim of stoning, a painful, gruesome, horrible death. Like most accused, he had been thrown into a shallow pit as his self-appointed executioners gathered around the rim. They had tossed off their outer garments, picked up stones the size of baseballs, and hurled them at the victim. Stones struck his back, arms, legs, and head. The pummeling continued until all were convinced he was dead.

That wasn't the end of the indignity. The assailants dragged the man's broken and bleeding body from the pit and carried it outside the limits of the city. It was what first-century Jews did with executed criminals. No Jewish burial for this victim. He would be left to rot in the sun and be ravaged by scavengers. Few things repulsed Jews more.

The man left in the dirt along the roadside was one of the most honored, best-known people in history. He, like many Jews of his day, was a man of multiple names: Saul and Paul. The stoning of Paul has a connection to another stoning, one in which he had participated. Approximately sixteen years before, Paul—better known then by his Jewish name, Saul—stood on the rim of a similar pit consenting, and perhaps orchestrating, the stoning death of a young man named Stephen, a deacon in the fledgling Jerusalem church.

Stephen was not an apostle. We have no idea how long he had been a Christian. Perhaps he was one of the outer circle of disciples who followed Jesus. We know very little about the man, but what we do know is impressive. The defense of the gospel that Stephen gave to the early persecutors of the church showed him to be logical and well-versed in Jewish history. So powerful was his message that it enraged many of the listeners—and led to his execution. As he looked up at the conclusion of his defense, Stephen saw a vision of Jesus.

A decade and a half later, Paul would be on the receiving end of a stoning for the same crime as Stephen: preaching the same kind of message in the same manner. Paul's stoning ended differently. The battered apostle, after being surrounded by his fellow Christians, rose—and continued his ministry. Had he been dead? Many scholars think so, and if so, then he experienced a resurrection; if not, then he was still the recipient of a miracle. Few people survived a stoning.

Lystra was a city in what is now Turkey. It was a Gentile region where belief in Roman gods like Zeus and Hermes thrived. Where Peter's ministry was aimed largely at his fellow Jews (although he did preach to the Gentiles), Paul took the gospel message to the non-Jews of the Roman Empire. It's possible Paul's journeys took him as far as Spain. He was an apostle in the truest sense. The Greek meaning of *apostle* is "sent out one" and its modern English equivalent is *ambassador* or *messenger*. Rome could be a hard taskmaster, often treating the inhabitants of conquered lands cruelly and taxing them heavily, but the Empire also provided roads and laws that made travel safer. Paul made good use of these, but the work was not easy and Paul endured much. By his own account (see 2 Cor. 11:23–29) he suffered imprisonments and more beatings than he could count; he faced death repeatedly, received thirty-nine lashes on five occasions, and was beaten with wooden rods three times; he endured shipwreck three times and was left to float a day and night in the ocean; he faced robbers, forded rivers, suffered persecution from his fellow Jewish leaders, and faced the same kind of persecution from Gentiles; he was oftentimes without food, drink, or sleep; and he suffered from exposure. These things he endured for people he didn't know; people he wouldn't even have spoken to a few years before. As a first-century Jew, he culturally would have had little use for Gentiles.

Down and Out In Damascus

How does a man go from being a person who persecutes the church to becoming its greatest promoter?

Sometime soon after the stoning of Stephen, Saul received permission and support from the Jewish religious leaders in Jerusalem to carry out the first wave of persecution of Christians, starting in Damascus, a city about 140 miles, a weeklong journey, from Jerusalem. It is doubtful that Saul met Jesus during his ministry. Most likely, Saul—who was born and reared in Tarsus, south-central Turkey—was not in the region during Jesus' three-year ministry. He did, however, meet Jesus in a most unexpected way. With Jerusalem behind him and Damascus to the north, Saul had led his team of thugs near the city when a blinding light surrounded him so suddenly, and apparently with such force, he was knocked to the ground (see Acts 9:1ff; 26:12–18).

"Saul, Saul, why do you persecute me?"

"Who are you, Lord?"

"I am Jesus, whom you are persecuting."

In today's language we might call this an eye-opening event, but in Paul's case it was an eye-closer. The light, apparently only seen by Paul, left him blind. Persecution is a difficult job for a sightless man.

"Lord, what do you want me to do?" He trembled as he asked the question.

"Arise and go into the city. There you will be told what to do."

Paul, leader of a band of persecutors with legal power granted by the high priests in Jerusalem to find, seize, and bring all Christians back to Jerusalem, now had to be helped to his feet and led by the hand into Damascus. Jesus had taken the fight out of the man.

We can only wonder about Paul's private thoughts during the days that followed. Certainly he weighed Jesus' words. "Why do you persecute me?" Paul was a Pharisee, a conservative religious leader. He was an "up-and-comer," a rising star in the religious world of Israel. His credentials were impeccable. He thought he was doing God a favor by attempting to stamp out the fledgling church. For three days Paul sat in his blindness, refusing food and drink. His depression must have been crushing. No doubt he thought about the Christians he had imprisoned and the accusations he had made. No doubt the image of Stephen's battered corpse came to mind. Paul's world had been turned upside down.

Three days later, a disciple named Ananias arrived at the home where Paul was staying. In a vision, Jesus had ordered him to deliver a message to the infamous persecutor. Ananias was not keen on the idea. What Christian would be? Paul's reputation had preceded him. However Ananias, despite his reservations, went and laid hands on Paul. A moment later Paul's sight was restored. His first sight was the face of a man whom Paul would have arrested had he not encountered Jesus on the road.

Saul of Tarsus became Paul the Apostle. Jesus would appear to him several times, and over the next few years Paul went about the arduous task of earning the trust of the people he had previously sought to persecute.

An Educated Man

Prior to his conversion, Saul used his misguided genius to cause harm; after his conversion, Paul used that same genius to help shape and expand the church throughout the known world. In many ways, Paul was the perfect choice to be an apostle.

Henry Van Dyke, Presbyterian minister, writer, and US ambassador in the early years of the twentieth century, said, "Genius is talent set on fire by courage."[3]

The more we study the life of Paul, the more we come to realize that he is to the Christian faith what Einstein is to physics, Jonas Salk is to medicine, and Charles Dickens is to literature. When the appearance of Jesus knocked Paul to the hard-pack road to Damascus, he was not only stopping a man intent on tormenting Christians, he was calling a man of enormous talent and expansive intellect. Today, Paul would be called a polymath. A polymath is a person of encyclopedic knowledge, an individual of wide-ranging learning. Can a first-century Jewish religious conservative living under Roman rule truly be called a genius? Paul certainly could. Growing up in Tarsus, a "university town," he had access to the finest of Greco-Roman education including its libraries. In the New Testament, evidence of this education is seen in Paul quoting ancient Gentile poets.

But his education was also Jewish. He was, after all, a member of a staunch Jewish family, one associated with the very conservative Pharisees (the group that gave Jesus so much difficulty and ultimately conspired to end his life). He studied under one of the most influential rabbis of the day, Gamaliel. Today, we would say Paul had an Ivy League education.

He knew several languages. As a Jew, he would have learned Hebrew, which was still spoken among Jews, especially during religious ceremonies. Aramaic was the common language of the Jews in Paul's time, and had been the dominant language for over five hundred years. Paul also showed a deep understanding of Koine Greek. Koine Greek is "common" Greek. We can think of it as "street Greek" or "everyday Greek." The New Testament was written in this form of Greek. Scholars can point out whose writing was "simple" and whose was "advanced." Paul's writing showed a deep familiarity with the language. He may have been adept at classical Greek as well. Paul was also familiar with Latin, as he lived and worked in Roman-occupied lands.

Paul was also a biblical scholar. In his days, the Jews studied the Tanakh, what most Christians today call the Old Testament. Paul's ministry focused on Gentiles but his writing was very Jewish, filled with references Jews would immediately recognize.

Paul was, at heart, a teacher. He studied to be a rabbi, someone responsible for teaching God's truth to others and guiding their spiritual behavior. That didn't change when Paul became a Christian. His theology did, however. Paul became a preacher. He is considered one of the finest communicators to have lived, which is ironic since he held his speaking skills in such low regard. He wrote in reference to himself, "His letters are weighty and powerful, but his physical presence is weak, and his public speaking is despicable" (2 Cor. 10:10 HCSB). Despite what shortcomings he saw in his preaching and teaching, history has shown that his words have changed millions of lives.

Writer, speaker, scholar, linguist, preacher, teacher, innovative communicator, church planter, defender of the faith, and more; Paul is worthy of the title *genius*.

If Henry Van Dyke is correct that "Genius is talent set on fire by courage," then could the second president of the United States, John Adams, also be right when he said, "Genius is sorrow's child"?[4] It was true for Paul. Being an intellectual giant and a spiritual dynamo didn't protect him from persecution, hardship, hatred, and martyrdom.

Earlier we listed some of the physical torments Paul endured in his ministry, but there were many emotional afflictions as well. Like Jesus, he was rejected by his people. Paul's method of operation was simple but difficult: visit a city situated at the crossroads of well-traveled roads, preach in the local synagogue. Get beaten and tossed out (most of the time), then take the same message to the Gentiles. Few men would have continued such a practice. Paul observed, "Apart from such external things, there is the daily pressure on me of concern for all the churches. Who is weak without my being weak? Who is led into sin without my intense concern?" (2 Cor. 11:28–29). Paul was a tortured man, physically and emotionally. He carried a heavy burden, yet he continued on until his death by beheading in the middle of the first century.

It's important to note that Paul was a Roman citizen. This was not common among Jews, but somehow his family had earned the right to be called citizens of the Empire and this gave Paul certain protections. It is why Paul was executed by beheading (a quick execution). Roman law protected her citizens from death by crucifixion.

Standing Up for the Outsiders

One of the greatest challenges Paul faced was ingrained racial prejudice. The early church was almost purely Jewish. Jesus was a Jew, as were all the apostles, and Paul was as Jewish as a man could be. Jews and Gentiles did not get along. One of the great sore spots in Jewish life was the constant presence of Romans on their turf. Tensions between Jews and Gentiles were often just a few degrees below boiling. A stone sign at the temple complex warned Gentiles that they faced death if they crossed a certain line. The warning read: "No foreigner is to enter within the balustrade and the embankment that goes around the sanctuary. If anyone is caught in the act, he must know that he has himself to blame for the penalty of death which will follow."[5] They were serious.

When it became clear that Gentiles were embracing Christ and his teaching, it caused confusion. It was difficult for Jews to believe that Gentiles could share in the same love and blessings of Christ that they did. Paul sided with the Gentile believers, and at a council in Jerusalem convinced the others that the inclusion of foreigners had always been a part of God's plan.

Paul would face other such challenges. Judaizers were a group who believed that Gentiles could be part of the church but only after they first became Jews through ritual cleansing and circumcision. Paul would have none of that.

Another group known as the Gnostics troubled the Gentile church, teaching Jesus was someone other than who he said he was and promoting behavior contrary to Christian teaching. Paul spent much of his energies writing letters showing that they were in error and that his teaching (and that of the other apostles) was correct.

False teaching is never a good thing, but it did require Paul to record what Christians believe. He became the church's first theologian, the first to list the basic doctrines that bind orthodox believers together.

Paul made great achievements in mission work, church planting, and the formation of Christian thinking, but his greatest work is work that is still touching lives and changing the world today: his writing. Paul shaped the church through the written word. After all, half of the New Testament was penned by him.

The persecutor became the preeminent preacher of love and acceptance. It is hard to imagine what the church would look like today had Saul of Tarsus not experienced Christ on the road to Damascus. The early church needed an apostle like Paul; the contemporary church has need of the same.

JOSEPHUS

Disinterested Historian

(37–100)

But for the agreement with the facts, I shall not scruple to say, and that boldly, that truth hath been what I have alone aimed at through its entire composition.

Flavius Josephus, *War of the Jews*

It may be surprising to find the name of Josephus listed alongside the great Christians of history. He was not a Christian, and the Jews of his homeland considered him a traitor, the Benedict Arnold of first-century Judaism. If not for the kindness of Vespasian and his son Titus, men who both served as emperor of Rome, Josephus' life might have been much more difficult and perhaps ended early by the business end of a sword.

Whatever his failings and questionable decisions, his accounts of first-century life, told in three volumes, are still read two thousand years later and are held as a reliable historical record of that day and age. As such, Josephus is one of the few "extrabiblical" writers to provide evidence to the historical accuracy of the New Testament. Such was not his intent, yet it is his legacy.

A Good Start

Josephus ben Matthias was born to an unknown mother and a father named Matthias. He was the younger of two sons, and his older brother was named after his father. Josephus could trace his bloodline through generations of priests, including High Priest Jonathan. His family was well-established and aristocratic. He was a descendant of Jewish nobility, born and reared in Jerusalem. Good family, good education, great lineage—it was the kind of situation most men longed for, but the historian lived in stressful, troubled times.

Rome ruled the land, and the tension between Jews and Romans grew daily. Romans found that Jews made poor captives. They did not bend the knee easily, refused to sacrifice their religious principles, and could not bear the idea that a Gentile nation ruled over them.

In his early adult years, Josephus had been selected to travel to Rome and negotiate with the emperor Nero for the release of some Jewish priests. While in the city, he got a firsthand view of Rome's splendor and power. His people had great determination, but Rome held irresistible might.

Returning to his homeland, he became a commander of Jewish fighters in the north region of the country called Galilee. Although Josephus didn't believe that Rome could be defeated, he fought alongside those who thought otherwise. It turned out badly. In 67 AD, after waging a month-and-a-half-long siege, the Romans—led by Vespasian and his son Titus, both whom would later lead Rome and become patrons of Josephus—took Jotapata (Yodfat). Forty thousand Jews lost their lives and twelve hundred women and children were taken captive as a result of the siege, including Josephus' wife and parents.

Josephus and others retreated, and continued to endure setback after setback. Roman soldiers pursued them until he and his men were trapped in a cave. Josephus devised a way to commit group suicide. One man would kill another, and they drew lots to determine the order. Of course, there was a problem with the plan: at the end one man would be left standing. It came down to Josephus and one other—and both men surrendered to Rome.

Once in captivity, he was brought before General Vespasian. Josephus declared he had the gift of prophecy and claimed to have had a vision that revealed Vespasian would become emperor.[1] Two years later, Josephus was proven right. Based on this, Vespasian released Josephus and arranged for his support. It was during those Roman years that Josephus produced the three works we remember him for.

Antiquities of the Jews was written to explain the Jewish way of thinking and to show the long and noble history of his people. It begins with the Genesis account of creation and ends with the great Jewish War that Josephus experienced firsthand. *War of the Jews* chronicles the battles of the Jews from the time of the Maccabees, a Jewish rebel army (167–160 BC), to the fall of Jerusalem in 70 AD. He also wrote a smaller work defending Jewish faith and philosophy called *Against Apion*.

These works give us a deep insight into life during the first century, filling in many gaps about events during and following the life of Jesus. Most consider his works valuable but acknowledge that he may have been kinder to his patrons than they deserved. Taken as a whole, his writings have benefited the church by painting the backdrop of the life and times of first-century Jews and Romans.

Three Passages

Specific to the Christian church, three passages in Josephus' *Antiquities of the Jews* are especially important. The first passage documents the reality of John the Baptist and his execution.

> Now, some of the Jews thought that the destruction of Herod's army came from God, and that very justly, as a punishment of what he did against John, who was called the Baptist; for Herod slew him, who was a good man, and commanded the Jews to exercise virtue, both as to be righteous towards one another, and piety towards God, and so to come to baptism; for that the washing [with water] would be acceptable to him, if they made use of it, not in order to the putting away, [or the remission] of some sins [only] but for the purification of the body; supposing still that the soul was thoroughly purified beforehand by righteousness.[2]

35

The second passage shows Jesus as historical fact, confirming the biblical account of his life, death, and the belief that he rose from the dead:

> Now, there was about this time, Jesus, a wise man, if it be lawful to call him a man, for he was a doer of wonderful works, a teacher of such men as received the truth with pleasure. He drew over to him many of the Jews and many of the Gentiles. He was [the] Christ; and when Pilate, at the suggestion of the principal men amongst us, had condemned him to the cross, those that loved him at the first did not forsake him, for he appeared to them alive again the third day, as the divine prophets had foretold these and ten thousand other wonderful things concerning him; and the tribe of Christians, so named from him, are not extinct at this day.[3]

The third passage mentions James, the half brother of Jesus and second leader of the church at Jerusalem, who was martyred for his faith.

> Festus was now dead, and Albinus was but upon the road, so he assembled the Sanhedrin of the judges, and brought before them the brother of Jesus, who was called Christ, whose name was James, and some others, and when he had formed an accusation against them as breakers of the law, he delivered them to be stoned.[4]

Josephus will always be a controversial character. To some, he is a traitor who chose the Romans over his own people; to others, he was a faithful Jew attempting to end bloodshed. His work opened the door of understanding to the Gentiles of his day. In the process, he shaped the church by showing what life was like for early Christians.

4

POLYCARP

Faith in the Fire

(69–155)

Pray also for kings, and potentates, and princes, and for those that persecute and hate you, and for the enemies of the cross, that your fruit may be manifest to all, and that ye may be perfect in Him.

Polycarp, *The Epistle of Polycarp to the Philippians*

There are approximately eleven thousand stadiums in the world that host events ranging from soccer matches to baseball games to rock concerts.[1] Gathering in stadiums is an ancient practice, with the oldest known stadium being the one in Olympia, Greece. Built nearly eight hundred years before Christ, the stadium held the first Olympic Games. Fifty thousand people could gather in one place to experience the excitement of athletic competition.

In ancient times however, stadiums were used for other, less pleasant events.

The man standing in the stadium on a fateful day in AD 155 was no athlete. His days of physical prowess were long gone. In his mid-eighties, Polycarp seemed a pathetic figure: aged, bent, gray-haired. Few in the first century lived as long as this bishop of Smyrna in western Turkey (now modern Izmir). Crowds filled the seating area of the local stadium and gazed upon this man, who was well-known to them. Polycarp had led the church in Smyrna for decades and he was known as a man of prayer and faithfulness, admirable qualities in another time and place. There, under Roman rule and with waves of persecution growing by the day, being a well-known Christian was unhealthy.

Later artists would depict this ancient church leader as thin, balding, and with narrow, sharp features. Sharpest of all were his wit and courage.

Ancient historian Eusebius gives the details of the story in his church history.[2]

Polycarp had been brought to the stadium for his refusal to sprinkle incense on a fire and say, "Caesar is Lord." People did it all the time. Three short words that had no meaning to most of the day. These words, however, meant a great deal to the aged bishop and he refused to follow the law of the land.

Over the years, a belief had spread among the Romans, a belief that Caesar's spirit was divine—that he was, on some level, a god. To polytheistic Greeks and Romans who were comfortable with the idea of many gods, one more made no difference. To Christians it made a great deal of difference. It was a line drawn in the sand they could not cross.

Eusebius wrote about the torture many early Christians endured in that part of Turkey, describing a type of scourging that stripped the flesh from the body, exposing nerves, blood vessels, and muscle tissue. Those who survived the whipping were forced to lay their raw flesh on broken sea shells. Many were thrown to starved, wild beasts. Polycarp was aware of what awaited those who defied the orders of Rome—what awaited him.

A Threshold Leader

Polycarp was a threshold man, one of the last church leaders who could say he had studied at the feet of the apostles, especially John, the only apostle to live into old age. His personal relationship with those who walked with Christ gave him a special standing in the

Christian community, and rightly so. It is possible that Revelation 2:8–11 was written to the Church of Smyrna while Polycarp was bishop. The passage mentions coming persecutions and ends with, "Be faithful until death, and I will give you the crown of life."

Word had reached Polycarp and his supporters that he was a wanted man. His followers convinced him, against his personal inclination, to hide. They moved him from his home to a farm outside the city. Perhaps they felt his death would discourage Christians throughout the region. Smyrna was one of the major cities of Christendom, and what happened there echoed throughout the community of believers.

Those searching for him arrived at his home and, learning he was gone, tortured one of the servants until they learned of the old man's whereabouts. Word of the event reached Polycarp, and his friends tried again to persuade him to flee to another place. He refused. He had spent the last few days praying, and one night had a vision of his pillow bursting into flame. This he took as a sign of his impending death. "The will of God be done," was his final word on the matter.

Those who searched for him came to the farm and were greeted by Polycarp, who called for a meal to be prepared. He entertained his captors as guests and asked only for an hour of prayer before leaving.

Back in the city, Herod son of Nicetes, the captain of the police, tried to convince Polycarp to give in this once. "What harm is there in saying 'Lord Caesar,' sacrificing, and saving your life?"

"I am not going to do what you advise me." Polycarp refused to be intimidated.

In the arena, the pastor stood in front of the crowds and before the proconsul Asiarch Philip. According to eyewitnesses, as he entered he heard a voice from heaven, saying, "Be strong, Polycarp, and play the man."

In the stands a few Christians stood in support, but in the arena Polycarp was alone.

"Are you Polycarp?" the proconsul asked.

"I am."

"Consider your age. Swear by the spirit of Caesar, repent, and say, 'Away with the atheists.'"

In one of history's great ironies, Romans considered Christians and Jews atheists because they refused to acknowledge Caesar as a god. It didn't matter that Christians believed in God, it only mattered that they *didn't* believe in Caesar.

Polycarp complied, but not as expected. He motioned to those who sat in judgment of him, to the crowd, and said, "Away with the atheists."

The proconsul gave him another chance. "Swear and I will release you; revile Christ."

"Fourscore and six years have I been serving him, and he has done me no wrong. How can I blaspheme my king who saved me?"

The government leader wouldn't let up and again ordered Polycarp to renounce Christ and swear by Caesar.

Polycarp wouldn't consider the demand. "Let me make this plain. I am a Christian. If you desire to learn Christian doctrine, then set a date to listen."

The official said, "I will throw you to wild beasts." This was not an idle threat. Christians had been mauled to death as punishment and as entertainment for the crowds.

"Call them. Turning from the better to embrace the worse is a change we cannot make; but it is noble to turn from wickedness to righteousness."

The proconsul was as determined to turn Polycarp as the pastor was to turn him. "If you disregard the wild beasts, then I will cause you to be consumed by fire. Repent."

The vision Polycarp had received before his arrest must have come to mind. He knew this was coming.

"You threaten me with a fire that burns for an hour and then is quenched. You know not the fire of eternal punishment that is reserved for the ungodly." If Polycarp felt fear, he didn't show it. "Why do you delay? Do what you will."

Finally, the proconsul had the elderly pastor's crime heralded to the people in the stands. "Polycarp has confessed that he is a Christian."

The crowd turned again, calling for the release of the wild animals. But Philip the proconsul chose to have Polycarp burned alive instead.

Wood was gathered; a pyre was built. The eighty-six-year-old man watched hate-filled enemies set up his place of execution. He waited for the work to be finished, then removed his clothing. Some

40

wanted to nail him to the stake in the middle of the pile so the old man couldn't flee. Polycarp promised them that such precautions were unnecessary. "Leave me as I am. He who has given me strength to endure the fire will also grant me the ability to remain in the fire."

They bound his hands behind his back while Polycarp prayed, thanking God for the honor to die for Christ.

They lit the fire and the flames rose—but they didn't touch his skin. Instead sheets of flame billowed around him like sails on the mast of a ship. Polycarp seemed to change. Instead of his skin becoming charred, he looked like metal in a refinery. It's difficult to tell from Eusebius' account just what that means, but the witness took it to be something miraculous.

Polycarp would die at last, not by fire but by a sword shoved through the flame and into the bishop's body.

A Short Letter

All that remains of Polycarp and his ministry is his short letter to the Philippians and the eyewitness testimony of his courage and death. The *Epistle of Polycarp to the Philippians* is a short book filled with reminders of what the apostles who came before him had said. Scholars consider it a "simple" work, not inspired or filled with new revelation. It is more a reminder note, calling to mind things Christians of the day already knew.

Nonetheless, the book is important. First, it shows the mind and heart of early church leaders. It also reveals how widely read the books of the New Testament were, and at such an early date. The full New Testament wouldn't be recognized (canonized) for another two centuries. Polycarp quotes sixty or so passages, over thirty of which are from Paul, showing his familiarity with him and the other apostles.

Polycarp shaped the church by his reliance on the writings of the apostles, by his insistence on doctrinal purity, and most of all by the powerful testimony of his martyrdom. When offered his freedom he turned it down, choosing to die a horrible death rather than say or do anything that might detract from Christ or stain the faith he spent his long life defending. He exemplifies Christian courage under fire. His death still instills courage in believers two thousand years later.

5

JUSTIN MARTYR

Christian Thinker

(100–165)

No right-thinking person falls away from piety to impiety.

Justin Martyr, *The Martyrdom of the Holy Martyrs*

When I was young, still shy of my teenage years, a head cold kept me home from school. Since both of my parents worked, I was left to fend for myself. I was passing the time by watching television when someone knocked on the door. It was a different time then, and I held no fears about opening the front door. On the other side of the screen door stood an elderly man. I had seen him many times. He was a fixture in the neighborhood, although I can't say he lived nearby.

The man was bent, his hair the white of snow, and the topography of his face showed deep creases and lines, the kind earned over decades of a hard life. He had other wrinkles that indicated he was a man who smiled a lot.

I looked past him and saw the handmade, plywood cart he pushed on his journeys around the neighborhood. The cart was simple, painted brown and rolled on small bicycle tires, the kind found on a child's bike. Every week or two, the man would walk the streets around my home, knocking on doors and collecting cast-off clothing for the poor. His visits were always short. "Collecting clothing for the poor," he would say. If we had nothing to give him, he would only say, "Thank you. God bless," then walk away.

He was the first person I recognized as a Christian. In some ways, he unnerved me. At the time, I couldn't say why. He just seemed different. Maybe it was his Italian accent. Maybe it was his extreme age. Maybe it was how he went through life without pretense and pride. Maybe it was because I sensed he knew something I didn't.

"Collecting for the poor . . ." He studied me for a moment. I could see questions in his eyes. "How come you not in school?" I can still hear his broken English.

"I'm sick."

"Sick?" He seemed stricken.

"It's just a cold."

"I will pray for you." With no hesitation, he pulled the screen door open, and before I knew what was happening, he placed a hand on my head. For the next few moments, I listened to his thickly accented prayer for my healing.

He smiled, then walked away.

It was my first encounter with a practicing Christian. I don't know what church he went to. I have no idea what happened to him. It took a few months for me to realize it when I no longer saw him make his rounds.

Because of a head cold, I had my first experience with a lifestyle Christian. I wouldn't become a believer until years later, but that event was the first real seed planted in my already skeptical mind.

Shortly after the turn of the first century, another encounter with an elderly Christian changed a man. That man was Flavius Justinus, later called Justin Martyr.

Lover of Philosophy

Justin could be described as a man searching for God in all the wrong places. Born on the cusp of the second century, Justin lived with his Greek parents in Palestine and developed a love for philosophy. He longed to wear the philosopher's cloak, a sign of respect and education. He tried several of the philosophical schools. First he attached himself to an unnamed Stoic teacher, but the man was found lacking in the knowledge Justin longed for; he then tried an Aristotelian teacher but was put off by the teacher's fixation on his fee. Then he tried Pythagoreanism—a philosophy based on mystical mathematics developed in the fifth century BC—but the instructor sent him away, telling him to study music and math first. Finally, Justin found his philosophical home in the writings of Plato. Still, it wasn't enough.

One day, while walking by the ocean and meditating, he encountered an elderly Christian. They talked. The elderly man suggested Justin study the ancient Hebrew prophets since they predated the philosophers. The suggestion changed Justin and the church. "But straightway a flame was kindled in my soul; and a love of the prophets, and of those men who are friends of Christ, possessed me; and whilst revolving his works in my mind, I found this philosophy alone to be safe and profitable. Thus, and for this reason, I am a philosopher."[1]

The courage of the Christians in the face of persecution added fuel to the fire that burned within this philosopher. These were life-changing events for a man reared in a pagan home. He would spend the rest of his life defending the faith and those who shared it. He did so by the spoken and written word.

Writer

Justin did not become a clergyman. He remained a philosopher, but one with a worldview based on biblical revelation. He may have done more for the church than any clergyman of his day. This was no easy task. Justin lived in a day when profession of faith in Christ was a criminal offense. Christians were executed in the most horrible ways simply because of their faith. Roman law defined Christianity as a secret society, and therefore illegal and punishable.

Seeing how fellow believers were being treated, Justin wrote his *First Apology* to Emperor Antonius Pius and his adopted sons. (A *Second Apology* was also written and is probably a supplement to the first.) His goal was to do away with the myths surrounding Christians and to demonstrate that Christians were not atheists (because they refused to worship the emperor), idolaters, or a threat to Rome. He argued that Christians were taught to respect their leaders.

The word *apology* needs explanation. In contemporary English, the word means to admit regret for an action, to say we're sorry for some offense. Justin's work has nothing to do with that kind of apology. Instead, the word draws its definition from the ancient Greek and means to make a reasoned argument. It's what lawyers did then and do now: present a case for or against something. Justin was arguing for humane treatment of Christians and explaining what Christians really did. It is here we learn how early Christians worshiped in church. It sounds very similar to what is done today:

And on the day called Sunday, all who live in cities or in the country gather together to one place, and the memoirs of the apostles or the writings of the prophets are read, as long as time permits; then, when the reader has ceased, the president verbally instructs, and exhorts to the imitation of these good things. Then we all rise together and pray, and, as we before said, when our prayer is ended, bread and wine and water are brought, and the president in like manner offers prayers and thanksgivings, according to his ability, and the people assent, saying Amen; and there is a distribution to each, and a participation of that over which thanks have been given, and to those who are absent a portion is sent by the deacons. And they who are well-to-do, and willing, give what each thinks fit; and what is collected is deposited with the president, who succors the orphans and widows and those who, through sickness or any other cause, are in want, and those who are in bonds and the strangers sojourning among us, and in a word takes care of all who are in need. But Sunday is the day on which we all hold our common assembly, because it is the first day on which God, having wrought a change in the darkness and matter, made the world; and Jesus Christ our Savior on the same day rose from the dead.[2]

The passage includes an interesting phrase: "memoirs of the apostles." Today we call those writings the four Gospels found at the beginning of the New Testament. *Memoir* is a good word, because the Gospels are indeed the recollections of those who traveled with Jesus. This shows that the Gospels were read in the churches long before the New Testament was compiled into its present form. It also shows that Christians met weekly and were concerned with biblical interpretation, prayer, and caring for one another.

Justin explains other aspects of the early church, something that was a mystery to its persecutors. He is to be admired for his zeal and courageous effort to defend the faith and those who held it.

He also wrote *Dialogue with Trypho the Jew*, where he contrasts Christianity with traditional Jewish thinking. Some of his other works, *Against Marcion* and *Against All Heresies*, are lost to time.

Ideas Worth Dying For

Justin was a millennialist, meaning he believed in a literal one-thousand-year reign of Christ on earth (a belief popular with today's evangelicals) and he also ascribed to what would later be dubbed dispensationalism, the belief that God's work in history changes over time, granting new "light" and calling for greater responsibility based on the newer revelation. For example, the knowledge and requirement of obedience for Noah was different than that for Abraham, and different still for Moses. Dispensationalism and millennialism are still debated today. Still, they show Justin's depth of study and foresight into issues the church would later face.

Justin Martyr earned the title that became his last name. He, along with six of his fellow Christians, were executed for their faith, dying by beheading. When told to disavow Christ and sacrifice to the Roman gods, Justin replied, "No one who is rightly minded turns from true belief to the false."

His last words were, "We desire nothing more than to suffer for our Lord Jesus Christ; for this gives the salvation and joyfulness before his dreadful judgment seat, at which all the world must appear."[3]

To Justin, Christianity was the most complete form of philosophy and the highest knowledge anyone could attain. His writing gives us glimpses into the earliest days of the church and the dangers Christians faced. He laid bare some of the doctrinal issues that would be discussed in the centuries ahead. He fought to defend the faith and the believers who pinned their hope to it, and he did so at the cost of his own life.

It is impossible not to admire his fearless devotion to the cause of truth and in the defense of the Christians against heathen criticisms and persecutions. He demanded justice for his brothers who were condemned, without trial, for simply being Christians.

CLEMENT OF ALEXANDRIA

The First Christian Scholar

(150–215)

Philosophers, then, are children, unless they have been made men by Christ.

Clement of Alexandria, *Stromata*

We live in an "us versus them" world. Everywhere we look, someone is drawing a line in the sand insisting that everyone on his side is correct while everyone else is wrong. This is true in many areas of life. Doctors argue over best treatment protocols, scientists debate origins, churches adopt labels to distinguish themselves from others, and politicians . . . well, politicians have raised divisiveness to a high art.

This, of course, is part of human nature. We tend to define ourselves as much by what we don't believe as by what we do. In 1913, poet Edwin Markham wrote the short poem "Outwitted!":

> He drew a circle that shut me out —
> Heretic, rebel, a thing to flout.
> But Love and I had the wit to win:
> We drew a circle that took him in![1]

Titus Flavius Clement would have agreed with that worldview. Better known today as Clement of Alexandria, he is remembered as being "the first Christian scholar."[2] He lived in one of the greatest cities of his day: Alexandria, a city known for its emphasis on learning and philosophy, a city that would become the center of the Eastern Orthodox Church. The metropolis may have had over one million inhabitants in Clement's day, and this Egyptian city, named after Alexander the Great, had the largest library of the ancient world. It rivaled educational centers such as Athens, Antioch, and Rome.

Clement took advantage of his educational opportunities. Traveling widely, and learning from the best teachers of the day in both ancient and contemporary philosophy, he eventually came to see the teachings of Christ and the apostles as the pinnacle of knowledge. Arriving in Alexandria, he became a student of Pantaenus, who had founded a school in the city. In Clement's day, it was not unusual for learned men to set up private schools and take in students. Clement stayed with the school as a teacher, and later became head of the institution. Like Pantaenus, whom Clement considered an expert in biblical interpretation, Clement taught the superiority of a Christian worldview.

Drawing a Wide Circle

He could have drawn a circle to embrace those who believed as he did and exclude those who didn't, but Clement took a different approach. Instead, he taught believers and nonbelievers alike. Jews, pagans, and Christians attended the school and learned side by side. The way he did this tells us much about the man.

Clement taught a "new philosophy," emphasizing the importance of knowing—of *gnosis*. The Gnostics were a heretical cult that troubled the church beginning in the days of the apostles. Many of the books in the New Testament, like Colossians, were written to combat their false teaching. Gnostics believed that they and they alone held special knowledge. They undermined the teaching of the apostles by changing the nature of Jesus, whom they believed was not a man but only *appeared* as such (some even believed that the Christ-spirit cloaked the human Jesus). And they departed from the apostles' message of the cross and the resurrection, believing salvation came through their special brand of knowledge. They also held to a dualistic world: light versus dark, physical versus spiritual. In their philosophy the two couldn't mix, therefore only the man Jesus died on the cross, the Christ-spirit having left prior to the crucifixion. In many ways, they were the New Age movement of the first two centuries.

Clement understood the appeal of the Gnostic philosophy and its dangers. Gnostics believed they held greater knowledge than the apostles and this undermined church teaching as handed down in the Bible. To them, church doctrine was incomplete.

Clement believed in the power of knowledge and its ability to point the way to Christ. Although he used many of the terms the Gnostics used, he was very different from them and held a biblical worldview. His way of spreading the gospel was to show how the philosophy of the Greeks and others were predecessors to the knowledge of Christ. As the Law of Moses was meant to prepare the Hebrews for a coming savior, so Greek philosophy was intended to prepare people for the gospel. Since Christ had come, it was time to move to a deeper, more accurate understanding of God's ways. Clement taught the superiority of Christian doctrine and tried to guide his students to an intellectual and heartfelt relationship with God. He wanted to show, in a scholarly way, that Christian faith was reasonable, the obvious choice for the thinking person. To do this, he had to challenge the Gnostic belief in two Gods—one good, one evil.

The pagan mind was comfortable with multiple gods and contradictory philosophies. Clement showed a better way.

A Christian Philosophy

The apostle Paul taught the members of the Galatian church, "Therefore the Law has become our tutor to lead us to Christ, so that we may be justified by faith. But now that faith has come, we are no longer under a tutor. For you are all sons of God through faith in Christ Jesus" (Gal. 3:24–26).

Clement seems to have adopted this approach, customizing it for the Gentile mind. To him the ancient philosophers were needed to prepare the mind for the higher philosophy of Christ. "The way of truth is one, but into it as into a perennial river, streams flow from all sides."[3] He believed that "understanding is sent by God."[4] That is not to say that he put human philosophy on the same level as divine revelation. Human reasoning could be faulty, but "the teaching which is according to the Savior is complete in itself and without defect being 'the power and wisdom of God.'"[5]

For many years, Dr. Joel Gregory taught preaching at Southwestern Seminary in Fort Worth. Many of his sermons are unforgettable, and he passed his knowledge on to hundreds of young preachers learning how to convey spiritual truth through the spoken word. In a sermon delivered in central California, he described the confusion many of his students encountered. They asked, "Dr. Gregory, when I preach should I begin with the human need and move to Scripture, or start with Scripture and move to the human need?"

He replied, "It doesn't matter where you start as long as you get to the truth in the Bible." Clement held the same idea. It didn't matter if his students began with Greek philosophy or the writings of Moses, as long as they ultimately came to the truth of Christ.

Clement wrote three books. In *Exhortations to the Greeks* he portrayed faith as reasonable for the thinking person, worthy of study and superior to everything that had come before.

In *The Instructor* he taught the need for proper Christian behavior. The Gnostics of his day cared nothing for individual behavior, but Clement believed it was one of the hallmarks of the Christian life. He included sections on eating, laughter, clothes, sleep, and even shoes. In each case, he tried to move the person of faith closer to God.

He left his last work unfinished. *Miscellanies* (also called *Stromata*) is a collection of topics for the "Christian Gnostic" (the educated Christian, not the heretical sect). The work is meant to bring people of faith to a greater knowledge and to living in a Christlike manner. Even incomplete, it is considered his major work.

Clement's goal was to reach the well-educated people of his time. Lovers of knowledge deserved a knowledgeable presentation of Christ and Christian living. He also cautioned the young church to choose its icons wisely, preferring images that represented some aspect of the faith. He wrote, "Let our emblem be a dove, or a fish, or a ship running before the wind, or a musician's lyre, or a ship's anchor. And if there be a fisherman, he will remind us of an apostle, and little children being drawn up out of the water."[6]

Clement had to abandon his school and flee Alexandria to escape the persecution ordered by Roman Emperor Septimius Severus in 202 AD. We have no information of his activities from that year on. He died around 215, and the cause of his death is unknown.

Clement had a strong influence on many church leaders, including many of his pupils. Origen was one of his most famous students. His lasting legacy will be his lifelong pursuit to portray Christian faith as worthy of serious intellectual study, and his willingness to draw a circle that included those outside the church in order to present the gospel in a way they could understand.

Clement of Alexandria helped give birth to the intellectual acceptance of faith—evidence that one does not have to sacrifice learning and deep thinking to embrace faith. In fact, Clement demonstrated the two work well together.

7

ORIGEN

Jesus Freak

(185–254)

The physical voice we use in prayer need not be great nor startling;
even should we not lift up any great cry or shout, God will yet hear us.

Origen, *Ante-Nicene Fathers*

Those who grew up in the late 1960s and 1970s are familiar with the term "Jesus Freak." Some used the phrase in a pejorative way, others wore it as a title of honor. The Jesus Freak movement was a subculture of Christianity, emphasizing love and pacifism. Members of this movement saw Jesus as a radical. Many were hippies with a deep faith. Several influential leaders came out of the movement. Those in the Jesus Freak movement were more interested in living a simple faith than in conforming to social norms. Origen, a scholar of the late second and early third centuries, would have likely found much in common with the Jesus Freaks of the '60s and '70s.

Origen—Origen Adamantius ("man of steel/unbreakable")—was born into a Christian home in Alexandria about AD 185. Origen was something of a child prodigy. Educated by his father, Leonidas, he showed a keen mind early on. Times were difficult for Christians. Persecution put many in prison, work camps, or the grave. Around

201, Origen's father was imprisoned under the persecutions of Emperor Septimius Severus. Origen encouraged his father not to deny the faith, not even for the sake of his family. He planned to join his father in prison by turning himself in and being martyred for his faith, but Origen's mother prevented him from leaving the house by hiding all of his clothing.

Leonidas was beheaded for his faith and his property was seized, leaving Origen to care for his mother and six siblings. He did so by teaching literature and copying manuscripts. The persecution that brought his family such grief ironically opened a door for him. Many teachers at the catechetical school (a place where Christians learned about the faith) in Alexandria had fled, leaving the school in dire need of teachers. Origen became head of the school—at the age of eighteen.

Origen cared only about serving Christ and defending the faith. His single-minded dedication caused him to do away with every creature comfort. He slept very little, instead choosing to spend that time in prayer and study. When he did sleep, he did so on a bare floor. He wore no shoes and possessed only a single coat. He fasted twice a week, drank no wine, and ate no meat. At one point, he sold his library to have enough money to buy what little food he needed.

Many, at that time, believed that Christianity was a belief only the uneducated could embrace. Some of that thinking persists today. Whether now or then, that assertion is untrue. Origen was anything but ignorant. He was a man of gigantic intellect and he demonstrated it in his writing.

A wealthy patron paid to make seven secretaries available to Origen, and he kept them all busy. When faced with the overwhelming volume of Origen's work, fourth-century historian and theologian Jerome is reputed to have asked, "Has anyone read everything that Origen wrote?" Most of what Origen wrote is lost to us today, but plenty remains that shows his startling wisdom and theological expertise. Of the hundreds of his works, three stand out as remarkable.

A Writing Machine

Perhaps most amazing is his *Hexapla*, a parallel Bible of the Old Testament in six columns, one in Hebrew and five in different Greek translations. There are about six hundred thousand words in the Old Testament, spread over thirty-nine books. Doing the math, this means that Origen compiled 4.2 million words. Add to that his meticulous notes comparing the various manuscripts, and the number soars. Modern writers typically use a manuscript format that has about three hundred words per page. If Origen used the same format (which he didn't), it would take over fourteen thousand pages to complete his work—and all had to be handwritten. Understandably, not many copies were made.

De principiis (*On First Principles*) is the first systematic theology in Christianity. In almost every pastor's library is one or more systematic theology, a set of books that organizes basic biblical doctrines by subject. Such books are part of every minister's training. Origen produced the first such work.

He also wrote a defense of Christianity. *Contra Celsum* (*Against Celsus*) is a top-notch defense of Christians and their lifestyle. It was often claimed that Christians were unpatriotic, refusing to serve in the military.

"We who by our prayers," he wrote, "destroy all demons which stir up wars, violate oaths, and disturb the peace are more help to the emperors than those who seem to be doing the fighting."[1]

Some Odd Doctrine

Origen was not without controversy. He favored an allegorical interpretation of the Scriptures, meaning he was prone to look for deeper, hidden meaning in Bible passages and interpreting certain events, comments, and people more than the literal reading allowed. This is not to say, however, that Origen couldn't take Bible passages literally. He was very strict in his interpretation of Matthew 19:12: "For there are eunuchs who were born that way from their mother's womb; and there are eunuchs who were made eunuchs by men; and there are also eunuchs who made themselves eunuchs for the sake of the kingdom of heaven. He who is able to accept this, let him accept it." Origen castrated himself, something church leaders of the day considered an inappropriate misreading of the verse.

Some of his doctrine veered from what was commonly accepted, causing a stir. He believed in the preexistence of the soul, and described the Trinity as a hierarchy rather than having God the Father, God the Son, and God the Holy Spirit as equals. He also suggested that even Satan and demons could be saved. His bishop excommunicated him, although other bishops showed support and gave him a new place to teach. Three centuries later (in 553), the Council of Constantinople formally declared him a heretic. Today, modern theologians are less severe in their treatment, even while acknowledging his doctrinal shortcomings.

Origen would suffer a similar fate as his father. As a teenager he had greatly wanted to die the martyr's death, and that desire eventually came to fruition. In 250, Emperor Decius imprisoned Origen and had him repeatedly tortured, keeping him alive in hopes the influential scholar would recant his faith. He didn't. Decius died and the scholar was set free. However, the torture had been so grueling that Origen's body was broken beyond repair and he spent his last days suffering, and died shortly after being released.

Origen shaped the church through his early scholarship. His writings defended the faith and gave the church material that would serve it for centuries. He was the first to offer a systematic theology and a deep analysis of biblical texts. His allegorical approach influenced the church well into the Middle Ages.

It is easy to show where Origen departed from what is now established orthodox doctrine, but still, he deserves at least an equal amount of praise as he does criticism—if not more—for furthering the church's insight into Scripture and showing the important role scholarship plays in our understanding of faith. He influenced countless scholars—including those who disagreed with him on some points—to excellence in their work.

8

DIOCLETIAN

Mass Murderer

(244–311)

The pagans themselves were sickened by so much bloodshed.

Philip Schaff, *History of the Christian Church*

For decades, the television show *Sesame Street* has used many creative approaches to entertaining and educating children. One segment that has endured teaches children to recognize what makes some items the same and others different. The segment is introduced with the song, "One of These Things Is Not Like the Others." Four items are presented, and children are encouraged to find the "one that doesn't belong." For example, there might be four bowls, three of which are the same size. The larger one doesn't fit.

Seeing the name Diocletian in a book dedicated to those who shaped the church seems out of place. After all, this Roman emperor is known for instigating the greatest persecution the church has known. So why include him in this work? Because just as people are shaped by the good and bad events in their lives, so it is with the church.

Diocletian was an able man in many respects, and successful in several areas of his life. His was a "rags to riches" story. He did much good for the Roman Empire, but the one thing he will always be remembered for was starting a campaign of horrific persecution against Christians. On the one hand there is a long list of achievements; on the other hand is blood.

A Mixed Bag

Diocletian was born in obscurity as Gaius Aurelius Valerius Diocletianus. He joined the military and rose rapidly through the ranks. His skill led to the role of governor of Moesia. This was during a time of rival emperors. Often armies selected their generals to be emperor in their region. Diocletian, however, focused on his military duties instead of glory.

The praetorian prefect Carus was proclaimed emperor in 282, and Diocletian quickly earned his favor. Two years later, during a military campaign against the Persians, Carus was, by some accounts, killed by a bolt of lightning. His two young sons took power, Numerian in the east and Carinus in the west. Both were killed. Diocletian succeeded them as emperor of the troubled Roman Empire in 284—all this before the age of forty. Recognizing the impossibility of one man effectively governing such a large empire, Diocletian created a tetrarchy, sharing leadership with three others. He and Maximan were *augusti*; Galerius and Constantius were titled *caesars*. All answered to Diocletian.

When Diocletian came to power, Rome was near anarchy. He was able to curtail the decline for a time, restore order, regain frontier land lost to others, and create an efficient form of government. However, despite these positive contributions, Diocletian is best known for a series of decrees he issued against Christians. These decrees led to the death of thousands of believers, often in horrible fashion, and succeeded in driving the church underground and into the catacombs.

From the time Diocletian took the emperor's chair until his first edict against the Christians on February 23, 303, he paid little attention to the still emergent religion. However, Christianity had grown rapidly since its inception. Some have estimated that the number of people calling themselves Christians was seventy-five million, or about 15 percent of the empire's population. The widespread growth of Christianity led to concerns within Roman leadership.

Christians were everywhere, including Diocletian's home and court. His wife, Prisca, and daughter Valeria were Christians. Many of his advisors and members of his administration were also believers. Church buildings were springing up across the empire. There was an increasing threat that Christians could form an empire within an empire. This, coupled with the knowledge that Rome was failing, compelled Diocletian to encourage the Roman Empire to rededicate itself to the adherence of its original pagan ways. The greatest danger to the Roman gods were the Christians who pledged allegiance to Jesus alone and would rather die than acknowledge any other god.

Around this time, Diocletian's palace endured two fires, one in early February 303 and another sixteen days later. As was often the case, Christians were blamed. No proof supporting arson by Christians was found but the accusation stuck. Horrible executions began.

Several edicts were issued, the first of which ordered the burning of the Scriptures and churches. The summer of 303 saw a second edict requiring the arrest of priests and bishops. So many were arrested the prison system could not hold them. In November of that year, a third edict was issued allowing clergy to be freed if they made a sacrifice to the Roman gods. Most would not and many were tortured. Early in 304, an additional edict called for corporate sacrifices to the gods be held in public places. Those who refused could be executed.

During the next eight years, Christians endured the worst kind of treatment. Diocletian's edicts gave the freedom to persecute. No Christian was safe. Churches were destroyed, Scriptures were made illegal and burned, and pastors were hunted down. Christians died by the sword, wild beasts, and fire. They were forced to swear an allegiance to Roman gods and make sacrifices or die. The violence was directed at men, women, and children. Many Christians were sent to labor in mines where they were worked to death. They were put in a position of deciding between starvation and faithfulness.

Year after year this continued, until the Romans themselves grew weary of the bloodshed and hatred. Executioners had to work shifts to keep up with their duties.

Galerius, one of the four leaders of Diocletian's empire and Diocletian's son-in-law, harbored a hatred for all things Christian. It is possible Galerius pushed his father-in-law to issuing the edicts. He persecuted with zeal even after Diocletian abdicated to return home and grow cabbage. The persecution continued until 311 when, on his deathbed, Diocletian put an end to it and asked Christians to pray for their leaders.

Can Any Good Come Out of This?

Yes.

A century before these persecutions, one of the early church fathers, Tertullian, wrote, "The blood of the martyrs is the seed of the church."[1] He also said that the more Christians the persecutors killed, the more Christians there were. The Christian faith could not be exterminated. He was right. As a result of Diocletian's persecution, Christians were driven from the cities and took the gospel message with them.

In April 1906, a 7.9-magnitude earthquake nearly destroyed San Francisco, California. It leveled many buildings but some of the greatest damage occurred later. Many buildings caught fire, and the thinking of the day was that dynamite could be used to snuff out the blazes. However, blowing up the burning buildings only made things worse, spreading the fire farther than it might have reached on its own.

Diocletian's edicts against Christians did the same. They didn't end the gospel message but rather ignited a blaze of growth.

Diocletian made it illegal to possess Christian Scriptures, what we would call the New Testament today. But the New Testament as we know it was not compiled by this time. All the New Testament books and letters were known and collected, but the process of canonization—choosing which books were inspired—was still incomplete. It was not unusual to have many Christian writings in circulation that were not inspired. What writings of the church were worth dying for? Which were truly God-inspired? The persecution forced church leaders to think about these questions, about which books had God's fingerprints on them and therefore were worth risking death to preserve for future generations.

Fire is refining. The persecution separated those with a casual faith from those willing to endure torture and die for it, leaving a purer, stronger, more committed body of Christians. The church was being purified.

None of this is to say that Diocletian's persecution was a good thing. It wasn't. It was horrible in every way. The martyrs—men, women, and children—endured indescribable pain and fear. Christians watched friends and loved ones executed. These are the unnamed heroes of the faith. However, despite the violence and slaughter, good did come out of it, a good that continues to make a difference today.

Diocletian would certainly chafe at this description, but like it or not, he was a shaper of the church he set out to destroy.

9

EUSEBIUS OF CAESAREA

Historian with Heart

(c. 264–c. 340)

> I am attempting to traverse as it were a lonely and untrodden path.
>
> Eusebius, *Ecclesiastical History*

It seems silly to say but, from a human perspective, there has always been history. History happens and much of it is soon forgotten. Humans have shown a well-developed ability to forget the past. Well, most humans. There is a special brand of people who find meaning in the present by studying the past. Some, like Martin Luther King Jr., have believed history to be important to civilization. "We are not makers of history," he said. "We are made by history."[1]

History has informed the decisions of world leaders: the wise learn from it and the unwise ignore it. We know how countries rose and fell because someone has jotted down their history; we know how wars were won and lost because some soul thought it important to study such events. The knowledge of history is crucial to every society. This is especially true of the church.

The contemporary church did not spring forth fully formed. It came about through persecution, discussion, fighting, and perseverance.

Making this information available are the historians, men and women trained to analyze yesterday so we can have a better understanding of today and anticipate tomorrow. One of the earliest historians, and certainly the earliest church historian, is Eusebius (his name meaning "worships well," or "pious"), a quiet, gentle man who preferred mending fences rather than breaking them down. Straddling the third and fourth century, this thinker penned *Ecclesiastical History*, the first and most important history of the church.

The writing of this book was no easy task. Being first at anything often means overcoming tremendous obstacles. As a trail-blazing historian, he acknowledged the difficulty before him with this humble admission:

> At the outset I must crave for my work the indulgence of the wise, for I confess that it is beyond my power to produce a perfect and complete history, and since I am the first to enter upon the subject, I am attempting to traverse, as it were, a lonely and untrodden path. I pray that I may have God as my guide and the power of the Lord as my aid, since I am unable to find even the bare footsteps of those who have traveled the way before me.[2]

It takes courage to attempt a work that no one else has tried to do. Fortunately, Eusebius had the right personality for it. He read everything he could and had access to the best libraries of the day, including one he helped develop with his mentor Pamphilus.

We know almost nothing of Eusebius' early life. Scholars assume he was born in Palestine, and was probably baptized in the oceanside city of Caesarea, where he became an elder in the church and later bishop in 315.

Eusebius thought highly of his teacher, calling himself Eusebius Pamphili—son of Pamphilus. During the great persecution of Diocletian, Pamphilus was arrested in 308 and killed in 310. It appears that Eusebius was also arrested for his faith but somehow suffered less than some of his contemporaries, something that would work against him later. Eusebius wrote a three-volume work about the life of his mentor. Sadly, those volumes are lost.

It was during the persecution that Eusebius set about writing his church history, revising it several times along the way. For over a decade, beginning around 303, he worked on the project, producing ten books on the topic and covering the years from the time of Christ and continuing into Constantine's reign as emperor.

Not all of Eusebius' life was that of an academic in an ivory tower. As bishop of Caesarea, he had church duties and became involved with the Arian controversy. Arius was a church leader from Alexandria, Egypt, who taught that there was a hierarchy among the three persons of the Trinity. Today, the Christian view describes God the Father, God the Son, and God the Holy Spirit as equals and always in existence. Arius taught that Jesus was created, and therefore beneath God the Father. The debate revolved around several issues, including the question, "Was there ever a time when Jesus wasn't?" In other words, was he created?

This idea spread and the church split into two groups. The division caught the attention of Emperor Constantine, who had legalized Christianity. He felt the two sides needed to be brought together and the rift healed, so he convened the Council of Nicaea. Eusebius not only attended but sat at the right hand of the emperor, a spot of prestige.

Constantine and Eusebius liked and trusted one another. The emperor invited the historian to his palace, told him of his battlefield vision of the cross (see chapter on Constantine), exchanged letters, and entrusted him to oversee the translation of fifty Bibles into Greek for use by churches in Constantinople (sometimes called the Fifty Bibles of Constantine).

Critics of Eusebius point to the circumstances surrounding his friendship with Constantine. He was kind in all of his writings regarding the emperor, leaving out material that might suggest that Constantine was not as noble as he wanted to be remembered. He justifies some of the emperor's actions that scholars today consider extreme, including Constantine having his son and wife put to death, or his attack and defeat of Licinius, his former coemperor and brother-in-law.

There is no evidence that Eusebius used his relationship with the empire's most powerful man for personal gain, nor did this relationship keep him from accusations made by other bishops. At the Council of Tyre (335 or 336), Bishop Potamon of Heraclea challenged him:

How do you, Eusebius, sit as judge of the innocent Athansius? Who can bear it? Why did you not sit with me in prison in the time of the tyrants? They plucked out my eye for my confession of the truth; you came out unhurt; you have suffered nothing for your confession; you are unscathed even now. How did you escape from prison? On some other ground than because you promised to do some unlawful thing, or maybe you actually did the unlawful?[3]

In an effort to bring the battling sides together, Eusebius had to endure such accusations. Being a man of peace can be painful. The accusation was unfair, and Eusebius' doctrine matched that of his accuser, but because he stood in the middle seeking compromise he drew fire from both sides.

Modern historians find many things to criticize in Eusebius' history, but we should remember that he was a pioneer. Today's historians are very systematic and scientific in their approach, but that technique was developed over time. Eusebius did the church a great favor by writing *Ecclesiastical History*. Not only do we know more about the early church than we would have otherwise, but he cites works that would have been lost to us.

Eusebius shaped the church by putting in its hands the story of its growth through the early centuries.

10

CONSTANTINE

The Christian Emperor?

(285–337)

> You are bishops whose restriction is within the church, but I also
> am a Bishop, ordained by God to overlook whatever is external to
> the church.
>
> Constantine, *The Life of Constantine*

Those who write novels or screenplays are familiar with the
three-act structure. It's a proven technique to convey a story
in a memorable, interesting way. Moving from one act to the next
requires some thought. These transitions are called "plot points" or
"turning points." In storytelling, it is a door the hero walks through
that changes everything that comes after. The story of the church
also has its "plot points," and if ever there was a turning point in the
story line of the church, it comes in the form of Emperor Constantine.

In a single act, the emperor overturned three centuries of persecution. Constantine became the first Roman leader to give rights to the
church, and the first to call himself a Christian. However, accounts
of Constantine's life bring his faith into question. He was certainly
no saint. In fact, many scholars doubt he had a Christian faith at all.

Flavius Valerius Aurelius Constantinus Augustus, better known as Constantine, entered this life a privileged child. His father, Constantius Chlorus, was coemperor and ruled the western portion of the Roman Empire. His mother was an innkeeper's daughter. He was declared emperor as his father lay dying, and he had the support of much of the army (a crucial requirement for one wanting to be head of the Empire). Still, things were not that simple. At least five others claimed the right to be emperor. The dispute could only be settled by battle. Constantine had distinguished himself in war as a leader of men during Diocletian's reign. He had led successful campaigns in Persia and Egypt, gaining the support of tens of thousands of soldiers, some of which he would need later in life.

Some of the most severe persecution occurred at the end of Diocletian's leadership. So severe was the persecution that few believed Christianity could survive. A few years later, Christians went from being hunted to being valuable citizens. Constantine would make popular what Diocletian had declared illegal.

The Vision

Constantine may have been sympathetic to Christians because of his father. Although a pagan until the end, Constantius Chlorus was monotheistic, worshiping just the Roman sun god. He also did not participate in the persecution ordered by Diocletian. Constantine went further, not just tolerating Christians but raising their profile throughout the Empire.

The catalyst for this appears to be a vision Constantine had while on his way to battle Maxentius, another man claiming the throne. Details of the vision are blurry and the story is told with conflicting details. Constantine, while marching with his troops, saw something in the sky that he took as a sign from God. It was an X-style cross with a Greek letter superimposed over it. In the sky (some accounts say it was in a dream) were two Greek letters: a chi and a rho (which looks like an English letter p). Together they form the first two letters of the Greek word *Cristos*, or Christ. There was also an inscription: "In this conquer." Constantine ordered his men to mark the symbol on their shields.

In 312, Maxentius had consulted a pagan oracle and was led to believe victory was his for the taking. It wasn't. Constantine won the day at Mulvain Bridge near Rome, and Maxentius lost his life, drowning in the Tiber River. To Constantine the rout was further proof of the power of the Christian God. In the winter of 312, Constantine wrote to one of his officers in North Africa, giving orders to supply money to the bishop of Carthage to cover the expenses of the clergy there.

The Edict

In 313, a man named Licinius married Constantine's half sister, making him brother-in-law to Constantine. Constantine and Licinius ruled the Empire together for a decade, but the relationship between the two ended badly. Constantine ruled in the West, Licinius in the East. One of their first acts was to enact the Edict of Milan, a law reversing the persecution of Diocletian and others. Christians no longer needed to hide in shadows.

Christians, under Roman persecution, had been stripped of property and of jobs, arrested, forced to work in mines, and made to witness their Scriptures being stolen and burned. Many had been tortured, often to death, for their faith. Now, with this new edict in place, they could worship safely and build churches, and bishops could sit as judges in civil lawsuits. Sunday became a day of rest; courts of law were closed. The cruel gladiator games were banned. Clergy were made exempt from military service.

Constantine funded the building of churches and appointed Christians as advisors. He even gave his own sons a Christian education. And he began referring to the church in his speeches as the "catholic (universal) church."

The Christian Behavior

The church of Constantine's time had many struggles over doctrine. It was still defining itself. Doctrinal lines were being drawn and the tension was serious enough for Constantine to call for a council of bishops to hash out the issues. Around 325 AD, three hundred church leaders from around the Empire met in Nicaea to settle the matter of Christ's nature. Constantine, although not likely able to follow or significantly contribute to the theological discussions, insisted on being a part of the proceedings. These first meetings began an era of church councils.

Constantine saw himself as more than emperor—as if that weren't enough. He also believed he had a religious role to play. That was to be expected, considering the vision he had received. He viewed his work and success as divinely ordained. Although he had no formal training to be a church leader, he adopted the role anyway, making a distinction between what went on in the church and what went on outside of it. He said to the gathered clergy, "You are bishops whose restriction is within the church, but I also am a Bishop, ordained by God to overlook whatever is external to the church."[1]

This idea that a man could be chosen by God to lead a nation was absolutely revolutionary.

The concept must have seemed strange to the Romans, who were used to their emperors claiming to be gods, but were unfamiliar with one claiming submission to a single deity, particularly when that god was the one worshiped by Jews and Christians. For Christians, however, it was a far more comfortable fit. The "theocracy" that God's people experienced before Christ must have prepared them for the concept. King David was selected by God to be king. If God could choose a shepherd boy to become king, then why couldn't he select a former pagan?

The Edict of Milan, which Constantine and Licinius signed in 313, was not specific to the freedoms of Christians only. It also allowed freedom of worship to people of all beliefs. But when Constantine became sole emperor in 324, he made Christianity the official religion of the Roman Empire.

The Pagan Behavior

Some scholars have voiced doubts about Constantine's vision and conversion, and with good cause. It would be a stretch to call Constantine a "good Christian." Despite his support of the church and his efforts to heal schisms by calling church councils, he remained very much the Roman emperor, quick to see conspiracy and condemn people to death. When rumors spread that his eldest son was having an incestuous affair with his wife, the son's stepmother, he had both executed.

A decade into his leadership, he and his coemperor, Licinius—the one who helped him come to power and who had signed the Edict of Milan with him—had a falling-out over several issues, most seriously an assassination attempt on Constantine by a man Licinius wanted elevated to high status, and then by Licinius' new persecution against Christians in the East (breaking the Edict of Milan). The two met in battle. Constantine defeated him and had him executed. It seems Constantine kept a foot in two worlds: one in the ever-expanding church, the other in Roman despotism.

He was a transitional catalyst, a man moving the world from past offenses and over the threshold into a new world that Christianity would help shape. Was Constantine's conversion genuine, or was it an action taken for political convenience? It's impossible to judge a man's heart 1700 years after he lived. Christianity, while centuries old, was still new to the likes of Constantine. Holding the position of power that he did pressed upon him challenges few can understand. This does not excuse his vicious actions, but it does lend a little understanding about the man.

His Baptism

Constantine died in May of 337 after serving the Empire as emperor for three decades. Shortly before he passed, knowing his end was near, he submitted to baptism. If the accounts of his conversion are true, he had become a Christian back in 312. Why put off baptism so long? In his day, many believed that a person could not be forgiven of sins committed after baptism. Leaders often delayed baptism until the end of their lives, fearing that some sin would cost them their salvation. This is not a doctrine held among Christians today, but it was a popular enough belief to make even someone with Constantine's indomitable spirit hesitate.

The Great

Constantine is often referred to as "Constantine the Great." The title is deserved. He not only ended persecution of the Christians and ushered in a government that allowed for the freedom of worship but he also aided in the building of many churches. He elevated the eastern city of Byzantium to "New Rome." In honor of their emperor, people called the city Constantinople ("Constantine's City"). It would serve as the center of the Eastern Empire for a thousand years.

He instituted other reforms as well, but he will be forever known as the first Christian emperor. We can never understand all that went on with Constantine and his faith. At times it seemed genuine, at other times less so. We are left to judge the man by what he *did* rather than who he *was*. The faith he defended, in some ways, had not changed him as much as we might have hoped, but it changed him more than anyone could have expected. Constantine, whatever the real cause and nature of his faith, pushed aside the Roman gods of old and opened the doors of the church for everyone.

11

ATHANASIUS

The Noble Champion of Christ

(295–373)

In these alone the teaching of godliness is proclaimed. No one may
add to them, and nothing may be taken away from them.

Athanasius, *Thirty-Ninth Festal Epistle*

Life is often difficult, full of peaks and valleys. People of faith
are no different. Even the most devout face rejection, opposition, and criticism. Such is life for most of us, and such was life for
Athanasius, who was bishop of Alexandria during a pivotal time
in the church's doctrinal development. Some years he was a hero,
others he was an outcast. He knew what it meant to fly like an eagle
and then plunge into despair. At one point, alone and despairing,
he declared, "Athanasius against the world."

Athanasius valued doctrinal purity above all else. Most people
who attend church today would not recognize his name, but Athanasius from Egypt had a dramatic impact on what the contemporary
church believes.

The church was born into difficulty. Persecution began with the arrest, torture, and crucifixion of Jesus. That persecution, led by Jewish religious leaders, spread to the church. The apostles, Peter in particular, were frequently arrested and tossed in jail. Although Peter and Paul served the church a great many years, both died a martyr's death.

The persecution of the church was then carried out by Roman leaders and continued for over two centuries. With the arrival of Constantine, things changed. The church gained respectability, and perhaps more importantly, legality. Christians could now meet and worship as they saw fit. This was, of course, a good thing, but as with many good things there came a price. The price the church paid was the newfound willingness of Christians to turn on one another.

The early centuries were spent in survival, followed by the painful process of defining the church's core beliefs. From its beginning, the church had to defend itself against heresy. In the first century the apostle Paul battled the Gnostics. He and Peter also faced off against the Judaizers, a group who taught Gentiles must first become Jews before they could become Christians. The lines of these battles were clearly drawn and the doctrinal issues easily recognized. Later, however, the task became more difficult as doctrinal concerns grew more complicated.

What Is Jesus?

One such issue dealt with the nature of Jesus Christ. There was little question about *who* Jesus was, but there was question about *what* he was. Exactly how does Jesus relate to God the Father? Certainly God is deity, but can the same be said of Jesus? Was Jesus created? And the biggest question of all: Was there ever a time when Jesus wasn't?

To some this may not seem an issue worth debating, but to the early leaders of the church, especially Athanasius, such questions were crucial. To Athanasius the whole concept of salvation rested in the answer. Jesus had to be fully man to die on the cross, and he also had to be fully God to bring about salvation. These arguments are tied to the Trinity, arguably one of the most difficult concepts for humans to grasp. It has no earthly analogy. The orthodox view of the Trinity is easy to state but hard for many to wrap their minds around: there is one and only one God, but there are three persons of the Godhead.

The whole debate comes down to three descriptive terms: coequal, coeternal, and consubstantial. Does Jesus have the same standing as God the Father (coequal)? Does Jesus have an eternal past and an eternal future the same as God the Father (coeternal)? Does Jesus have the *same* essence (not *similar* essence) as God the Father (consubstantial)?

For those with no theological background this might seem confusing and even insignificant, but it was a divisive issue in Athanasius' day.

Athanasius was a young and, by all accounts, brilliant deacon in the church in Alexandria, Egypt. He felt, as did his bishop and many others, that such distinctions were worth fighting for. Counter to Athanasius' view was the teaching of an elderly priest in the Alexandrian church named Arias, who was soon to embark in a number of heated debates with Athanasius.

In 325, Constantine, in an effort to put an end to the squabbling, called for a gathering of bishops. By convening the council, Constantine demonstrated his power over the church. As many as eighteen hundred bishops were invited to the city of Nicaea, but only about three hundred came. This Council of Bishops, under the emperor's order, set about to determine the truth of the matter. Although not himself a bishop, Athanasius was granted permission to press his case before them. When the debate was over, his view prevailed and Arius was exiled. The final verdict? Jesus was Creator, not created, and this decision is summed up in the approximately forty-six words (in English) of the Nicene Creed:

> And in one Lord Jesus Christ, the only-begotten Son of God, begotten of the Father before all worlds; God of God, Light of Light, very God of very God; begotten, not made, being of one substance with the Father, by whom all things were made.

The nature and position of Jesus had been defined for the church.

More Tension

Athanasius became bishop of Alexandria in June of 328, but would spend much of his time in exile.

Arius signed an altered version of the first Nicene Creed, and Constantine ordered Athanasius to restore the man to fellowship in the Alexandrian church. Athanasius refused. Soon rumors and trumped-up charges were leveled against him, including murder, sorcery, and treason. Constantine was forced to exile Athanasius. This was the first of five exiles he would endure, including two years in Germany, seven years in Rome, six years in the Egyptian desert, followed by nearly another year in the desert, and then four months living in his father's tomb. He was exiled by four different emperors. Political influence played a large role in his returns and subsequent exiles. It is estimated that of the forty-five years he served as bishop of Alexandria, seventeen years were spent in exile. At the age of seventy, he was able to return home. He died in peace. Ultimately, the church would uphold his theological arguments about the nature of Christ.

Athanasius shaped the church in yet another way. In one of his annual letters to the churches in his diocese, he listed the twenty-seven books he believed were inspired and appropriate for the church to read. He wrote, "In these alone the teaching of godliness is proclaimed."[1] It's the same list of books as those in the current New Testament.

12

AMBROSE OF MILAN

Of Music and Emperors

(337–397)

> When we speak about wisdom, we are speaking about Christ. When we speak about virtue, we are speaking about Christ. When we speak about justice, we are speaking about Christ. When we speak about truth and life and redemption, we are speaking about Christ.
>
> Traditionally attributed to Ambrose of Milan

Be not afraid of greatness; Some are born great, some achieve greatness, and others have greatness thrust upon them."[1] Those words of William Shakespeare could describe Ambrose of Milan.

Ambrose was a multifaceted man, garnering respect and achieving power at an early age. At just age thirty, he was appointed governor in Italy's northern provinces. Before his life would end, he would count among his accomplishments those of biblical interpreter, political theorist, eloquent speaker and teacher, musician, and bishop of Milan.

"Ambrose for Bishop!"

Ambrose's transition from governor to minister was unexpected and unplanned. By 380 the church had grown in prominence and Christians were no longer social outcasts. By Ambrose's day, non-Christians were more likely to be penalized for their choices than Christians.

Emperor Theodosius made Christianity a requirement. He wrote:

> It is our will that all people we rule shall practice that religion which the divine Peter the apostle transmitted to the Romans. We shall believe in the single deity of the Father, the Son, and the Holy Spirit, under the concepts of equal majesty and of the Holy Trinity. We command that those persons who follow this rule shall embrace the name of Catholic Christians. The rest, however, whom we adjudge to be demented and insane, shall sustain the infamy of heretical dogmas, their meeting places shall not receive the name of churches, and they shall be smitten first by divine vengeance and secondly by the retribution of our own initiative, which we shall assume in accordance with divine judgment.[2]

Christianity was not only protected by the law, it had *become* the law. Christianity had moved from a personal choice to a government mandate. Many of those attending churches were not doing so out of a longing for worship and greater knowledge of Christ but rather out of compulsion. Christianity as a mandated religion led to many un-Christian acts by the "church." Where once matters of doctrine were fought with words, they were now, in some places, being fought with violence.

One such battle pitted orthodox Christians against members of the Arian heresy. Arianism began with an Alexandrian priest named Arius. It was his contention that Christ was not divine and not equal with God, and while important, was not to be confused with the Father. To the Arians, Jesus was a created being and therefore not coeternal with God. By this time the orthodox church had an abiding belief in the Trinity, the belief that there is one God in three persons, distinct but equal. Emperor Theodosius had made the orthodox view mandatory; Auxentius, however, was an Arian and therefore out of step with accepted doctrine of the church. He was declared a heretic. To this day, he is not listed as a bishop of Milan in the Roman Catholic list of bishops. Nevertheless, he was able to hold his position as bishop of Milan until his death.

Auxentius had many supporters who held him and his doctrine in high regard. When he died, conflict erupted, leading to violence between the Arians and the orthodox Christians.

Ambrose, as governor, attended the meeting to select the new bishop of Milan. As a representative of the empire, he hoped his presence would curtail further violence. Both Arians and orthodox believers filled the hall to select their next leader, and both sides of the argument held Ambrose in high regard—one of the few things they could agree on. Someone shouted, "Ambrose for bishop!" No one knows who that "someone" was, but this single declaration was joined by a chorus of others.

Ambrose had no desire to serve as bishop, but he was clearly the favorite of those on both sides of the dispute. Still, he resisted. After all, although a believer, he had never been baptized. How could he assume the role of church leader? It didn't matter. He had been chosen and that was that. The people wrote the emperor asking for help in persuading Ambrose. He responded in true imperial fashion: he placed Ambrose under arrest until he agreed to become the new bishop of Milan.

Ambrose had been drafted.

Subsequently, his baptism followed, as did a rapid sequence of promotions through the established church hierarchy. Eight days later, Ambrose became bishop—an unlikely outcome for a governor who was simply trying to quell violence after the death of Auxentius.

Ambrose threw himself into the work, applying his keen mind to the task of Scripture study and a reading of the church fathers. He began preaching, and the oratory skills that had served him so well in the public sector now brought him fame as a preacher.

The Bishop of "No"

While it is nice to be loved and entrusted with an important work, Ambrose's life was not free from turmoil. The debate between the Arians and their orthodox counterparts continued to rage. If the

Arians who helped usher Ambrose into his new role thought he might be sympathetic to their cause, they were doomed to disappointment. Ambrose was no Arian and he resisted their heretical teachings, even writing several works against them: *On the Faith*, *The Mystery of the Lord's Incarnation*, and *On the Holy Spirit*. Under his leadership, Arianism lost influence, but not without a battle. Many leaders in politics and the military subscribed to the Arian views, including the mother of the emperor. The Arians in Milan demanded two churches for their congregations, one in the city and one in the suburbs. This demand came from local authorities and the members of the emperor's family.

Ambrose refused this request, saying, "If you demand my person, I am ready to submit: carry me to prison or to death, I will not resist; but I will never betray the church of Christ. I will not call upon the people to succor me; I will die at the foot of the altar rather than desert it. The tumult of the people I will not encourage: but God alone can appease it."[3]

He then turned away those who had come to prepare one of the churches for the arrival of the emperor's mother. In so doing, he showed for the first time that the church could stand up to the government.

A Bloodbath

Ambrose's dedication to truth was tested to the extreme when an arrest of a local athlete led to murder and, eventually, something much worse. In 390, the governor arrested a popular chariot racer in Thessalonica for homosexuality. Those spectators loyal to this popular athlete demanded his release. When the governor refused, the people took up arms and freed the athlete themselves, and in the process killed the governor and others.

Word reached Emperor Theodosius. He devised a plan that would achieve vengeance for the death of his governor, calling for a chariot race to be held in the city. The day of the event came and thousands filled the arena. Once the spectators were inside, the gates were locked and Theodosius' soldiers descended upon the crowd. Seven thousand spectators were slaughtered over the course of three hours.

Ambrose was not only appalled but furious. Although no longer possessing political power, he did have the power of the state-sanctioned church. He wrote a courteous but direct, two-fisted letter to Theodosius:

> Listen, august Emperor. I cannot deny that you have a zeal for the faith; I do confess that you have the fear of God. But you have a natural vehemence, which, if anyone endeavors to soothe, you quickly turn to mercy; if anyone stirs it up, you rouse it so much more that you can scarcely restrain it. Would that if no one soothe it, at least no one may inflame it! To yourself I willingly entrust it, you restrain yourself, and overcome your natural vehemence by the love of piety.
>
> You are a man, and it has come upon you, conquer it. Sin is not done away but by tears and penitence. Neither angel can do it, nor archangel. The Lord Himself, Who alone can say, "I am with you," if we have sinned, does not forgive any but those who repent.
>
> Do not add another sin to your sin by a course of action which has injured many.[4]

Ambrose didn't stop with a letter: he excommunicated the emperor. Theodosius was not allowed to attend church or receive the sacraments until he came before Ambrose, humbled himself, repented, and asked forgiveness of God.

Theodosius did so, stepping before the altar, removing his purple robes, and prostrating himself. But Ambrose was not satisfied until the most powerful man in the country had repeated this action several times. On Christmas day, Ambrose accepted the emperor's evidence of repentance. Later, Theodosius would say, "The only man I know worthy of the name Bishop is Ambrose."[5]

In what must be one of his most significant acts of humility and forgiveness, Ambrose held Theodosius in his arms as the emperor died. At Theodosius' funeral, Ambrose said, "I confess I love him, and felt the sorrow of his death in the abyss of my heart."

Ambrose's willingness to confront power proved to be a turning point in the church. Once the empire "became Christian," it placed itself under the authority of church leaders. Ambrose was the first to use the power of the church to sway the actions of a country. This would happen many times in the decades ahead.

Hymns

In light of these acts of bravery, these monumental stands against heresy and government abuse, it might be easy to overlook another major change in the church: music. Congregational singing is common in the contemporary church. It's hard to imagine attending worship where singing doesn't take place. In most evangelical churches, music makes up a significant portion of the service. That hasn't always been the case. It was Ambrose, a lover of music, who brought singing to the churches. He wrote as many as eighteen hymns that influenced the church in the East and the West. The exact number is debated by scholars, but Augustine links Ambrose with church music.[6] According to Augustine, the music provided spiritual relief for the church during the stressful times it endured in Milan, and the custom continued.

A man of Ambrose's stature and accomplishment had many opportunities to directly influence the lives of others. After hearing one of Ambrose's famous sermons, a skeptical man sought Ambrose afterward, and eventually became one of his students. Ambrose mentored this student for four years. This student of Ambrose, Augustine of Hippo, would soon change the church in ways that surpassed his famous teacher.

Ambrose never set out to be a church leader. His was the world of politics and public service. In the end, however, he became a church-shaper through his courageous stand for doctrinal purity, obedience of state to the church, the introduction of music in worship, and in the mentoring of one of the greatest church shapers and theologians of all: Augustine of Hippo.

13

JEROME

A Thousand-Year Influence

(342–420)

Ignorance of Scripture is Ignorance of Christ.

Jerome, *Commentary on Isaiah*

How often when I was living in the desert, parched by a burning sun, did I fancy myself among the pleasures of Rome! Sackcloth disfigured my unshapely limbs, and my skin long neglected had become as black as an Ethiopian's. And although in my fear of hell I had consigned myself to this prison, where I had no companions but scorpions and wild beasts, I often thought myself in the company of many girls. My face grew pale, and my frame chilled with fasting; yet my mind was burning with desire, and the fires of lust kept bubbling up before me when my flesh was as good as dead. Helpless, I cast myself at the feet of Jesus.[1]

Does this sound like a man who is considered one of the most revered Christian scholars of his time and for centuries to follow? Nonetheless, these words are found in a letter Jerome wrote to a trusted friend and are informative about his character.

A Mind at Work

Eusebius Hieronymus Sophronius—better known as Jerome—was born in what is now Ljubljana, Slovenia, to a wealthy Christian family. He received an excellent education in Rome, studying what most scholars of the day did: grammar, rhetoric, and philosophy. At the age of nineteen he was baptized, beginning a life of service in the church, although decidedly not a typical life.

Some believe that genius comes at the cost of civility. This might be impossible to prove, but there are plenty of examples indicating the greater the intellect, the greater the social awkwardness. Albert Einstein was brilliant in many ways but biographers indicate he was not particularly adept as a husband and father. Isaac Newton wrote abusive letters and made critical accusations about other scientists. At times it seems as if mental brilliance dims other aspects of life, and Jerome fit that category.

A Nightmare

Jerome was a man driven by a desire to obey, to live a life of purity and righteousness. He was plagued by the same sensual desires as men with lesser intellect and training and he hated himself for it. That and his desire for learning drove him to an ascetic lifestyle—a lifestyle of self-denial. He first encountered asceticism while continuing his education and during his travels, and he became a believer in the spiritual power and discipline of monastic living.

Jerome had received training in the classics and loved them, especially the writing of the Roman writer, orator, and statesman Cicero, who lived a century before Christ. One night, during Lent of 375, he had a nightmare. He saw himself at the judgment seat, but instead of receiving praise for living a life of sacrifice and choosing to give up the wealth he was born into, he instead heard scathing condemnation: "You are a follower of Cicero, not Christ." The dream so hurt him he swore off reading classic writings. He moved to the Syrian desert to live as a hermit. The life was hard and lonely. He begged for letters. He spent lonely days praying, fasting, copying manuscripts, and learning Hebrew from Jewish Christians.

Jerome's gift with languages and translation were quickly recognized and Bishop Paulinus of Antioch ordained him as a priest—only after it was agreed that he would never have to do priestly duties. He wanted to serve God through the church but knew that he would make an inadequate parish priest.

He continued his studies, listened to lectures by famous theologians, and met with other scholars. Then came a summons to Rome, where he would serve as secretary to Bishop Damasus. This was a highly esteemed position and put him in place to be Damasus' successor.

A New Translation

It was Damasus who set in motion a work that would span centuries. The church had grown in two directions: the Eastern and the Western Church. The Western Church would become known as the Roman Church. Damasus felt a Bible in the common language of the West would strengthen the church and further the spread of the gospel. The problem rested in the original languages of the Bible: Old Testament Hebrew and New Testament Greek. The Old Testament had already been translated into Greek six centuries before and was in popular use. This translation was called the Septuagint because it was the work of seventy (some say seventy-two) translators. When the apostle Paul quoted the Old Testament in his letters that would become part of the New Testament, he quoted from the Septuagint.

While Greek was fine for the East, Latin was the predominate language in the West. What was needed was a good Latin translation of the Bible. Other translations existed but they were considered inferior and the result of poor scholarship. This fact bothered Jerome. He wrote to Damasus:

> If we are to pin our faith to the Latin texts, it is for our opponents to tell us which; for there are almost as many forms of texts as there are copies. If, on the other hand, we are to glean the truth from a comparison of many, why not go back to the original Greek and correct the mistakes introduced by inaccurate translators, and the blundering alterations of confident but ignorant critics, and, further, all that has been inserted or changed by copyists more asleep than awake?[2]

Here is Jerome's genius. Instead of embarking on what could have been a lengthy revision process of comparing one Latin Bible with another and then determining which most accurately reflected the original Greek, Jerome decided that a direct translation was needed. He put aside the many flawed earlier works and started from scratch. And he didn't stop with the New Testament. It would take over twenty years for him to complete the work. The New Testament, being smaller, came about fairly quickly. The Old Testament was more demanding. Jerome, while versed in Hebrew, sought the advice of Hebrew scholars in the Holy Land. He had moved there from Rome when Damasus died in 384. Jerome had not been selected as his successor after all, probably for many reasons, including his sharp tongue. He settled in Bethlehem and continued his work.

Here Jerome's brilliance shines again. He started his work the same way others had, but then decided the translation should be based on the original Hebrew, not the Greek rendition. He saw no sense in making a translation of a translation.

Today, scholars have many tools available to them that were undreamt of in Jerome's time. There are many more manuscripts available, as well as many tools made possible via the advent of computers. Jerome had to use the best Hebrew manuscripts he could find and, with the help of Jewish scholars, convert from Hebrew to Latin.

Jerome's translation work became known as the Latin Vulgate. *Vulgate* comes from the Latin for "common." It would endure for a millennium. When it was finished the Western Church had a uniform translation, free from frequent error and poor scholarship.

Jerome wrote many other works, including commentaries, but the Vulgate was his pinnacle. He has been called the greatest Christian scholar of all time. Few would argue.

He was a man born into wealth but preferred the hermit's life. He was ordained a priest but only after the bishop agreed he wouldn't have to do priestly duties. He preferred books to people, held women and marriage in low regard, and wrestled with his physical passions. He was curt and at times verbally abusive. He was often intolerant of others' scholarship. Still, he was aware of his problems and sought only to serve the church.

14

JOHN CHRYSOSTOM

The Man with the Golden Voice

(347–407)

I know my own soul, how feeble and puny it is: I know the magnitude
of this ministry, and the great difficulty of the work; for more stormy
billows vex the soul of the priest than the gales which disturb the sea.

John Chrysostom, *Treatise on the Priesthood*

Few people can claim a riot as the stepping-stone to a successful career. Almost every major city in the world has seen its citizens up in arms over some cause. Many such riots turn violent, and in countries with fewer freedoms and safeguards, government retribution is certain. John of Antioch—better known as John Chrysostom—rose to fame partly because of a riot in his city of Antioch.

Chrysostom was born in 347 to a fairly wealthy family, but one not immune to disaster. His father was a successful military man who died shortly after John was born, leaving his twenty-year-old wife, Anthusa, with the obligation of the house and the rearing of their children. Although still very young and attractive, Anthusa shunned all suitors and devoted herself to her son and daughter, taking special care to make sure Chrysostom received the best education.

The Man Who Could Have Been Anything

A fellow student introduced Chrysostom to the idea of ministry with the monastics, something that immediately appealed to him. He desired to become an ascetic, to withdraw from society and focus on purely searchable thoughts. However, this desire had to be set aside because he would not leave his mother alone. In the meantime, he studied rhetoric with one of the most famous teachers of the day, a pagan named Libanius who considered Chrysostom one of his finest students. When Libanius was close to death, he was asked which of his students should succeed him as teacher. His response: "John, if only the Christians should not have carried him away."[1]

Chrysostom had no thirst for fame, only for godly service. After his mother's death he withdrew from the city and its temptations to live in a cave. For almost a decade he lived in this harsh environment until his health could take no more. Worn and ill, he returned to Antioch and was immediately welcomed into the church, first as a deacon, then as a presbyter, and finally as a priest.

During those days the emperor of the Eastern Empire, Theodosius, levied a new tax to fund a celebration of the tenth anniversary of his ascent to power. The citizens of Antioch, in protest, defaced statues of Emperor Theodosius I, the deceased Empress Flacilla, and her two children Arcadius and Honorius. These acts of vandalism were more than the emperor could bear. He threatened to destroy the city.

In an effort to avoid the slaughter, Bishop Flavius of Antioch left for Constantinople to plead with the emperor for mercy. While he was away Chrysostom attempted to settle the angry mobs. He delivered a series of twenty (some say twenty-one) sermons now known as the *Homilies on the Statues*. The sermons were effective and the power of Chrysostom's words kept a bad situation from becoming worse. These were sermons that saved lives and helped keep a city from being destroyed.

The Golden Voice

We know John of Antioch today as John Chrysostom. *Chrysostom* comes from the Greek meaning "golden mouth." Chrysostom was given this name to honor him for his skill in public speaking. To this day people study his technique of oral communication.

Chrysostom's sermons were long and powerful. He spoke plainly but with an oratorical beauty that touched the mind and the heart of his listeners.

> Who, beloved, has bewitched us? Who hath envied us? When has all the change come over us? Nothing was more dignified than our city! Now, never was anything more pitiable! The populace so well ordered and quiet, yes, even like a tractable and well-tamed steed, always submissive to the hands of its ruler, hath now so suddenly started off with us, as to have wrought such evils, as one can hardly dare mention.[2]

He then called them to higher, nobler, more Christian behavior:

> Confident then in these hopes, let us beseech Him continually; let us be earnest in prayers and supplications; and let us with all strictness give our attention to every other virtue; that we may escape the danger that threatens, and obtain the good things to come; which God grant we may all be worthy of.[3]

Chrysostom labored on his sermons so they might convey the truth in a way his listeners would receive. His oratory skill was so impressive that his sermons were often interrupted by applause and the stamping of feet. During one of his sermons, he even condemned the practice of applauding during a sermon. He did so with such great conviction that, ironically, the people broke into spontaneous applause.

While many preachers in his day took an allegorical approach to the biblical text, Chrysostom believed that sermons should be based in literal interpretation. This practice has endured through the centuries and helped guide the leaders of the Protestant Reformation.

Chrysostom's fame reached far and wide, and when the bishop of Constantinople died, he was selected to replace him. Chrysostom was content where he was and did not seek higher office; however, the emperor had made up his mind—Chrysostom would be bishop of Constantinople, and he sent soldiers to retrieve the preacher.

Chrysostom took this in stride and threw himself into the work, apparently more seriously than had been done before. Priests in Constantinople during this time were known to be hypocritical and immoral. Chrysostom was not about to follow in those footsteps.

A Message Made of More Than Words

His commitment would cause him trouble and ultimately lead to his death. Chrysostom was one of those preachers who "meddled" in the lives of his parishioners. He was not the kind of preacher who offered just sweet and comforting words but rather pointed out sin and demanded obedience to Christ. He showed no hesitancy in confronting those living in sin, whether they be ordinary men or leaders in society. Chrysostom lived a simple life even though he was surrounded by prosperity and was given an enormous amount of money to run his house. He gave most of that money to the poor. He continued to live a private life, preferring to give to the needy rather than give to himself. He was described as making himself poor so that the poor might be richer. This frustrated many powerful people of his time, including Empress Aelia Eudoxia and Bishop Theophilus of Alexandria. Eudoxia felt that John had been critical of her extravagant lifestyle. Theophilus was jealous and felt Chrysostom should be subservient to him. Together they caused him a great deal of trouble.

Theophilus and Eudoxia trumped up twenty-nine charges, including heresy, requesting the Synod at the Oak to oust Chrysostom. The synod was a council of three dozen hand-selected bishops—a kangaroo court. They heard the false charges of treason and immorality, and in 403 Chrysostom was deposed and exiled—but he returned soon after. An earthquake struck near Eudoxia's palace and frightened her. She took it as a sign of pending doom because of her part in having Chrysostom exiled. She begged the emperor to have the banishment lifted. He concurred, and Chrysostom was back in Constantinople doing the work he felt called to do.

However, it didn't last long.

After Chrysostom criticized Eudoxia for erecting a statue of herself near the cathedral where he preached, she arranged for him to be exiled again. This time permanently. He was banished to an isolated region in Armenia.

Chrysostom died in 407 while in exile there. The banishment proved too much for his frail health, but his sermons and literal approach to the biblical text live on to this day.

The Eastern church sees John Chrysostom as one of the great church fathers and as the greatest preacher the church has ever known. He preached with word and with action and left the church changed for the better.

15

AUGUSTINE OF HIPPO
From Delinquent to Theologian

(354–430)

> Instantly as I reached the end of the sentence, it was as if the light of peace was poured into my heart, and all the shades of doubt faded away.
>
> Augustine, *Confessions*

An elderly man lay upon his deathbed. From beneath the covers he could see selections from the book of Psalms affixed to his walls. In the last ten days of his life, he pondered these words and his existence. The frail figure of Augustine teetered on the edge of the grave, awaiting his transfer from the pains of the earthly world to the joys of the heavenly kingdom. All around him was trouble. The city he loved was under siege. And shortly after his death, the city would fall and the attackers would find that most of the city's inhabitants were dead or dying of starvation. Aurelius Augustinus, or Augustine, lived a life that forever changed the church. He is one of the few theologians and ministers revered by both Protestants and Catholics.

Augustine was an intellectual giant. Historians and theologians hold him in high regard, yet those who knew him when he was a young man could never have guessed how the troublemaker would change. Early in his life, he was a poor student and found more pleasure in causing trouble than in learning. Born to a minor Roman official father and Monica, a devout Christian mother, Augustine preferred thrills and pleasure over education. He and his friends would steal pears from a neighbor's orchard not because they were hungry, but because they enjoyed the thrill of it. In most cases, they fed the stolen goods to pigs. His poor work ethic in school brought reprimands and even beatings, but Augustine didn't care. He was a rebel, a delinquent, a young man addicted to fun and pleasure.

Then came an opportunity to study in Carthage. Carthage was a much larger city than Augustine's small community of Tagaste, and he was ready to leave behind small town life for the "city lights." Once out of his Christian mother's reach and care, Augustine did what many young people do when initially freed from the restrictions of home life: he partied. While still in his teen years, Augustine took a lover and became a father. Marrying the woman was out of the question, as this would damage his future career.

While he was indulging his passions, Augustine also developed a love for philosophy and rhetoric. His past actions troubled him, and now on his own, free to do whatever he chose, he began to reflect on his life choices. Perhaps he was growing up, or perhaps having a child of his own sobered him. Regardless, he set aside some of the frivolity that had consumed him. His intellect grew hungry. Where once he had to be punished and beaten to learn, he now did so because of his growing love of knowledge. The fervent prayers of his mother were also certainly a factor in the changes taking place in Augustine's life. She prayed for him constantly and her greatest desire was to see him commit to Christ.

Yet Augustine was not a converted man. He wanted nothing to do with his mother's faith. To him Christianity was the religion of the uneducated and simpleminded. But despite Augustine's resolute pursuit of his education and apparent disdain of his mother's faith, he was profoundly unhappy. He had freedom. He had a mistress.

He had his learning, and he was gaining a following of students. Still, he was unhappy. Worse. He was miserable and had no idea how to fix himself. It was a struggle he'd endure for years, even as he maintained a successful vocation as a teacher in Carthage, then Rome, and then Milan.

Unhappiness, although unpleasant, can lead to something beneficial. Augustine had what he wanted, but it wasn't enough. Guilt dogged his steps. He sought truth, and although he had mastered the great philosophers and the demanding art of rhetoric, there remained a hole in his life. He was a man who didn't like to be controlled, something he certainly proved in his teen years, but he was honest enough to acknowledge that he was a captive—not to a person but to his own lusts and passions. He was a man at war with himself. This idea of the good waging war with the bad drew him to a doctrinally twisted offshoot of Christianity: Manichaeism. Founded by a man named Mani, this belief system saw everything as distinctly black and white, light and dark. This resonated with Augustine. He longed for the light but sensed his soul was in the dark. Augustine began raising questions about certain aspects of Manichaeism, and his fellow followers told him to wait for Faustus of Mileve (modern-day Algeria), who was the current leader of the movement. He did, but he was disappointed in the man's answers. Faustus and Manichaeism didn't measure up to Augustine's intellectual expectations, and ultimately failed to answer the deep yearnings within him for truth. Augustine would eventually write a treatise against Manichaeism, exposing it for the faulty religion that it was.

Manichaeism had failed to help. And philosophy, as much as Augustine loved it, didn't satisfy his deep hunger. So he continued his search. He traveled to Rome to teach, and eventually found his way to Milan. There, he met a man of powerful reputation: Ambrose.

Ambrose was renowned for being an excellent speaker, and as a lifelong student of rhetoric, Augustine wanted to see if the man was everything he was reputed to be. He was. In Ambrose, Augustine found a man in whom Christianity and supreme intelligence lived in peace. Ambrose proved that Christianity was not only compatible with intelligence and learning but complemented them.

However, Augustine was not a quick convert. He still had powerful passions that drove him. In his book *Confessions* he admits to a youthful prayer, "Give me chastity and continence—but not yet."[1]

There was also another influence in his life: Christian monks. The monks had given up all their worldly possessions and surrendered normal life with wives and family for the monastery or, in some cases, for living in isolation in desolate places like the desert. How could monks, many uneducated in Augustine's view, show so much discipline and self-control when he was a puppet of his own desires?

A Child's Voice

In 386, Augustine was in another wrestling match with himself. He paced the garden outside his home, grappling with a nagging spiritual need. Internal struggles can be as vicious as physical ones. Augustine knew this. He was not a man just walking the garden and "thinking things through." He was deep in an emotional and spiritual quagmire. As he fought through the despair and the agony, he heard a child's voice: "Take up and read. Take up and read." It was songlike. He assumed it came from the neighbors, but was unable to tell if it was the voice of a young boy or girl. Regardless of the source, Augustine saw it as a direct message from God.

Nearby was a copy of Paul's epistle to the Romans. He opened it and his eyes fell on two verses: Romans 13:13–14.

> Let us behave properly as in the day, not in carousing and drunkenness, not in sexual promiscuity and sensuality, not in strife and jealousy. But put on the Lord Jesus Christ, and make no provision for the flesh in regard to its lusts.

The world receded from him and Augustine could only focus on Paul's words. These words, at this moment, struck him as if they were written just for him. "The instant I reached the end of the sentence, it seemed the light of peace was poured into my heart, and all shades of doubt faded away."[2]

The interplay of the garden setting, Augustine's inner turmoil and regrets for a misspent life, the singsong voice of a child chanting a simple line, and immediate access to just the right words at just the right time brought forth an immediate and permanent change in Augustine. He was, at that moment, made new in right relationship with Christ—a Christian.

Loss

Augustine's mother, Monica, had recently joined him in Milan. It was a different person who walked back into the house and told his mother about what had just happened. For Monica, the years of ceaseless prayers made on behalf of her son were answered. Augustine then withdrew from Milan to a villa in Cassiciacum with his mother, son, some students, and a few others, and stayed there for about seven months. It was in this villa that he prepared himself for his new Christian life. On Easter, Bishop Ambrose, the man who proved to Augustine that a Christian could be an intellectual, baptized Augustine and his son, Adeodatus.

In 387, Monica fell ill with a fever and died in Augustine's presence. She was fifty-six and he thirty-three. His record of her passing is heartrending:

> I closed her eyelids, and sorrow beyond measure filled my heart and would have overflowed in tears. But by a strong effort of will I had no tears.
>
> It was not fitting that her funeral should be conducted with moaning and weeping, for such is normal when death is seen as only misery or as the complete end of existence. But she had not died in misery, and death was not her end.
>
> Of the one fact we were certain by reason of her character, of the other by our Faith.[3]

After her death, Augustine and his son returned to Rome for a time. This was followed by travels to previous homes in Carthage and Tagaste. It was on one of his many trips that Augustine's personal world would be upended again. His son, just seventeen (the same age Augustine was when Adeodatus was born), died of unknown causes. Despite the tragic loss of his mother and son so close together, and despite dealing with his own debilitating illness, Augustine remained faithful.

Pressed into the Priesthood

He returned to North Africa and adopted a monastic life. In the city of Hippo, he attended services led by Bishop Valerius. On one such visit, the bishop preached a message laying out the church's need for priests. Augustine had no plans to be a part of the clergy, but the congregation had a different idea. They insisted he be ordained. The thought of this brought Augustine to tears. Still, he had no desire to be a priest. Yet, at age forty-three, and despite his initial resistance, Augustine found himself at the threshold of what would become thirty-three years of service as a priest of the church.

Soon after his ordination, at the request of Valerius, Augustine became the assistant bishop. When Valerius died, Augustine became the bishop of Hippo.

Augustine threw himself into the work, writing unceasingly, and preaching as often as twice a day, five days a week.

Augustine was tremendously influential in his years of service. He stood with one foot in the classical world of philosophy and the other in the changing world of the church. As a teacher he had debated heresies, but as a bishop he had to confront them. Much of his writing focused on defending right doctrine and challenging the teaching of several cult groups and unorthodox sects.

His first battle was with the Manichaeans, the group he had once been a part of. Manichaeans were similar to the Gnostics, dividing the world into light and dark, spiritual and physical. This sect taught that Jesus had no physical body (because physical was bad) and therefore did not die on the cross. To them God was neither omnipotent, nor fully Creator. These ideas contradicted the Bible.

Augustine also took a stand against the Donatists, who saw the church as filled with flawed priests and felt there should be a separate, pure church. The movement began almost a century before, when Emperor Diocletian persecuted the church and demanded, among other things, the burning of the Scriptures. Christians could avoid persecution by turning in Bibles. Some did, including some church leaders. After the persecution ended, some returned to their positions in the church, infuriating those who had suffered and lost loved ones to the persecution. It raised a theological problem. Could such flawed church leaders administer the sacraments? Augustine argued against the idea of a separate, pure church. He wasn't opposed to pursuing purity, but because perfection was not possible, he could not align with the notion of a "pure church." More importantly, he argued that God's blessing was not dependent on the priests' purity but on God's faithfulness. There would always be a mix of faithful and flawed priests. He drew on Jesus' parable of the wheat and tares. A tare is a plant that looks very much like wheat until it matures. In Jesus' day it was impossible to remove the tares without uprooting the wheat. The separation occurred only after the harvest. Augustine's point was simple: God will do the judging, not the Donatists.

Additional important doctrine was defined when Augustine faced off with Pelagius. Pelagius was a British monk who came to North Africa via Rome. Augustine took issue with Pelagius' belief that sin was not transmitted from Adam to all men and women. Pelagius believed that everyone sinned, but purely by choice. He denied a connection between sin and humankind's condition. He taught (and some still do) that a person could live a sinless life without the grace of God.

Augustine argued that original sin was passed from Adam to everyone, man needed the help of God to come to salvation (he felt that this was what happened to him in the garden in Milan), and no one came to faith unless God first called him. The Catholic Church would later declare Pelagius' teaching as heresy at the Council of Carthage (418), and it was denounced.

Augustine's Pen

Augustine faced much more than doctrinal turmoil. In 410, Alaric and his German Visigoths led forces against Rome. Overwhelmed, city officials asked for terms of surrender. Alaric wasn't shy: "All your gold; all your silver; all your German slaves." He and his men plundered the city but then, because he considered himself a Christian—belonging to a sect called Arianism—Alaric returned all valuables taken from churches. He died shortly after Rome fell. His army, however, continued to North Africa. The Visigoths would later take Augustine's beloved Hippo.

Many had fled Rome, traveling to North Africa and to Hippo. Augustine ministered to these displaced people the best he could. The most difficult task was answering a question they all asked. The pagan residents of Rome believed that the ancient gods were punishing them for allowing Christian emperors to rule and the church to thrive. It was more than an idle thought. Some called for a return to the gods who were worshiped when Rome was great.

Augustine decided to answer this prevailing and culturally relevant question, spending sixteen years in writing an answer in the form of the classic book *City of God*. He wanted Christians to understand that they now lived in the City of the World but would eternally live in the City of God. It was a tale of two cities, the one that awaits and the temporary one in which we all live. The book is one of the most beloved of all ancient literature and remains a reminder that this life is not the end of the story but only the beginning. He encouraged Christians not to dwell on what is but on the city that is to come. Augustine couldn't stop the Visigoths, but he could focus Christian minds on something greater than what they were losing.

Augustine penned other works, over one hundred books, five hundred sermons, and two hundred letters. Like many of the great church leaders, he changed the world of his time and the world to come through his writing.

Perhaps his best-known book is *Confessions*, which tells his life story and conversion. He wrote it as if penning a letter to God. If *Confessions* is his autobiography, then *Revisions* (*Retractions*) can be called his intellectual autobiography. In *Revisions* he reviews and corrects his earlier writings.

He also wrote books on doctrine, philosophy, biblical interpretation, and the history of heresies. Augustine filled the world of his day with his intellect, his presence, and his written words—words still read today.

Protestants are fond of Augustine because he emphasized the grace of God; Catholics love his support of the church and the sacraments.

Some of his teachings would later be abused, but that was through no fault of his own.

His life story is also an inspiration. His rebellious days, his constant search for truth, his misdeeds and his admission of them, his inner turmoil, and his struggles with his desires speak to many believers today, people who struggle with many of the same sins and compulsions. He was a fractured man made whole by Christ. He did not seek power, but when it was thrust upon him he was dedicated and passionate in fulfilling his duties.

16

POPE LEO I

The Pope Who Roared

(c. 400–461)

One is ashamed to say this, and yet one dares not be silent. You value the devils higher than the apostles.

Pope Leo I, sermon to the Romans, 455

The Cullinan diamond is considered the largest gem quality diamond ever discovered. It weighs in at over 3100 carats (over 600 grams). Several large diamonds were cut from the stone. Only after being cut by diamond experts could the Cullinan diamond begin to shine. This can be a fitting metaphor for the church. The contemporary church is like a cut diamond. Each cut diamond is unique. It shares some common characteristics of the original it came from but also has distinctions that set it apart. The problem with the church has been that in the process of such cutting, creating, and refining, there have been instances where shattering has occurred.

A man at the center of one of these "diamond cuttings" was Leo, the bishop of Rome. We know nothing of his early life. He just appears on history's stage. It is assumed that he had a noble birth in Tuscany. Beyond that, his early life is lost to us. His later work, however, is much better known. He would prove he was a talented man, able to preach mind-grabbing sermons, influence emperors, face down invading kings, prosecute heresy, and make theological arguments for his belief.

Emperor Valentian III sent Leo to Gaul to mediate a dispute. While there, Sixtus III died and Leo, although absent from Rome at the time, was elected to replace the bishop. And replace him he did.

Early in the church's history, bishops oversaw local congregations. Bishops of larger cities were considered more influential. As the church grew in size, and as more cities came under the influence of Christianity, more bishops were needed. At times they would gather to debate and refine a questionable bit of doctrine. Some bishops rose to prominence based on their scholarship, preaching, or administration, yet there remained a conviction that all bishops stood on an equal footing. Some, however, referred to the bishop of Rome as the "first among equals." Leo wasn't comfortable with that. To Leo, the bishop of Rome held a higher position than anyone else, and all other bishops should follow the leadership of the Roman Church.

Saving Rome

In 452, Attila the Hun had brought havoc to the Roman Empire and now threatened the city of Rome. A delegation from the city went to meet him—not a delegation of politicians, or rulers, or military leaders but of priests including Leo, the bishop of Rome. Bruce Shelley described it this way: "Man-to-man, the contest seemed unequal. On the one side, the law of conquest; on the other, the law of faith. On the one side, triumph over the wounded, the ravaged, the dying; on the other, submission to the divine mysteries of the church. A foreign king and a ruling pope."[1]

Behind Attila the Hun—"the scourge of God"—stood countless soldiers; next to Leo, a couple of priests. It was Daniel in the lions' den. Attila had left many dead in his wake. He was a man to be feared. While he could appear humble before invited guests, he had no qualms about putting people in their graves. A man of short stature, a broad chest, a large head, a thin graying beard, small eyes, and a flat nose, he may not have looked fierce, but any soldier who faced him knew otherwise.[2]

Had Leo come with an offer of surrender, there may have been less danger, but his mission was not that easy, nor his message that welcome. Leo faced the feared conqueror and made a simple request: "Go away." He spoke not as a military man but as the bishop of Rome, a spiritual man.

Attila's army had suffered from an onset of disease and a lack of food. Some historians believe the Hun was already thinking about leaving the city alone. Even so, Leo faced the man Roman soldiers feared and prevailed. Attila not only retreated from Rome, he left Italy entirely.

This remarkable act of bravery and conviction raised Leo's standing with the people and with secular leaders.

Three years later, he would have to do it again.

Saving Rome a Second Time

The glory days of Rome were long gone. Once it had ruled the world with shield and sword, but now it struggled to keep what little dignity it had. Outside forces like Attila plagued the Empire and its glorious city. Rome would endure a series of attacks over the centuries: in 410, 455, 546, 846, 1084, and 1527. In Leo's day, the Roman military was a shadow of its previous self. Once, no force could stand before them. Now they seemed unable to stand by themselves.

The Vandals, an east Germanic tribe, approached Rome in May of 455 to continue their practice of looting, pillaging, and murdering citizens. The Vandal king, Genseric, agreed to meet with Leo. Once again, the bishop had taken it upon himself to intercede on behalf of his city and people. Genseric and Leo were the same age: sixty-five. The Vandal leader moved with a limp, the result of a fall from a horse when he was young. Leo offered money and, perhaps sensing that he could not expect the king to give up the plunder, asked that the city and its citizens be spared. The Roman army could no longer be counted on. Even the emperor had been killed by one of his bodyguards and dragged into the streets, where he was torn to pieces. Leo's goal was to save the citizens and buildings.

Genseric nodded, then made a single statement: "Fourteen days of looting." He kept his word. The city was stripped of its wealth, although most of the churches were spared from plundering. Genseric also took senators and Empress Licinia Eudoxia and her daughters for ransom. He even took the gilded roof off the capital. When his ships were loaded, the Vandals left. Rome still stood. Most of the citizenry survived. All because Leo once again put faith against power.

A solemn thanksgiving ceremony was held but few attended. It would take some time for the fear to subside. At the service Leo was direct and pointed.

> One is ashamed to say this, and yet one dares not be silent. You value the devils higher than the apostles. Who has restored security to the city? Who has liberated, preserving it from massacre? Turn to the Lord, acknowledge the miracles he has manifestly wrought on our behalf, and describe our liberation not, as the goddesses do, to the influence of the stars but to the ineffable mercy of the Almighty, who has softened the rage of the barbarians.[3]

Once again, the people knew who had interceded on their behalf.

Peter and Leo

Leo had strong opinions about how ecclesiastical authority should trickle down to the churches. While many claimed the bishop of Rome held a special authority, Leo clearly stated the scriptural mandates justifying the church's authority:

1. Peter, when asked about who he believed Jesus to be, proclaimed, "You are the Christ, the Son of the living God" (Matt. 16:16), and received Jesus' blessing for his bold and accurate statement.

2. Jesus said he would build his church upon that statement and upon Peter, to whom he gave the keys to heaven and hell.

3. Jesus prayed for Peter: "Simon, Simon, look out! Satan has asked to sift you like wheat. But I have prayed for you that your faith may not fail. And you, when you have turned back, strengthen your brothers" (Luke 22:31).

4. Peter is seen as the chief of the apostles.

5. It was to Peter that Jesus said, "Feed my sheep" (John 21:17).

6. It was by God's direction that Peter ministered and died in Rome, and that his body was buried there.

According to Leo, authority was transferred from Peter to the bishop of Rome. All authority rested with the church, and the pope (*pope* comes from the Greek and Latin for "papa") was to lead the church. Whoever was not a part of the church in Rome was outside of the faith. To challenge the pope's authority was to court hell. Obedience to the pope was necessary for salvation.

He was successful in furthering this belief, but not everyone was so agreeable. In the end, the diamond fractured, with the head of the Eastern church in Constantinople seeing his power as equal to that of Leo's. Over time there would be other factions—factions that remain to this day. In the centuries ahead, the papacy would grow in power and the Roman church would expand around the world. It would do much good, but also be plagued by troubles from within. Groups would continue to split and new denominations would be born.

Leo shaped the church through his dedication to a pure doctrine, defending it from heresy, and by showing courage and strength born of faith when he faced Attila the Hun and later the Vandal king Genseric. His leadership and determination strengthened the authoritative posture of the Western church. Ultimately the idea of the supremacy of the Roman bishop would drive a wedge between East and West. But Leo's force of will and his stated beliefs have moved Roman Catholics, Eastern Catholics, Eastern Orthodox Churches, and Anglicans to venerate him through the ages.

17

THE VENERABLE BEDE

Changing the World with His Pen

(c. 673–735)

I really don't work night and day, but it is quite true that I do toil hard to reach a right judgment on all that I read.

Bede, in response to a letter from Acca of Hexham

There is a scene in the movie *Amadeus* that is difficult to forget. Wolfgang Amadeus Mozart is propped up in bed, dying. He is only thirty-five. Around the room candles cast a golden glow and flicker as if mimicking the fading life of the musician. Longtime nemesis Antonio Salieri has decided to help Mozart with the last parts of his *Requiem*. He jots down what Mozart says, barely able to keep up with the maestro's machine-gun delivery. Soon after, Mozart dies with the work unfinished.

Long before the great composer lived, another man would be faced with a similar situation. He was a British monk named Bede, a man of unique ability, gentle disposition, and relentless drive. Bede was to scholarly research and history what Mozart was to music. He was a master.

Born in northern England, seven-year-old Bede found himself in the care of monks, perhaps as an orphan. He lived with the monks of Wearmouth Abbey, eventually moving with them to a new monastery a short distance away. He seldom left the grounds and the few times he did it was to visit nearby friends. Bede would live the rest of his life behind the walls of that abbey.

His first teacher was the abbot, or head of the abbey, Benedict Biscop. Biscop was a nobleman who gave up everything to become a monk at the age of twenty-five. One thing he didn't surrender was his love of books. He often returned from his trips with new tomes and Bede wasted no time learning from them.

Bede loved to study Scripture, and learned Greek, Hebrew, and Latin. He was not just a scholar with a particular interest in history, but he was also a man of faith. Of the forty books Bede wrote, thirty-two of them deal with biblical matters. Considering this, it is somewhat odd that he is best remembered for his historical accounts.

Bede was ordained as a deacon at the age of nineteen. Usually a man could not be ordained to that office until he had reached age twenty-five. This was rare and is a testimony to the high regard he had earned. At the age of thirty, Bede was ordained as a priest. Each day he would carry out his duties as a monk: prayer, worship, teaching, and, in his case, study. He was so dedicated to his work that he turned down the opportunity to become abbot because its demands would take him away from what he considered his true calling.

"It has ever been my delight to learn or teach or write."[1] For some, deep study is boring and difficult. For Bede it was the purpose of his life. If the libraries of the day used the Dewey Decimal System, then Bede's books would be in at least seven categories. He wrote educational works for his students, expository works on the Scriptures, letters, sermons, poetry, biographies of the saints, and history. It was his work in the last category that had the greatest impact on the world and Christian community.

The Ecclesiastical History of England covers the span between 55 BC to 73 AD. Bede also made use of "BC" (before Christ) and "AD" (anno Domini, "year of our Lord"). Prior to this, there had been no formal, unified history of Britain. By creating this work, he recorded many stories and accounts that would otherwise have been lost. He researched and interviewed, and did so with the goal of finding the facts. He wanted real accounts, not fabricated stories. The heroes were not warriors, as was common in the oral histories of the day, but people of great faith. He consulted and cited over 140 sources. Much of what we know about the history of England during that time we know because of Bede's work.

To His Dying Breath

In 735, Bede grew ill. He sensed that his days were numbered. He had been working on a translation of the Gospel of John, translating it from Latin to English. As he felt his life slipping away, he pushed his pupil Cuthbert to write faster, fearing like Mozart did that he would die before the work was completed.

Some of his last words tell us much about the man.

> I have some little articles of value in my chest, such as pepper, napkins and incense: run quickly, and bring the priests of our monastery to me, that I may distribute among them the gifts which God has bestowed on me. The rich in this world are bent on giving gold and silver and other precious things. But I, in charity, would joyfully give my brothers what God has given me.[2]

He also said, "It is time that I returned to him who formed me out of nothing: I have lived long; my merciful judge well foresaw my life for me; the time of my dissolution draws nigh; for I desire to die and be with Christ."[3]

Bede finished his work. Back in his monastic cell, he knelt at his bed and began to sing the *Gloria Patri*: "Glory be to the Father, and to the Son, and to the Holy Spirit . . ."

His fellow monks found him dead on the floor of his room.

Bede lived in an age not known for great scholarship. Yet he undertook the monumental task of writing a history of the English church, and did so in a time when gathering accurate information was difficult. This he did, and his other works as well, as a gift to God and the world. He raised the level of religious scholarship in his day. And he introduced a concept we use without question today: BC and AD.

He, like a handful of others, believed that what had happened in the past mattered in the present. Much of what we know about the early English church, we know because of a monk living behind the walls of an abbey.

18

ANSELM

The Reluctant Archbishop

(1033–1109)

I believe that I may understand.

Anselm, *Proslogion I*

Three thousand years ago, King David wrote a psalm that states, "A fool has said in his heart, 'there is no God'" (Ps. 14:1). Atheism is not a new "religion." Not so long ago as David, another man wrote about the existence of God and did so with such clarity and logic that he could be considered the atheist's worst nightmare. His name was Anselm.

Anselm's life was punctuated with the word *no*. When he was fifteen, he wanted to join the local abbey in northern Italy, but Gundulf de Candia, his father, had other ideas. He wanted his son to go into politics, but Anselm wasn't so inclined. Not wanting to take his father's advice, he personally approached the abbot to plead his case. However, without Anselm's father's permission, the abbot would not allow Anselm to join the abbey.

Anselm didn't give up easily. He prayed about the matter, but not in the usual way. He prayed that he would become severely ill, hoping that the abbot would then feel compelled to take him in. He indeed became ill, but he endured his sickness outside the walls of the monastery.

He left home at last at the age of twenty-seven and spent several years traveling. In Normandy, he came upon the monastery at Bec. The abbot, Lanfranc, took him in and trained Anselm to become a monk. Within three years of Anselm arriving at Bec, Lanfranc was appointed archbishop of Canterbury, a significant church position across the English Channel.

Unwanted Recognition

There's a problem with being very good at what you do: you get promoted. Soon after Lanfranc left Bec, Anselm was given his role as abbot. Under his leadership, the abbey gained a reputation for scholarship. Still, Anselm appeared to resent the time he had to spend on administration, which deprived him of opportunities to study. He asked his bishop to relieve him of some of his pressing duties as abbot, but instead of being granted relief, he was told that he should prepare himself for greater work. That greater work came in 1093, when he was appointed archbishop of Canterbury.

It was not an easy appointment. King William II of England didn't want Anselm, and Anselm didn't want Canterbury. Both men were happy to keep their distance from one another. But several years passed and William became extremely ill. Not wanting to die in his sin, he tried to make amends for some of his behavior by installing Anselm as archbishop. Anselm believed his age, health, and disposition would keep him from being a good archbishop and so resisted the appointment. However, William insisted and, at that time, it was his decision to make. Anselm had little choice but to relent, but in his acceptance he put forth three conditions: King William had to return land taken from the church; he had to acknowledge the authority of Pope Urban II, with whom he had been at odds; and he had to accept Anselm's spiritual authority. Those requirements were accepted by the king.

Anselm would live out his days in the position, and be buried on the church grounds in 1109.

Contributions

Anselm's two greatest contributions during his long ministry have endured through the centuries. First, while still at the abbey in Bec, he developed what has come to be known as the "ontological argument." His goal was to prove the existence of God. Anselm's approach is highly philosophical and a tad difficult to comprehend for those not trained in philosophy. The heart of the ontological argument is that God is the greatest being we can conceive; we can't conceive of a being greater. In Anselm's worldview, that meant there must therefore be a God in reality. In our age, which depends upon evidence rather than arguments of logic, this sounds a tad iffy. Still, it had a great influence on theology for years.

Anselm's other great contribution is the theological proclamation that Jesus, as God in the flesh, did for humankind what it could not do for itself. During the early centuries of the church a view of the atonement—the reconciling of humanity with God—called the "ransom" view was the accepted doctrine. This view taught that when Adam and Eve sinned, all humankind became Satan's hostage. When Jesus came and died on the cross, he ransomed us from the dominion of Satan. So, Jesus' death paid the price for our freedom from Satan—a ransom.

Anselm believed this view to be wrong. Satan wasn't owed anything by God. Sin offended God, not Satan. God was loving but it was also his nature to be just. In *Why God Became Man*, Anselm argued that Christ's death was not a payment of ransom to Satan but rather a way of satisfying God's perfect and just nature. People lacked the ability to do anything to be forgiven, so Jesus did for them what they could not do for themselves. Of course, in Christian thinking, Jesus is God in the flesh. "No one," said Anselm, "but the God-man can make the satisfaction (sacrifice) by which man is saved."[1]

Nearing death, Anselm told his monks that he was ready to leave this life. He just wanted to do one more thing: address Augustine's questions about the soul's origin. He could not think of anyone else who could do the work. But it was not to be. He died only a few days later.

History is often changed by war, by disaster, or by great discoveries, but sometimes it is changed in quiet ways, by men who shun the power and trappings of politics or powerful business. Anselm's revolution was one of the mind, of Christian thinking. Anselm made a contribution to the defense of God's existence and to our understanding of the achievement made on the cross. Most contemporary Christians may not understand Anselm's ontological argument, but most do understand that Christ died to pay for humankind's sin, a payment made to God.

19

FRANCIS OF ASSISI

Simple Faith

(1183–1226)

I have done my duty, may Christ teach you yours.

The last words of Francis of Assisi, recorded
by his biographer, Bonaventure

In the late 1960s the hippie movement was in full swing. A segment of this group, especially those in the San Francisco Bay Area, were called "flower children." They were easily identified by the flowers in their hair and the clothing they wore. These young people had turned their back on the hustle and bustle of the world to live a simpler life. There have been many such movements in history, where groups of people separated themselves from a society that they felt had lost its way. Historically, most of these groups were interested in finding new ways to satisfy their base wants and needs.

Approximately eight hundred years ago, someone else decided to drop out of society and forge a new way of living, but what he did and why stands in stark contrast to the hippies of the '60s or any number of other radical movements through the ages.

Giovanni Bernardone was born to a wealthy family in a small town eighty-five miles north of Rome. Today we call him Francis of Assisi, and he is, without argument, one of the more intriguing figures in church history. Several movies have been made about his life and an equal number of classical music pieces are associated with him, including work by Franz Liszt. Scores of books and many more articles have been written about him as well. What is particularly ironic about his fame is that he was the kind of man who abhorred such attention. He dropped out of society, leaving behind his inheritance and a father who disowned him, not to seek personal pleasure but to serve God in the most humble of ways.

Francis was not always self-sacrificing. His father's wealth provided young Francis the means to pursue with abandon all the pleasures he coveted. And his father, Pietro Bernardone, hoped his son would one day be knighted. When Assisi went to war with another city-state, Perugia, Francis signed up. He was twenty years old when he, in knightly array, marched off to war.

Whatever glory he imagined war contained was lost when he was captured and held prisoner—an imprisonment that lasted a year while his father struggled to raise ransom money. When peace returned, Francis was released but returned home very ill, perhaps from a fever he had endured during his imprisonment. His illness was lengthy and recurrent.

During his recovery, Francis questioned the meaning of his life and its purpose. As time passed he became more earnest in his search for meaning and direction. It was a slow transformation, but his self-questioning led to prayer and meditation. During this time he began to experience dreams and visions. One such dream came as he undertook another stab at a military career in 1205. In his dream, he traveled with a knight headed to Apulia to join papal forces there. He saw a hall with armor hanging on the walls. All the armor bore the emblem of the cross. A voice in the dream said, "These are for you and your soldiers." This he took to mean he would become a great soldier, and began his journey to Apulia to join a battle, but his progress was stopped in Spoleto by another illness—and another dream, one he could not misunderstand.

"Francis, Francis!" the voice said. "Who can bring you further, the Lord or his servant, the rich man or the beggar?"

"Why, the Lord, the rich man, to be sure," he answered.

"Then why are you following the servant instead of the master, the beggar rather than the Lord, your God? The saddles and weapons of last night's dream are for a spiritual battle, not an earthly one."

Still asleep, Francis pleaded, "Then, Lord, tell me what the battle is. What is it you want me to do?"

"Return to Assisi at dawn, and there it will be revealed to you what you are to do."[1]

This dream changed his direction and his life.

With the goal of being a well-known knight behind him, Francis began giving to the poor and searching for God's will. His gradual transformation took a long step forward when he faced one of his greatest fears: lepers. The sight and smell of lepers had always unhinged him, and he went out of his way to keep his distance. He would not give money to a begging leper unless someone else handled the exchange for him.

While traveling outside his city, he came across a leper. Although his first reaction was to look the other way, he did something few others would. Seeing, perhaps for the first time, the person behind the disease, he dismounted his horse, stepped close, knelt, and kissed the diseased skin. Francis would later clean the wounds of many lepers as part of his ministry.

That same year another formative event took place in a small, rundown chapel in San Damiano near Assisi. While in prayer, Francis heard the voice of Jesus speaking from a crucifix in the church. "Francis, repair my church which you see is decaying." The voice repeated the command three times.

Francis took this to mean that Jesus wanted him to repair the church building where he'd been praying. He was happy to do so. Unfortunately, the task would require materials, so he sold some of the family goods to fund the repairs—without permission. His father was furious. A confrontation took place in front of the bishop of Assisi. Francis decided it was time to break ranks with the family. He disrobed, folded his fine clothing, set it on the floor, then walked away from the building.

Embracing Poverty

From that day in 1206, Francis would spend the rest of his life in poverty—by choice. He had come to believe it was the duty of the Christian to care for those less fortunate. His way of accomplishing this was to give away everything he had. He donned the robe of the poverty-stricken and used a rope taken from a scarecrow as his belt. He begged for food—not just for himself but for others too.

Francis' greatest shame was encountering someone poorer than he. His approach to ministry was in stark contrast to what was common for the day. Most monks lived in monasteries with walls between them and the outside world. As we've seen, some of them achieved remarkable scholastic and intellectual accomplishments, but Francis was of a different mind. He believed the monk's work should be on the outside of the abbey, where the people were, where they could see with their own eyes and touch with their own hands the pain and the poverty of the land. To do this Francis took poverty upon himself.

It would seem that, given the hardships and sacrifice, few would follow him, but that assumption would be wrong. Francis never set out to create a new order of ministers. His goal was to live a solitary life helping the disadvantaged and repairing churches. Still, others were moved by his dedication to living life as described by Jesus in the Sermon on the Mount. The life Francis chose was severe and filled with pain, but by all appearances it gave him joy. He found satisfaction simply by being in nature. He preached to the animals, speaking to them as if they understood every word.

"Brother birds," he once said, "you ought to love and praise your Creator very much. He has given you feathers for clothing, wings for flying, and all things that can be of use to you. You have neither to sow, nor reap, and yet he takes care of you."[2] In some ways he was the first flower child, but one with a heavenly view. He presented a simple gospel but always included the need for repentance, something he never watered down. To Francis the greatest preaching a man could do was live a simple, godly life.

Francis didn't set out to create a movement or establish a religious order. His goal was to live the way Jesus did, moving from place to place; performing acts of compassion, kindness, and grace; preaching a very simple gospel; and meeting the needs of the poor and disenfranchised. Soon, Francis had followers. Eleven men joined him, selling what they had, embracing poverty, leaving behind a normal life for the hardship of an itinerate, missionary existence.

Francis had no desire to leave the Roman Church. He had not trained as a priest. He was a merchant's son and little more. For Francis to be comfortable with the addition of others to his group, he needed the approval of the church. He wrote a simple set of "Rules," guidelines used by religious groups in the church dictating their mission and motivation. Francis based his Rules on three passages of Scripture, all dealing with the sacrifice of material goods. Francis took these verses in the most literal sense and made them the game plan for his life.

> Then Jesus said to His disciples, "If anyone wishes to come after Me, he must deny himself, and take up his cross and follow Me. For whoever wishes to save his life will lose it; but whoever loses his life for My sake will find it. For what will it profit a man if he gains the whole world and forfeits his soul? Or what will a man give in exchange for his soul?" (Matt. 16:24–26)

> And someone came to [Jesus] and said, "Teacher, what good thing shall I do that I may obtain eternal life?" And He said to him, "Why are you asking Me about what is good? There is only One who is good; but if you wish to enter into life, keep the commandments." Then he said to Him, "Which ones?" And Jesus said, "You shall not commit murder; you shall not commit adultery; you shall not steal; you shall not bear false witness; honor your father and mother; and you shall love your neighbor as yourself." The young man said to Him, "All these things I have kept; what am I still lacking?" Jesus said to him, "If you wish to be complete, go and sell your possessions and give to the poor, and you will have treasure in heaven; and come, follow Me." But when the young man heard this statement, he went away grieving; for he was one who owned much property. (Matt. 19:16–22)

> And [Jesus] said to them, "Take nothing for your journey, neither a staff, nor a bag, nor bread, nor money; and do not even have two

tunics apiece. Whatever house you enter, stay there until you leave that city." (Luke 9:3–4)

These verses were revolutionary to Francis and exerted such a hold on him that he walked away from everything—things others longed to have—and into the world fully dependent upon God and the kindness of others. Those who wished to be part of his group had to make the same commitment.

The twelve men arrived in Rome to seek the blessing of Pope Innocent III, to whom Francis presented his followers and their Rules. When the pope heard the request, he decided to test Francis' sincerity. "Go, Brother, to the pigs to whom you are more fit to be compared than to men and roll with them, and to them preach the rules you have so ably set forth."[3]

Francis did as he was told, and when he returned, Innocent III gave his blessing to the group. The movement we now call the Franciscans was born. Soon, two other Franciscan groups formed, including one for women. A young girl named Clare, just sixteen, heard Francis preach and was drawn to the message and the lifestyle. Two years later, in 1212, she and Francis were granted permission to form an order for women. The group became known as the Poor Clares.

A third group arose for those who, because of family or business ties, could not leave their homes or work. They took the same vows and supported the work of others. These were the Tertiaries—the "third order."

Francis had left home in 1206; twelve years later he had as many as three thousand followers. His message and lifestyle offered something very different than what people witnessed in typical church life. Francis didn't just speak of Christ's life, he reflected it.

Many of these followers, or "Minor Brothers" (Friars Minor), traveled as missionaries. Years after Francis' death, the missionary monk John De Monte Corvino traveled to China. By 1300 he had baptized thousands and had seen thirty thousand conversions.

Francis' approach to spiritual service differed from what was practiced in his day in yet another way. Many monks, as we have seen, spent their lives in academic pursuits and study. They made significant contributions to the growth of the church through their writing, but Francis was a creature of a different stripe. He was dubious about learning. He considered himself untaught, an *idiota*. He did not consider himself stupid, just uneducated compared to the scholastic monks.

He had reservations about too much learning. He feared that too much focus on books would take the eyes of spiritual leaders away from the needy. He never lost sight of the painful lives others lived. He would rather walk from place to place and live on donated bread and water while ministering to lepers than spend his days stooped over books and ancient texts. Prior to the work of Francis, the poor had largely been overlooked in the ministry of the church. Francis brought their needs for spiritual and physical help back to the forefront of faith practice.

Francis' life, in many ways, is the stuff of legend. Accounts of his life are rife with miracles, humility, sacrifice, and amazing encounters. One of his biographers tells of an event in Spoleto, Italy, where Francis met a man with a face deformed by cancer. The man tried to throw himself at Francis' feet but the monk wouldn't allow it. Instead, he took the man's face in his hands and kissed him on both cheeks. The man was healed.

Another account goes a long way in supporting the idea that Francis and nature were closely tied. A vicious wolf had been terrorizing the Italian town of Gubbio, leaving people fearful to leave their homes. One day, Francis encountered the snarling wolf, which charged him with jaws snapping. Unexpectedly and suddenly, the beast came to a stop, ceased his attack, and lay at Francis' feet. Francis spoke to the animal. "Brother Wolf, in the name of Jesus Christ, I command you to do no evil to me or to any man." It is said the wolf lowered his head in agreement.

Of all the strange events surrounding Francis, none is so remarkable as the stigmata he endured toward the end of his life. In 1224, on Mount Penna, while in prayer and fasting, he had another vision: an image of Christ nailed to the cross. When the vision ended, he felt pain in his hands, feet, and side. He was bleeding. The term *stigmata* is based on the Greek word *stigma*, which refers to a mark, like a dot made by the point of a pen. Later, stigma came to mean a mark associated with some particular event and is often used in a negative way. Stigmata refers to marks on the human body that correspond to the wounds of Christ on the cross: pierced hands, pierced feet, and a spear wound in the side. Francis came out of the vision bleeding as if he had been crucified. In many Christian circles this is taken as a sign of deep religious fervor and a desire to suffer as Christ did. Francis fit that description.

Latter Years

Francis' health declined through the years. The stigmata was painful and a life of hardship and poverty had taken its toll. Eventually, he went blind. Not long before he died, he wrote *The Canticle of Brother Sun*, again showing his love for God's creation. "Be praised, my Lord, through our Sister Bodily Death, from whose embrace no living person can escape."[4]

Two years later, Francis of Assisi, worn by a long, hard life of service to others, died singing to his Lord. Francis is not remembered as a great thinker or theologian; he was, however, a great doer. He was not a scholar, he was a champion of the poor. When he was a young man he busied himself having fun and dreaming of exploits as a knight, but everything changed after his imprisonment, illness, and subsequent personal calling from God. Respect came his way, but not as he planned. By the end of his life, he was respected, revered, and so loved that he was canonized as a saint in two years, unusually fast for the Roman Catholic Church of the day. Francis became known as St. Francis of Assisi, leaving behind an altered church and a society open to helping the needy.

Francis is often pictured with birds and other wildlife. His love of creation was genuine, but his love for those in need was greater. Francis is a reminder of how Christ lived and worked.

20

THOMAS AQUINAS
The Not-So-Dumb Ox

(1225–1274)

Reginald, I cannot, because all that I have written seems like straw to me.

Thomas Aquinas, in response to Reginald
of Piperno's urgent request he return to work

During our school days, we all saw the poor souls who were so different from other students face constant ridicule. Maybe they stood out because they were smarter, more dedicated, shorter, awkward, socially inept, or just looked or sounded different. For many of them the daily grind of school was an unending chain of ridicule. Every generation has a percentage of people who serve as targets for the mockery of others. Some would go on to achieve great things; others would drop out.

Some may not have fit in during their school years but blossomed in their adult years. I went to school with several such people. One was hopelessly awkward, and he endured more emotional hardship than anyone his age should have to. Another of my classmates cared little what others thought. He had a gift for the sciences, and spent some of

120

his nonschool hours working at a prestigious cancer research department of a nearby medical school. In his adult years he has dedicated his time and efforts in the fight against diseases such as diabetes.

The Tough Beginning

Around 1225, in the family castle in Lombardy, in the kingdom of Naples, a noble Italian family welcomed the birth of their ninth child, a son. His father, Landulf, the count of Aquino and his mother, Theodora, the countess of Teano, named him Thomas.

Even as a child Thomas Aquinas showed a devout nature, and so his family sent him to school at a nearby abbey. He would go from there to study at the finest schools of his day. Those days were not easy. At the University of Naples, his fellow students called Aquinas "the dumb ox," most likely because of his physical heft, his less than handsome appearance, and his quiet, taciturn nature. Although he might have appeared as a dumb ox to his classmates, he was not. He had a keen intellect, a dedication to study, the ability to think in the abstract, and the ability to formulate answers to complex questions. His teacher, Dominican monk Albertus Magnus, predicted the young man would change the world: "We call this young man a dumb ox, but his bellowing in doctrine will one day resound throughout the world."[1] This echoes a statement made by a "holy hermit" before Thomas' birth: "He will enter the Order of Friars Preachers, and so great will be his learning and sanctity that in his day no one will be found to equal him."[2]

Albertus Magnus so impressed Aquinas that he decided he too would join the ranks of the Dominicans, but despite the pre-birth prediction of the holy hermit, his parents did not share Aquinas' spiritual enthusiasm. Monks lived a harsh life and took a vow of poverty, something his parents, people of nobility, did not want to see their son endure. They tried to persuade him to seek positions in the church that provided greater comfort and more esteem. They even offered to buy him the position of archbishop of Naples, but Thomas had no interest in this and remained determined to become a Dominican monk. His parents, apparently out of desperation, had him kidnapped and held him against his will for well over a year. In addition to this unorthodox act, they even went so far as to tempt

121

him with a prostitute in hopes that he would leave behind the idea of being a monk. Their efforts failed. Thomas Aquinas, in spite of the wiles of his parents, would become a Dominican monk.

An Old Philosophy Made New

Aristotle, the ancient Greek philosopher, lived fifteen hundred years before Thomas Aquinas. While his work was well-known in some parts of the world, much of it had been lost in Europe. When the thinking of Aristotle was reintroduced, it made a splash. Thinkers of every kind studied the old philosopher. Thomas Aquinas was one of them.

In the church of that day, however, ancient philosophies that emphasized reason and observation were not well-received. Aquinas did not let that stop him. He made it his goal to understand Aristotle and to see how much of the philosopher's thinking could be applied to Christianity and what should be dismissed. His ruminations would lead to one of the most famous writings in church history: the *Summa Theologica*—summary of theology. Although he wrote other material, this book is by far his best known.

"In sacred theology, all things are treated from the standpoint of God," Thomas states in the beginning of his work, thus establishing his Christian approach. The book is structured into three parts (Part I: Theology, Part II: Ethics, Part III: Christ) and contains 3000 articles, 38 tracts, 631 questions, and 10,000 objections and answers. Thomas introduces each subject with a question, raises objections that others had voiced or might bring up, and replies to those objections.

It was a monumental work. One recent translation runs five volumes and more than three thousand pages. Impressive as that is, it is even more stunning to realize that the work is unfinished. Thomas died in 1274, leaving the work he had spent the last nine years composing incomplete.

Reason and Revelation

Thomas was a controversial scholar, and his use of a pagan philosopher in his reasoning created a few enemies. Thomas made no attempt to show human philosophy as greater than the Bible. Quite the contrary. He did, however, acknowledge that human reason was useful. Thomas' scales had reason on one side and revelation on the other. To him, the two were complementary.

Reason, he argued, could lead a person to a belief in God but lacked the ability to provide the details necessary for the person to act on that faith. A person might see the endless universe and realize a Creator must be involved. From such observations, generalizations could be made, but those concepts lacked sufficient detail to paint a full picture. For that, one needed revelation. Revelation is the act of God whereby he reveals what would otherwise be unknown.

Today, theologians speak of "general" (sometimes called "natural" revelation) and "specific" revelation (sometimes called "special" revelation). General revelation describes how God is revealed through observation of nature; specific revelation is the information God made available through the Bible, prophecy, and Christ. General revelation might suggest that there is a God who loves us, but specific revelation is needed for us to know it as a fact (John 3:16, for example) and to see how that love was displayed through Christ. Reason is limited to sensory knowledge, what we learn by observation; revelation is detailed and personal. Reason is good, Thomas believed, but revelation was necessary. Understanding always came back to God. His teaching on reason versus revelation is appreciated by Protestants and Catholics alike.

First Cause

Thomas also offered five arguments for the existence of God. He called them "ways." Three of the "ways" are forms of the cosmological argument, a reasoning based on Aristotle's belief that every effect has a cause, and that cause has a cause, and that cause has a cause, and so on until we reach the First Cause—God—who started everything. Another one of his "ways" is now called the "teleological argument." Although *teleology* might not be a familiar word, the concept is simple: if we see a design, then there must be a designer. The interstate freeway system did not come about by accident or a confluence of coincidence. Someone conceived of the system of roads and designs were made. Thomas saw design in the universe as well as concepts unique to humanity (beauty, truth), and said those things could only come about if there is a God.

Thomas Aquinas was Roman Catholic through and through. He believed the church was a channel of salvation, and salvation could not be had apart from the church. Although many of the concepts of the Roman Church came about before Thomas' day, his writings gave them greater weight and would become some of the hallmarks of the world's largest church.

Purgatory was one concept Thomas defended. He believed that those who are evil went straight to hell after death, while the godly went to heaven and less dedicated believers went to purgatory. *Purgatory* comes from a Latin word meaning "purifying." It was believed (and still is in the Roman Catholic Church) that the bulk of the deceased, who are not holy enough for immediate entry into heaven, pay for their sins in purgatory until such time that they can be received into the joys of heaven. He went even further in this thinking by teaching that the living could pray for the dead and those prayers would be beneficial to those being purified. In other words, the church's influence could impact the souls of the dead. Purgatory is a doctrine rejected by Protestants and similar groups who find no evidence for it in the Bible.

Thomas also defended the sacraments as having the power to impart grace to the participant—that is, to help maintain salvation. He believed in the seven sacraments: baptism, confirmation, Eucharist (Lord's Supper), extreme unction, marriage, penance, and ordination. Perhaps the most significant of these is the Eucharist. For Catholics then and now, the Eucharist is very special and miraculous. Thomas taught "transubstantiation," a belief that the elements of the Lord's Supper changed physically from wine and bread to the blood and flesh of Christ. Again, this is an idea Protestants reject.

Thomas defended the supremacy of the pope, salvation through the church alone, and grace received through the other sacraments.

All of this makes what Thomas Aquinas represents a conflicting bundle of ideas for Protestants, who appreciate his powerful arguments for the existence of God but who can't accept his ideas about salvation through the church, purgatory, and transubstantiation.

124

To Roman Catholics, however, he is one of the great teachers of the church.

Unfinished Work

Thomas' work is central to the Roman Catholic Church, but he was not immediately elevated to the rare position of Doctor of the Church (*doctor* meaning "teacher"). Just thirty-three men hold that title, and getting on that list takes time. In Thomas' case it took 314 years.

His greatest work—the book he gave nearly a decade of labor to—was never finished. Thomas told those close to him that he had received a vision and saw things that caused him to consider all his work as "straw." He put down his pen and, despite the encouragement of others, refused to take it up again. The *Summa* sat incomplete. We don't know what Thomas saw in the vision, but whatever it was, it took the wind from his sails.

Three months later, he died. It was March 7, 1274. He was forty-nine years old. One church history sums up his life this way:

> The influence of Thomas Aquinas even today is profound and widespread: it is seen in theology, philosophy, ethics and in major issues facing government and other branches of society. The Christian of such a deep, broad, and lasting impact is a kind of thinker with the kind of vision that the church needs in every age.[3]

Whether we agree or disagree with certain aspects of his doctrine, one thing should be acknowledged: Thomas Aquinas must be numbered among those who shaped the church.

JOHN WYCLIFFE

The Protestant in Catholic Clothing

(c. 1320–1384)

I am ready to defend my convictions even unto death. . . . I have
followed the sacred Scriptures and the holy doctors.

John Wycliffe, *Protestatio*

Morning Star of the Reformation." That's what historians
call John Wycliffe: English priest, scholar, teacher, translator, and thorn in the side of popes and bishops. He had been such a
problem that anger against him boiled for years after his death. At
the order of church leaders, his bones were dug up, removed from
the grave, burned, and the ashes scattered on the river Swift—four
decades after his death.

What could one man, a priest, do to deserve such treatment? In
the fourteenth century, the Roman Church was powerful and ever-
present. In many countries, it was joined at the hip with governing
officials. The church had come a long way from its first days in Jerusalem and the years it spent under persecution. By Wycliffe's time, the
roles had been reversed. What had once been an organization under
attack was now itself waging war against those who disagreed with

it. Wycliffe disagreed with many things taught in the organization that had ordained him.

We know nothing about his early years, and we can only guess at his year of birth. He was born on a sheep farm about two hundred miles from London. We get our first glimpses of him at Oxford University. He left home in 1346 for the university but didn't earn his doctor's degree until 1372 due to delays in education caused by the bubonic plague that affected so much of Europe. Still, he made a name for himself and many considered him Oxford's finest theologian and philosopher.

Although he remained a Roman Catholic all his life, he had no reservations about criticizing the church on many key issues, all of which stemmed from his belief that the Bible should be the source of authority in a Christian's life. The church of his day taught that salvation came through it and the sacraments. Wycliffe didn't see it that way. He believed the Bible fully revealed the person and work of Christ and the instructions necessary for salvation and should, therefore, be available to all people, not just priests.

If he had confined his comments to this one issue, they may have been tolerated more, but Wycliffe had other ideas that were equally disturbing to the church. He denied the authority of the pope, he spoke out against the sale of indulgences (a way of purchasing a pass out of purgatory), he criticized church hierarchies, and he denied the claims of transubstantiation (the belief that the wine and bread of the Eucharist physically transform into the blood and body of Christ). These were commonly held tenets of faith, taught by the church for a long time. To debate or question these tenets was to call the Roman Church into question.

An Angry Church

Wycliffe also meddled in other affairs of the church. Rome was demanding financial support from England, but England was struggling with financing their ability to defend themselves from a possible attack by France. When consulted on the issue, Wycliffe advised John of Gaunt, Duke of Lancaster and one of the sons of King Edward III (and therefore a powerful figure in English government), to persuade

Parliament to say no to Rome's demands. Wycliffe said the church was rich enough and needed to be reminded that Jesus called his followers to poverty, not wealth. England needed what Rome demanded. In providing this advice, Wycliffe was not only calling into question doctrines of the Roman Church but was also questioning its need for and methods of financial support.

In 1377, Wycliffe was called from Oxford to London to stand before the bishop of London and answer charges leveled against him. He went, as did his protector John of Gaunt. One of the attendees described Wycliffe as, "A tall thin figure, covered with a long, light gown of black color . . . the head, adorned with the full flowing beard, exhibited features keen and sharply cut; the eye clear and penetrating; the lips firmly closed in token of resolution."[1] During the proceedings, an argument erupted over whether Wycliffe should be seated or remain standing. Chaos soon followed. John of Gaunt had to flee, and friends of Wycliffe had to spirit him away. A few months after this dustup in London, Pope Gregory XI issued five papal bulls (edicts) accusing Wycliffe of eighteen counts of heresy and wrongdoing. Wycliffe was dubbed, "The Master of Errors."

Wycliffe was dedicated to his beliefs and responded in his written *Protestatio*. "I am ready to defend my convictions even unto death. . . . I have followed the sacred Scriptures and the holy doctors."[2] Wycliffe believed the Bible to be the sole authority for the believer and the instrument to introduce the lost person to Christ. Everything else—councils, decrees, writings of the saints—was secondary.

"Neither the testimony of Augustine nor Jerome, nor any other saint should be accepted except in so far as it was based on Scripture."[3] This is a very Protestant belief.

Wycliffe also wrote:

> The New Testament is of full authority, and open to the understanding of simple men, as to the points that be most needful to salvation. . . . He that keepeth meekness and charity hath the true understanding and perfection of all Holy Writ [for] Christ did not write his laws on tablet, or on skins of animals, but in the hearts of men.[4]

"Mumblers"

Wycliffe so valued Scripture and so desired it be made available to everyone that he, with the support of other scholars, created the first English translation of the Bible derived from the Latin text. To help put the Bible in the hands of people, he recruited and sent out men he called "poor priests," individuals who wore simple robes, carried large staffs, walked the countryside barefoot, and preached the gospel. They also carried pages of the Wycliffe Bible and read from it so people could hear the Bible in their own language. What Wycliffe called "poor priests," detractors called Lollards—the name means "mumblers." The name stuck.

Wycliffe ultimately was a polarizing figure, seemingly with an equal number of supporters and detractors. He was "The Master of Errors" to some and "The Morning Star of the Reformation" to others. He was a reformer who worked within the church, but his efforts at reformation cost him his position at Oxford. He fought to make the Bible accessible and reintroduced the idea that Christ is all one needs for salvation.

In many ways, John Wycliffe was a Protestant in Roman Catholic clothing. Later, reformers would call upon his teaching to bolster their own claims. Wycliffe refocused the attention of the church on Jesus, promoted a simpler form of Christianity, one not clothed in riches or position, and was instrumental in providing an English translation of the Bible. For this, his body was exhumed and his remains burned, yet he lives on as an influential character in the shaping of the church.

22

NICOLAUS COPERNICUS
Amazing Résumé

(1473–1543)

O Lord, the faith thou didst give to St. Paul, I cannot ask; the mercy
thou didst show to St. Peter; I dare not ask: but Lord, the grace thou
didst show unto the dying robber, that, Lord, show to me.

Nicolaus Copernicus, his chosen epitaph

Nicolaus Copernicus is an ironic figure in history. Check almost any biography of him and he will be listed first as an astronomer. He was certainly that, but science was not his chosen profession. It can be argued that, although very important to him, astronomy was a hobby. So what then did one of the most famous men of science do? He was a clergyman. Although never ordained a priest, he spent his adult life as a canon in a cathedral where his uncle was bishop. As a canon he helped minister to the poor, guided the church, and did administrative work. It was a demanding occupation.

Copernicus was one of the most learned men of his day. He had an impressive educational résumé. He studied at Kraków University, Bologna University, the University of Padua, and the University of Ferrara. For a time, he lectured in math and astronomy in Rome.

130

He was a mathematician, an astronomer, a medical doctor, a lawyer (he took a doctorate in law), and much more. He was multilingual. He was the kind of man others called *genius*.

With his vast education, he could have chosen any of a number of careers. He could have been a physician in private practice, he could have lectured in the sciences at the best universities, he could have practiced law. Instead, he chose a life in the church.

All the Same to Him

Most of us compartmentalize our lives: work, family, entertainment, and social life. We might look at Copernicus' interests and say he was a man of many facets. True as that is, he did not distinguish between faith and science. In his words, "I regard my research as a loving duty to seek the truth in all things, insofar as God has granted."[1]

Working among the poor was his occupation; math, physics, and astronomy were his avocations. One amplified the other. When he looked to the stars and planets he saw the handiwork of God. He was a creationist in general and—using today's nomenclature—an advocate of intelligent design. Of course, in his day most people were. Yet he was a free thinker when it came to explaining the motion of the planets in the sky.

Most intellectuals of the day believed the earth was the center of the solar system (geocentric); Copernicus and others before him could only explain planetary motion if the sun was at the center (heliocentric). This went against the logic of the day. The earth was heavy and dense while stars and planets appeared as specks of light and so must therefore be lighter than the earth. How then could something less dense than earth be at the center?

There were other long-held ideas, theological ideas, that made a sun-centered solar system unbelievable. The general theological belief said man was the object of creation, therefore man must be the center of God's attention. His earth would not be placed in a subservient role to the sun. Such thinking, however, couldn't explain what was being observed. Convoluted and tortured math had to be used to explain the motion of the sun and stars in the sky. That was a problem for Copernicus, and he attacked it with math. He was able to explain most of the motions and prove his ideas with mathematics.

Copernicus preferred quietly going about his ministry. He wrote *On the Revolutions of the Heavenly Spheres (De Revolutionibus Orbium Coelestium)* but was reluctant to publish it. He knew attacks would come from all sides, and although he was willing to fight it out with other mathematicians who challenged his work, he was less willing to upset the church. The church feared such an idea might destroy the image of God as Creator. But the fact that the earth orbited the sun as did the other planets didn't bother Copernicus' theology, as "God is the Best and Most Orderly Workman of all."[2] He saw the system as a proof of creation, not as a threat.

Copernicus had to be convinced to publish his work, which he did shortly before his death. Someone, maybe the book's editor or publisher, wrote an anonymous preface stating the book did not teach an alternate view of the solar system, which, of course, it did. This was evidence of the fear of reprisal. Despite this preface, Copernicus' views were seen as harmful to the Roman Church, and his book remained on the Catholic *Index of Forbidden Books* for over two hundred years.

Copernicus, while not the first to suggest the sun-centered solar system, did give it credibility by proving many of the points with math rather than philosophical or theological arguments. In the end, his views did not undermine the concept of God the Creator. Many scientists believe that life could not exist on the earth if the solar system functioned in any way other than it does. Copernicus demonstrated by his lifetime of ministry that science and faith need not be enemies.

MARTIN LUTHER

Lightning Strikes Twice

(1483–1546)

> My situation was that, although an impeccable monk, I stood before God as a sinner troubled in conscience, and I had no confidence that my merit would assuage him.
>
> Martin Luther, preface to Latin writings, 1545

The copper miner's son walked a bleak path near Stotterheim in Germany. Overhead thick blankets of black clouds robbed the area of light. Wind blew and rain struck the face of this twenty-one-year-old like gravel. Thunder rattled the trees and shook the bones of anyone daring to be out on a day like this. Lightning cracked like cannon fire, and a bolt struck near the young man, knocking him to the ground. Terrified, he cried, "Help me, Saint Anne! I'll become a monk!" He survived the near strike, but the course of his life was changed from that moment on. He kept his promise to the saint of miners and two weeks later, Martin Luder, better known as Martin Luther, entered an Augustinian monastery.

Later, that same young man was in Rome on business for his monastery. He knelt on the first of twenty-eight marble steps that make up the *Scala Sancta*, the Holy Stairs. Tradition holds that the stairs were brought to Rome from Jerusalem by Saint Helena, mother of Constantine the Great, the famed collector of Christian artifacts. These stairs, it was believed, were the ones Jesus ascended to stand before Pontius Pilate. The young man ignored the pain the stone caused his knees. Bending forward, he kissed the tread before him, then—still kneeling—climbed the next step. Kiss, climb, kiss, climb. Twenty-eight times.

All Martin Luther ever wanted was to be loved by God. It would take years before he would recognize and embrace God's unmerited favor.

There are few people more famous than Martin Luther. This is especially true in church history. More books have been written about this German priest than any individual in the church other than Jesus. He takes up more pages in most church history texts than anyone else. Understandably. He not only shaped the church, he changed the entire Western world.

Brilliant monk, priest, university professor, writer, composer of hymns, theologian, preacher, but most of all, Reformer—Martin Luther rose from obscurity to take on the Roman Church he served for so many years.

Before Greatness

Martin Luther lived much of his life under two clouds: guilt and fear. His words and actions reveal a man who hated himself for his sin and feared the wrath of God. His early efforts as a monk and a priest were to atone for his sin. He fasted for days. He slept in the cold without a blanket. He prayed for hours. He stood in the snow for hours as penance. As much as the lightning bolt had frightened him as a young man, God terrified him far more.

Luther was miserable. The idea of God's pending wrath assaulted his mind and heart. He could find no hope for his soul. He confessed—as was part of the priestly life—his spiritual pains to one of his superiors. When encouraged to love God, he admitted to not only lacking love for God but also hating him.

He felt so sinful and unworthy that he could barely perform his first mass. He punished himself frequently, often whipping himself.

He abused himself in an attempt to gain God's forgiveness and never felt he obtained it. One wonders if a more miserable, self-hating man ever lived.

The Trip to Rome

Around 1510, his order sent Luther and another monk to Rome. While there he visited churches and relic sites, but he did not leave comforted by the power and prestige of the church. Just the opposite. He saw wealth, immoral priests, and a general lack of piety. Doubts about the church he served were born. Here he was, a man struggling to work for the salvation of his soul to appease an angry, vengeful God, and church leaders he observed lived in luxury and walked among churches of great splendor.

The Rome trip altered Luther's view of the church and its work. He kept his dissatisfaction to himself, where it ate away at his conscience and ultimately became the first crack in the foundation of respect he held for the church. Other insights would widen those cracks until the entire structure would fall.

Early Days

On November 10, 1483, Martin Luther was born to harsh parents. His father worked in mining and had a financial interest in several operations. He was a severe disciplinarian and could be cruel. He punished Martin by making him stand barefoot in the snow. His mother shared her husband's harsh parenting style. Luther once described being whipped by his mother until he bled—for stealing a nut.

Luther's father pressed his son to become a lawyer, and Martin had started down that path until the incident with a lightning bolt frightened him into a life of faithful service to the Lord. He told his father that he was giving up the study of law to become a monk, and over his father's objection, Luther began his spiritual journey. He had started college in 1501 at the age of nineteen. He excelled academically, showing a talent for learning and teaching. He earned his bachelor's and master's degrees in the shortest time allowed by the school. He was sent to teach a course at the new University at Wittenberg, and soon after continued his own education. He obtained a Doctorate of Theology and became a full-time professor at Wittenberg, teaching Bible. He prepared his courses with the same diligence he applied to the other areas of his life.

It was during such preparations that the teacher became his own student. While working on a series of lectures on the Psalms, Romans, and other epistles of Paul, he came across a verse that changed his thinking. Romans 1:16–17 (especially verse 17) struck at his mind and heart:

> For I am not ashamed of the gospel, for it is the power of God for salvation to everyone who believes, to the Jew first and also to the Greek. For in it the righteousness of God is revealed from faith to faith; as it is written, "But the righteous man shall live by faith."

That verse and others kept him awake at night. He pondered this over and over until, in the process, he came to understand that a man was saved not by good works but by faith. This idea in Martin Luther's day was not at all common, nor seen as orthodox. Salvation required faith, yes, but it was shown in good works and obedience to the Roman Church.

"Night and day I pondered until I saw the connection between the justice of God and the statement that the just shall live by faith. Then I grasped that the justice of God is the justice which through grace and sheer mercy God justifies us through faith. Thereupon I felt myself to be reborn and to have gone through open doors into paradise."[1]

This realization began an avalanche of understanding that caused Luther to challenge everything he believed about the church he served.

The implication of Luther's discovery was enormous. If salvation came through faith in Christ alone, the need for interceding priests was gone. Since the Word of God could provide everything a believer needed for spiritual life, there was no need for priests, monks, or the Mass, and no need to pray to saints for help. In Luther's mind, the Roman Church as it existed was not needed, was found wanting, and was crumbling.

No to Indulgences

Even in the fifteenth century, there were those who understood the selling power of a jingle. One such man was John Tetzel, a Dominican friar who had been appointed to preach a message of indulgences. Indulgences had become a popular way for the church to raise money. Tetzel would chant, "As soon as the coin in the coffer rings, the soul from purgatory springs."

Catchy, but Luther considered it immoral and unbiblical. Tetzel was raising money to help complete the Saint Peter's Basilica in Rome. He broadened the idea that a person could contribute money to the cause and thereby free a loved one from purgatory.

Luther was furious.

In what is considered one of the most famous and pivotal acts in all of history, Luther nailed a list of ninety-five theses (propositions) to the door of the Wittenberg church. It was October 31, 1517. The act in itself was not unusual, as many people used the door as a public bulletin board. It was a place where a scholar could invite debate, which was Luther's goal. He wanted to expose the truth about the danger and heresy of buying indulgences. He argued indulgences could not remove guilt, did not apply to purgatory, and were harmful because they gave the donor a false sense of security.

With that list, a nail, and a hammer, Martin Luther set in motion the Reformation.

In 1519, Luther was granted a debate with theologian John Eck, a debate that would last for eighteen days. They met in Leipzig. During the debate, Luther stated, "The Council may sometime err. Neither the church nor Pope can establish articles of faith. These must come from Scriptures."[2]

Luther had just attacked two of the church's sources of authority. The church of Luther's day drew its authority from Scripture, the pope, councils, and traditions. Luther was trying to knock some of those pillars down. His efforts met with angry opposition.

Through much agonizing thought, study, and meditation, he had come to the belief that salvation came through faith in Christ and Christ alone (*sola fide*: "by faith alone"). In addition, Luther stated that Scripture and Scripture alone set the standard for Christian behavior. Not the pope. Not a system òf cardinals. Not councils and synods. This became known as *sola scriptura*: "by Scripture alone."

More Than Indulgences

The church taught that its seven sacraments were channels of grace; that is, they brought additional salvation. This was unacceptable to a man who believed that salvation came through the work of Christ, not the work of the believer. A sacrament could only be valid, Luther argued, if it came directly from Christ. That left only two sacraments: baptism and the Lord's Supper. No sacramental system meant no priestly system was needed.

In an effort to further his cause, Luther presented his declarations to the people of Germany. Beginning in 1520, he wrote three pamphlets. *The Address to the German Nobility* took on the church hierarchy. *The Babylonian Captivity* criticized the sacramental system of the Roman Church. The third pamphlet, *The Freedom of the Christian Man*, argued for the priesthood of the believer, meaning that every believer was a priest, not just those ordained by Rome.

The pamphlets were widely read by both his supporters and his enemies. Luther had become a theological outlaw.

Pope Leo X had had enough. It was time for Luther to go. Because of the implications of Luther's ideas to the power structure of the Roman Church, Pope Leo X excommunicated him in June of 1520. He did so by issuing the papal bull *Exsurge Domine* ("Arise O Lord"). A papal bull is a document issued by the pope. "Bull" comes from the Latin *bulla*, which referred to the seal on the document. In the document, Leo likened Luther to a wild boar and listed forty-one of Luther's beliefs as false, offensive, seductive, repugnant, heretical, and scandalous. It took three months for the document to be placed in Luther's hands, but he had already heard what it contained. He was unshaken.

Luther was given two months to recant his heretical positions. He waited for the grace period to expire, then on December 10, 1520, he burned the document along with several books by Catholic theologians. Luther was fearless and not to be intimidated.

Emperor Charles V, all of twenty-one years of age, had the duty of "protecting" the church from danger and heresy. It was part of his oath. The young ruler summoned Luther to appear at the Diet of Worms (*diet* refers to a legislative assembly; Worms is a town in Germany). Having been promised safe passage, Luther appeared before the assembly in the spring of 1521, but refused to back away from his statements unless someone could prove from Scripture that he was wrong.

Here he made his famous statement that has been quoted for the past five hundred years: "My conscience is captive to the word of God. I will not recant anything, for to go against conscience is neither honest nor safe. God help me. Amen."[3]

Charles V was not moved. He said of Luther, "The devil in the habit of a monk has brought together ancient errors into one stinking puddle, and has invented new ones."

Stinking puddle or not, Luther stayed the course, but now he stood condemned by both church and state. Fearing for his safety, his friends smuggled Luther away and delivered him to Wartburg Castle, where he lived dressed as a nobleman and under the protection of Duke Frederick the Wise for nearly a year. The Diet had condemned Luther, and the subjects of the emperor were ordered to seize Luther and hand him over. It became illegal to read his books. Luther was no longer a monk, no longer a priest. He was a man in hiding. A theological fugitive. It's not difficult to imagine what would have happened to him if his friends and supporters had not kept him safe.

Luther did not waste his time while hidden away in Wartburg Castle. Believing the Bible should be available to anyone who could read, he undertook translating the Bible from the original languages into German. He finished the New Testament in six months. The Old Testament followed.

Charles V tried to crush the growing Lutheran movement but failed. Tired of skirmishes with Luther's supporters and many of the German princes, he forged an agreement between the church and the growing number of people aligned with Luther. Each prince could select Catholicism or Lutheranism for the area under their control. No other Reformer group would be allowed.

Lutheranism was now a state religion.

Luther's Tarnished Halo

In spite of his positive impact on the church, Luther was not without his warts. Even his most favorable biographers are at a loss to explain some of his statements and actions made in his later years. He could be cruel, disparaging of others, and often used language that could not be printed in a book like this. He spoke against Jews, railed against other Reformers, and was extremely critical of those who criticized him. Perhaps some of this can be explained by the rough treatment he endured at the hands of his parents. Or perhaps the many years he spent in fear of hell and judgment, and the countless times he punished himself for sins real and imagined, had left him emotionally compromised.

One of the most puzzling actions on his part involves the Peasant Revolt of 1525. Germany maintained a serf class system, with families laboring for their princes. Luther's writing said all men were equal in the eyes of God and peasants took that to heart. If they were equal before God, then didn't they deserve better treatment from their lords? Battle broke out, and when the peasants resorted to violence Luther encouraged German princes to use force to maintain the current order. They did, and some estimate that as many as one hundred thousand peasants died. Historian Bruce Shelley noted, "Luther's conservative political and economic views arose from his belief that the equality of all men before God applied to spiritual not secular matters."[4]

In short, Martin Luther was not a perfect man.

The beginning of the Reformation can be traced back to a copper miner's son who, in a moment of sheer terror, offered to serve God his whole life. Other Reformers had laid the tracks for significant change in the church, but when an angry monk hung a series of propositions on the door of Wittenberg disputing the selling of indulgences, true Reform was ignited. Martin Luther became the irresistible force striking the immovable object of the church. The shockwaves still reverberate today.

24

ULRICH ZWINGLI

Bible and Sword

(1484–1531)

> Whenever we give heed to the word, we acquire pure and clear knowledge of the will of God and are drawn to him by his Spirit and transformed into his likeness.
>
> Ulrich Zwingli, *Sixty-Seven Articles*

The Reformation spread over the Alps and poured into Switzerland where it found Ulrich Zwingli—a willing advocate and messenger.

Zwingli was born in Wildhause, Switzerland. His father was the village mayor. Zwingli chose a life in the church and attended school in Basel, Bern, and Vienna. He returned to Basel where he earned his bachelor's degree in 1504 and a master's degree in theology two years later. In 1506 he was ordained and served as a parish priest in Glarus.

Twice, in 1513 and 1515, he served as chaplain to Swiss mercenaries. Swiss soldiers were often dispatched to foreign armies as part of political pacts. The French, the pope, and the emperor all drew on Swiss soldiers. This meant young soldiers were being traded as a commodity. Zwingli abhorred the practice, but as chaplain he could at least provide spiritual guidance to the soldiers.

The Slow Awakening

Zwingli didn't set out to be a Reformer. Unlike Martin Luther, who as a monk feared God, death, and judgment, and routinely made himself suffer for his sins, Zwingli struggled with disenchantment.

Many priests in Zwingli's time knew very little about the Bible. They were taught many things through tradition, with an emphasis on earning salvation through good works. Biblical scholars like Luther discovered a different salvation doctrine than what had been taught them by their teachers. And so it was with Zwingli, who fell in love with the Bible, especially the New Testament in Greek.

He studied a copy of Erasmus' Greek New Testament. As he learned the Greek language and studied the New Testament, he began to see conflicts between what he had been taught and what the New Testament revealed. Many of the practices and devices of the Roman Catholic Church did not align with New Testament teachings. Zwingli came to believe that every church practice and doctrine had to be supported by the Word of God. If no support for a particular practice or doctrine could be found, it was to be set aside as unbiblical. This is one of the areas where he disagreed with Martin Luther. Luther was a biblicist too. It had been a study in Romans that led to his nailing the *Ninety-Five Theses* to the Wittenberg door. Yet, in some respects, Luther was a little more lax. Luther's approach was that if the Bible didn't prohibit it, then it was allowed. Zwingli, on the other hand, believed that if the Bible didn't allow it, it was to be avoided.

Migrating from Catholicism

On New Year's Day of 1519, the parish priest of Glarus became the pastor of Grossmünster, an important church in Zurich. That day he made a surprising announcement. Instead of preaching the prescribed lectionary provided by the Roman Catholic Church, he was going to deliver a series of sermons from the Gospel of Matthew. This was an act of defiance. Zwingli wanted his congregation to hear the Word of God from the Bible itself.

The Bible became his only source of authority, and this put his conscience in conflict with Catholic practices. In 1522, a few of his parishioners defied the ban on eating meat during Lent, a time of penance and self-denial. Unable to find a biblical foundation for abstaining from meat, he joined his parishioners by eating sausage in public, something no priest would do. He also preached a sermon on freedom to accentuate his point.

Like many city-states in Europe, church and state were intertwined. There was no separation between them. Defying church doctrine often brought down the fist of the government. The pope demanded Zurich expel Zwingli, but they were not so inclined. Zwingli arranged to appear before the leaders of the city to defend his doctrine. He presented his *Sixty-Seven Articles*, arguing that his beliefs were biblical. Article 1 stated: "All who say that the Gospel is invalid without the confirmation of the church err and slander God."[1]

In the *Sixty-Seven Articles*, he established that Christ should be the center of all teaching, denied that popes had a special standing, rejected Mass as a part of salvation, explained that Christians were to pray through Christ and not through saints, argued that salvation comes from Christ and not through good works, endorsed the privileges of marriage for priests and nuns, ridiculed vows of chastity, and dispelled the idea of purgatory. No one in that meeting could have walked away thinking Zwingli was still a Roman Catholic priest.

On January 29, 1523, the city council of Zurich threw their support behind Zwingli, thus disappointing the pope. They stated Zwingli could continue his work and preaching as before.

The next few years saw radical changes in Zurich. In what had once been a Catholic city, priests and nuns began to marry; icons, statues, and images were removed from the churches; and preaching became the focus of the Sunday service. Also eliminated were the Mass and the Catholic version of the Eucharist. A break with Rome had been made, and Zwingli's influence and doctrine spread to other cities including Bern, Schaffhausen, Basel, Glarus, and others.

So Close, Yet So Far

Two men, very similar yet very different, met in Marburg. It was 1529 and Philip of Hesse, a supporter of the Reformation, wanted the two champions of the Reformation movement, Ulrich Zwingli of Switzerland and Martin Luther of Germany, to meet and join forces. Could the two agree on key church doctrines? Zwingli and Luther discussed fifteen key beliefs, agreeing on fourteen of those doctrines. The one doctrine that was disputed: the Lord's Supper. Zwingli taught that it was a memorial with the wine and bread representing the blood and body of Christ, whereas Luther believed in consubstantiation—the real blood and body of Christ mingled with the elements. Luther was somewhere between Roman Catholic doctrine in which the elements were entirely transformed and Zwingli's view that the wine remained wine and bread remained bread. Fourteen areas of agreement and just one topic in dispute, yet that one theological difference was enough to kill any hope of working together. Luther, who was known to mock other Reformers, left convinced Zwingli was of the devil. Much later, when word reached Luther that Zwingli had died, he rejoiced.

This Means War

In 1529, conflict eventually broke out between armed Catholic and Protestant forces. This was not just a battle over doctrine but over the authority of the district, the definition of church property, and more. Zwingli rode off to the battlefield, leading the troops in prayer and preaching sermons to the Protestant soldiers who were his congregation. Catholic and Protestant forces met on the border between Zürich and Zug. Milk soup was cooked and shared by the parties, and a peace was negotiated. The Catholics provided the milk; the Protestants the bread. This, the First War of Kappel, was resolved through discussion, although tensions remained high. But the peace wouldn't last.

Zwingli's country was a Swiss Confederation made up of thirteen cantons (states). These cantons had a great deal of autonomy. Some chose to side with the Catholic Church and others chose to side with the Reformation. In 1531, a group of five cantons declared war on Zurich, resulting in the start of the Second Kappel War. Many pastors did as Zwingli did in the first campaign, yet this time a battle ensued and there was bloodshed. In a battle that lasted only an hour, five hundred men died. One of them was Zwingli. His body was dismembered, his remains burned, and his helmet taken as a trophy. Twenty-four other Protestant pastors died that day. This was just the beginning of a religious war that would continue for decades.

25

KING HENRY VIII

Breaking Up Is Easy to Do

(1491–1547)

> Alas, how can the poor souls live in concord when you preachers
> sow amongst them in your sermons debate and discord? They look
> to you for light and you bring them darkness. Amend these crimes,
> I exhort you, and set forth God's word truly, both by true preaching
> and giving a good example, or else, I, whom God has appointed
> his vicar and high minister here, will see these divisions extinct,
> and these enormities corrected.
>
> King Henry VIII, last speech to parliament, December 24, 1545

We might be led to believe by the quote above that Henry VIII was a deeply spiritual man, concerned about the souls of his subjects. Perhaps, in his own way, he was, but Henry is better known for making breaks than mending hurts. Charles Dickens called him "a most intolerable ruffian and a blot of blood and grease on the history of England."[1]

Not very complimentary.

As a prince he enjoyed the pastimes of royalty: hunting, tennis, archery, and other sports. Considered handsome, he was popular with his father's subjects. As king, he was a larger than life figure and ruled with a strong hand. But responsibility for a country, as well as his difficulty in bringing an heir into the world, took its toll on Henry.

While a queen could take the English throne, Henry seemed to think that the country needed a stronger, male hand in dealing with the pressing issues facing England. Despite the great power that came with being the sovereign of a major country, it didn't come with the ability to predict the gender of his children.

While he was yet a prince, Henry's brother died, leaving Catherine of Aragon—the daughter of Spain's ruler—a widow. Henry's father, Henry VII, did not want to return the dowry. He arranged for Henry to take his sister-in-law as his wife. That decision would haunt the younger Henry.

Henry and Catherine had a child whom they named Mary. He came to believe that no male child would come from his union with Catherine because God was punishing him. He cited Leviticus 20:21 as his proof text: "If there is a man who takes his brother's wife, it is abhorrent; he has uncovered his brother's nakedness. They will be childless."

Of Wives and Churches

Henry sought a divorce from Catherine, sending Cardinal Wolsey to present his case to Pope Clement VII. But there was a problem. The pope was under the thumb of Charles V, king of Spain and emperor of the Holy Roman Empire, and nephew to Catherine, Henry's wife. Fearful of offending Charles, the pope refused the divorce. Henry was beside himself, accusing his advocate Cardinal Wolsey of high treason. The man died before he could be executed.

In the meantime, Henry had fallen in love with the beautiful Anne Boleyn and wanted her as his wife. So, if the church in Rome wouldn't grant the divorce, he was sure an English church would. Parliament, at Henry's urging, declared Henry the head of the Church of England, thus opening the door for Henry to gain a divorce in 1533. Henry and Anne married on January 25 of that year, and she was already pregnant. This act was the first of many wedges that Henry would drive between the Church of England and the Roman Church.

Next, Henry convened the clergy in a national meeting so they could agree to the *Submissions of the Clergy*, an act that forbid the sharing of any papal decree without the king's permission. The 1534 *Act of Supremacy* officially made the king the head of the Church of England. Henry VIII had now formally cut ties to the Roman Church.

This break seems odd in light of Henry's dedication to Roman doctrine. Years earlier, in a reaction to Martin Luther's declarations that most of the sacraments held by the Roman Church were unbiblical, Henry wrote a *Defense of the Seven Sacraments*, taking Luther to task and calling him a "poisonous serpent." For this the Roman Church bestowed the title "Defender of the Faith" on the king, a title that has followed every English monarch since.

Henry closed most of the monasteries, seized their property, and then gave it away (or sold it for very little money) to the middle class, garnering their support and creating a healthier treasury. In part, his motivation was a disciplinary act against the behavior of some of the monks who routinely ignored biblical morals. Henry wasn't particularly attentive to biblical morals either, but in his mind this mattered little since he wasn't in the rank of monks.

In early September in the same year of her marriage, Anne Boleyn gave birth to a girl, Elizabeth, but a male heir was still wanted. In July of 1534, Anne gave birth to a stillborn son. In 1536 she miscarried. Henry's attention then moved to Jane Seymour, whom he married in May of 1536. To make way for his new wife-to-be, Anne was accused, tried, and executed on trumped-up charges of adultery and incest. She was executed by beheading while Henry played tennis. Jane Seymour became Henry's new wife and soon bore the son he had been longing for. Jane died two weeks later, probably from difficulties related to the birth of baby Edward. Her son, Edward VI, would become king at the age of ten—and die at age sixteen.

In January 1540, Anne of Cleves became Henry's next wife. The German noblewoman would be "queen" for about six months, but the marriage, according to Henry, was never consummated. He asked for and received an annulment. She outlived all of Henry's other wives.

Catherine Howard became Henry's wife almost immediately following the annulment of his marriage to Anne of Cleves. Within two years, she was convicted of adultery and executed. Catherine

Parr was next to the altar with Henry in 1543, four years prior to his death in 1547.

Henry VIII shaped the church with a wedge, splitting the English church from the Roman Church. Ironically, he had no dispute with Roman Catholic doctrine, unlike the Protestants of the Reformation movement. Yet the pope and the inconvenience of Roman Church politics stood in the way of his desires. Henry wasn't seeking the establishment of a Protestant church but envisioned an English Catholic Church, one with the same sacraments as Rome. Despite the nefarious motivations behind the establishment of an independent Church of England, today the Church of England (the Anglican Church) numbers close to three million members and has about eighteen thousand ordained clergy.

Henry was also influential in his allowing an English translation of the Bible, based on the work of William Tyndale and Miles Coverdale, to be completed. The Roman Church was opposed to translations made from the original languages of Hebrew and Greek. Many of the doctrines of the Roman Church were built on verses that could not be supported by a more literal translation of the original language.

Henry's lifestyle was hardly an example of Christian living, but his actions, despite being born of selfish motivation, changed the shape of the church in England.

26

IGNATIUS OF LOYOLA
Exchanging Kings

(1492–1556)

Soul of Christ, make me holy.

Ignatius of Loyola,
Spiritual Exercises

Few things can cause a man to reassess his life like a cannonball in the leg.

At least that was true for Iñigo Lopez of Loyola, who went from soldier to priest after being crippled in war.

Iñigo Lopez de Loyola (later Ignatius of Loyola) was born into a privileged Basque family of noble means. He spent many of his youthful years in the court of King Ferdinand in Spain, where he lived a materialistic and lustful life of sword fighting, gambling, and womanizing. He loved the "vanities of the world" and desired fame most of all. However, his experiences on the battlefield would radically alter the direction and priorities of his life.

In 1521, a battle between the French and Spanish erupted in the town of Pamplona in Spain near the border of France. During the skirmish, a fist-sized cannonball struck Iñigo in the leg, shattering bone. He was carted back to Loyola for surgery to fix his knee and remove protruding bone. In that day, such a surgery was messy and excruciating. He would spend nearly two months recuperating. To pass the time, he read about the spiritual adventures of Francis of Assisi. He also read a book by a Cistercian monk, who portrayed the holy life as a life of chivalry, something that appealed to Iñigo. The accounts of these men inspired him to take a different course in life, one spent on godly pursuits rather than carnal ones.

When he was well enough to travel, he said good-bye to his family and friends and made his way to an area in Montserrat, where he spent three days confessing his previous sins. Once done, he left his sword near a statue of Mary. His life as a Spanish knight was over. He replaced the clothing of the Spanish court with coarse sackcloth.

At thirty years of age, and for the next three years, he determined to live as a beggar, at times living in a cave, letting his hair and fingernails grow, and spending days on end in unceasing prayer. During these days he formulated a practice of severe self-discipline, resulting in what he claimed were supernatural visions. He also began work on his book *Spiritual Exercises*, a work designed to lead a person to understanding God's will. The book is still in print today.

When he was thirty-three he decided to prepare for the priesthood and began what would be twelve years of study, taking him from Barcelona to the University of Alcala and from there to the University of Paris. His life centered on two things: studying and helping the ill and the poor. He visited hospitals and ministered to the dying.

He also gained a small following of men who admired his dedication and approach to life. He was committed to helping others in their spiritual experiences, something that earned him an appearance before the Spanish Inquisition. Determined to keep the church pure, the inquisitors challenged his actions. The problem was that he was not an ordained priest. He was acquitted of all charges, but would have to endure similar inquisitions in other cities.

In 1534 he and six others formed a small band, taking vows of poverty, chastity, and unswerving obedience to the pope and the church. The official forming of a religious order would not come about for another three years.

A Vision Becomes Reality

Iñigo, now Ignatius, had a remarkable vision. He saw God and Jesus walking together. Jesus was carrying a cross. God said to his Son, "I want you to take this man as your servant." He was speaking of Ignatius.

Jesus spoke directly to Ignatius: "It is my will that you serve us."

He was told the name of the followers would be, "The Company of Jesus."

In 1540, Ignatius received papal authority from Pope Paul III to form the Society of Jesus, better known as the Jesuits. Ignatius was selected as leader. He would spend the next fifteen years in Rome.

The Jesuits focused on service to those in need: the poor, the sick, and the lost. This they did by building hospitals and orphanages and by doing missions work. They preached wherever they traveled. In 1551, Ignatius, who had spent so many years in study, founded Roman College, the first Jesuit institution of higher learning.

The Society of Jesus spread from Rome and Spain, eventually even reaching across the Atlantic Ocean and into the New World. Their work continues to this day.

27

WILLIAM TYNDALE

Smuggling Truth

(c. 1494–1536)

> I have perceived by experience, how that it was impossible to [establish] the lay people in any truth, except the Scripture were plainly laid before their eyes in their mother tongue, that they might see the process, order, and meaning of the text.
>
> William Tyndale, preface to *The Pentateuch*

The man with the neatly trimmed beard, serious brow, stately forehead, and piercing eyes stood motionless. A wood post stood at his back. He was tied to it. At his feet men piled logs, brush, and kindling. They then poured gunpowder over the dry wood. Nearby, a city official stood by with a torch, its flames flickering, licking the air as if hungry for the pyre. The October sun seemed to stop its transit to watch the drama unfold.

The man shifted his weight, feeling both the chain around his neck that bound him to the pole and the rope noose beneath the chain. He could feel each movement of the rope as the executioner continued his preparations. He knew what awaited him.

A representative of his prosecutor gave him the opportunity to recant. There, in the middle of the gathered crowd, he refused. He was then given an opportunity to pray. He accepted that offer. "Lord, open the king of England's eyes."[1]

The ranking town official gave the signal and the executioner yanked the noose tight, strangling the forty-two-year-old to death. Then the fire was lit. His body burned. His ashes were scattered to the wind.

William Tyndale, British subject living in exile, died a criminal, expelled from the church, his priesthood stripped from him for his heinous crime: making an English translation of the Bible so any common English person could read and study the Word of God. The task cost him time, effort, his homeland, and his life. The one thing the execution of William Tyndale failed to kill was the man's cause.

Passion for the English Word of God

> For the worde off god is quycke & myghty in operacion and sharper then eny two edged swearde: and entreth through, even unto the dividynge asonder of the soule and the sprete and of the joyntes, and the mary: and judgeth the thoughtes and the intent of the herte.

The above verse looks strange to the eye, but it is a familiar passage from the New Testament. Here it is again:

> For the word of God is living and active and sharper than any two-edged sword, and piercing as far as the division of soul and spirit, of both joints and marrow, and able to judge the thoughts and intentions of the heart. (Heb. 4:12)

The first passage is taken from the 1526 version of William Tyndale's English translation of the New Testament and, of course, uses spelling of the day. The translation, like all worthwhile translations, would undergo many revisions and would serve as the basis for several other English works.

Let's move beyond the archaic spelling and look at the meaning of the passage. It speaks of the power of God's Word in the life of the individual. For William Tyndale, this was more than just an interesting verse. It was the foundation of his passion to place in the hands of English-speaking people a Bible they could read in their own language. Such a goal was neither original, nor limited to England. Martin Luther had translated the Bible into German for his people many years before.

Tyndale lived his life with sacrificial allegiance to the cause of making the Bible available to all. Years before, Erasmus, who had compiled the New Testament from the Greek that Tyndale (and Luther in Germany) used to make his translation, said, "Christ desires His mysteries to be published abroad as widely as possible. I would that [the Gospels and Epistles of Paul] were translated into all languages of all Christian people, and that they might be read and known."[2]

Tyndale had the same desire for his people, but the king and the pope were against it. At the time, churches in England were still tied to Roman Catholicism, although the break arranged by King Henry VIII between the English and Roman Church was at hand. Ironically, King Henry VIII would later, a few years after Tyndale's execution, sanction the release of an English Bible.

A Personal Mission

Tyndale did not begin as a reformer or rebel. He was born in western England around 1494 and took the path to priesthood. He studied in Oxford and Cambridge. He had a remarkable intellect and was able to speak seven languages and work in both biblical Hebrew and Greek. He grew increasingly disappointed in the lack of biblical knowledge held by priests of his day. Most priests at that time rarely read the Bible.

In his early thirties, he approached the bishop of London seeking funds and a place to make an English translation of the Bible. The bishop refused outright, a stance Tyndale found consistently throughout the church in England. What Tyndale was proposing was considered a criminal act.

In 1524, Tyndale traveled to Germany, where he lived in Hamburg, Cologne, and Worms, carrying out his translation work. In 1525 he finished his first translation of the New Testament. Over the next five years, six editions were done and fifteen thousand copies made and smuggled into England.

Tyndale's translation caused quite a stir, infuriating King Henry VIII, Cardinal Wosley, and Sir Thomas More. More captured the rage of those in church leadership over the translation and its distribution when he stated: "Not worthy to be called Christ's testament, but either Tyndale's own testament or the testament of his master Antichrist."

Tyndale became a wanted man and his translation an illegal item. Efforts to keep it from the English people included buying up all the stock, which of course provided the funding for additional publishing and distribution of the translation. It took the help of friends to smuggle Tyndale from place to place, keeping him out of the hands of his enemies and allowing him to continue his work. He managed to translate the first five books of the Old Testament and a few other books from the Hebrew into English before his capture.

Despite the demands of his translation work, Tyndale still considered himself a priest of the people and structured his workweek to include time helping the poor, visiting religious refugees who had fled England, and visiting the homes of merchants, joining them for supper and reading the Scripture before and after the meal.

It may be that his servant heart was what ultimately led to his capture and execution. Several agents from different sources searched for Tyndale, but he had been able to avoid them all—all except Henry Phillips. Phillips came from a prestigious family but was a scoundrel who had gambled away his money. He found Tyndale in Antwerp and befriended him, worming his way into the translator's confidence. He even became one of the few who had the privilege of seeing Tyndale's papers.

In May of 1535, Phillips had things set in motion. He was able to convince Tyndale to cancel a previous lunch engagement and have lunch with him. Tyndale agreed. Phillips led him into the arms of arresting soldiers.

He was taken to the Castle of Filford, where he spent the next year and some months imprisoned. He was tried by ecclesiastical authorities as a heretic and found guilty. He was stripped of his priesthood and was handed over to civil authorities for execution.

The Dream Remains

Tyndale's enemies had finally succeeded in putting an end to the person William Tyndale, but they failed to stop the movement Tyndale had birthed. Miles Coverdale, another Cambridge graduate, published the first complete edition of Tyndale's translation. In 1537 the Matthew Bible appeared from "Thomas Matthew," a pseudonym for John Rodgers, a clergyman who would also be executed at the stake on February 4, 1555 under Queen Mary I—"Bloody Mary." In 1539, Henry VIII, who had opposed an English Bible, was convinced by Thomas Cramner, Archbishop of Canterbury, to release the "Great Bible," which was based on Coverdale's work that had itself been based on Tyndale's translation. Since Tyndale's death, there have been hundreds of translations, versions, paraphrases, and revisions of the English Bible. The Bible has also been translated into over two thousand languages.

28

MENNO SIMONS

Afraid of the Bible

(1496–1561)

> True evangelical faith cannot lie dormant. It clothes the naked, it feeds the hungry, it comforts the sorrowful, it shelters the destitute, it serves those that harm it, it binds up that which is wounded, it has become all things to all people.
>
> Menno Simons, *Why I Do Not Cease Teaching and Writing*

It has been said that there are three great persecutions of the church: persecution waged by the first-century religious leaders, then persecution by the Romans, and finally—and sadly—persecution *by* the church *on* the church. Menno Simons lived in this third wave of persecution. Although his name may not be familiar to most, he is well-known to hundreds of thousands of Mennonites around the world.

Menno Simons was born in 1496 in Witmarsum, Friesland, in the Netherlands. Little is known about his childhood, but his early days were spent as a peasant in a war-torn land. Somehow he found his way into the Roman Catholic Church, where he was educated and trained as a priest and spiritual advisor.

158

Afraid of the Bible

We wouldn't think of hiring a plumber who hasn't studied plumbing, or go to a doctor who has never read a medical text, but Menno Simons served as a priest without ever opening the Bible. "I feared if I should read them they would mislead me," he wrote.[1]

Imagine that. A priest who feared being misled by the Scriptures. The two priests who served with him in the town of Pingjum had only read parts of the Bible. In his later writings Simons admitted to a love for gambling, drinking, and "diversions as, alas, is the fashion and usage of such useless people." In other words, he was a spiritual man in name only.

"I spoke much concerning the word of the Lord, without spirituality or love, as all hypocrites do, and by this means I [made] disciples of my own kind, vain boasters and frivolous babblers, who, alas, like myself did not take these matters seriously."[2]

A Puzzled Priest

How does such a man become a shaper of the church? It started when Simons observed a break between what he had been taught about the Eucharist and what he experienced during Mass. The word *Eucharist* refers to the church ordinance that recalls the body and blood of Christ. Wine (or grape juice) and bread are shared with worshipers as Jesus shared with his disciples in the upper room shortly before his betrayal and crucifixion. Other church groups call it communion or the Lord's Supper. The church has practiced it since the first century in a belief that to do so follows the command of Christ (Luke 22:19–20). As has been mentioned, the Roman Catholic Church taught the doctrine of transubstantiation, a belief that the wine literally turns into the blood of Christ and the bread literally turns into his flesh. Lutherans adopted consubstantiation, which teaches that the blood and flesh of Jesus *mingle* with the wine and the bread.

As a priest, it fell to Simons to distribute the elements of the Eucharist to his parishioners, but as he did, questions arose. The elements, as far as Simons could tell, never changed. Bread remained bread; wine remained wine. This created for him a spiritual crisis. He first assumed the devil was misleading him. He prayed for God's intervention, but he could not shake the questions swirling in his mind. To settle himself, he turned to the Bible he had previously ignored, studying the New Testament to look for biblical evidence that confirmed the sacramental practice of the Eucharist.

"Finally, I got the idea to examine the New Testament diligently. I had not gone very far when I discovered that we were deceived, and my conscience, troubled on account of the aforementioned bread, was quickly relieved."[3] Simons felt led astray by the church. He could find no biblical evidence for transubstantiation.

Simons, who had before avoided reading the Bible, became one of its greatest spokesmen. His newfound love of the Bible and its teachings produced in him a passion for preaching and made him a popular teacher. But despite this newfound love, and in spite of all outward appearances, Menno Simons still felt spiritually empty. Then news of a tragic event sent him searching the Scriptures again.

Among the Dutch there was a growing spiritual movement, the Anabaptists, who were drawing the attention and ire of the Roman Catholic Church and some Protestant groups. The term "anabaptist" comes from two Greek words; *ana* meaning "again" or "re-" and *baptizo*, referring to immersion. Anabaptists taught "believers baptism," the idea that baptism followed conversion. This meant that they rejected infant baptism, which was part of Catholic teaching and the prominent baptism practice of the day. Remarkably, this view of rebaptism was considered punishable by death, with executions being carried out by local authorities. One such execution took the life of an Anabaptist in Leeuwarden. He was beheaded, and he wasn't the only Anabaptist to die for being rebaptized.

News of the execution led Simons to reconsider the practice of rebaptism. "It sounded very strange to me to hear of a second baptism. I examined the Scriptures diligently and pondered them earnestly but could find no report of infant baptism."[4]

Simons did not have a natural proclivity or zeal for any cause. It troubled him to think of people being willing to die for their beliefs. He had preached to secure his comfortable lifestyle, but to hear that Anabaptists were willing to face death by beheading in order to practice biblical faithfulness brought him intense spiritual conviction.

"My soul was troubled and I reflected upon the outcome, that if I should gain the whole world and live 1000 years, and at last have to endure the wrath of God, what would I have gained?"[5]

The persecution of Anabaptists grew. Over three hundred Anabaptists were executed at Old Cloister at Bolsward. Simons' brother Peter was one of those executed. The knowledge of this sent the priest into a spiritual depression. They had given everything; he had given so little.

> Pondering these things, my conscience tormented me so that I could no longer endure it. My heart trembled within me. I prayed to God with sighs and tears that He would give to me, a sorrowing sinner, the gift of His grace, create within me a clean heart, and graciously through the merits of the crimson blood of Christ forgive my unclean walk and I might preach His exalted and adorable name and holy Word in purity.
>
> Then I, without constraint, of a sudden, renounced all my worldly reputation, name and fame, my unchristian abominations, my masses, infant baptism, and my easy life, and I willingly submitted to distress and poverty under the heavy cross of Christ. In my weakness I feared God; I sought out the pious and though they were few in number I found some who were zealous and maintained the truth.[6]

For the better part of a year he used his Catholic pulpit to preach the gospel, which for Simons meant repentance, the narrow path, and the power of Scripture to change lives. It was not enough for him. The differences he saw between the Roman Catholic dogma he had been taught and what he was learning from Bible study became too pronounced. After twelve years as a priest, Menno Simons turned his back on Rome and joined the Anabaptists, who gladly received him.

As if the troubles of the Anabaptists in defending rebaptism were not enough, a fanatical, end-times group called the Munsterites arose. Led by Jan Matthijs, this spin-off group of Anabaptists were fanatical about bringing in the one-thousand-year reign of Christ. Catholics and Lutherans alike feared the radicals, and armed men were sent against them by the area bishop. The Munsterites fought back, something peace-loving Anabaptists were not expected to do. In 1534, the more extreme Munsterites took control of the town and, claiming divine revelation, ruled with a heavy hand. Jan of Leiden seized power and ruled like a tyrant, instituting polygamy. But in June of 1535, the bishop's army prevailed against them.

The damage, however, had been done. The term *Anabaptist* no longer stood for peaceful people who longed to follow the New Testament pattern. The label came to represent something abhorrent. Menno Simons' ministry now included repudiating violence and encouraging the peaceful Anabaptists to persevere despite having to endure this second wave of persecution brought about by the Munsterites. The priest who had once lived a comfortable life found himself and his family—he had married a woman named Gertrude and had at least three children—constantly on the run. As Simons traveled, he ministered to Anabaptists who were also on the move. Offers of pardon or monetary reward were made for information leading to his whereabouts. No one gave him up. On one of his trips to Friesland, he stayed in the home of Tjard Reynders. In January 1539, Reynders was arrested, tortured, and executed. All for having given Menno Simons and his family a place to sleep for the night.

Life on the Run

Charles V, emperor of the Holy Roman Empire, distributed an edict against Simons and offered gold to anyone who turned the preacher in. It became illegal to provide food and shelter to him. The earthly quality of his life deteriorated while his spiritual life blossomed. In his words, "For this I, my poor, feeble wife and children have for eighteen years endured extreme anxiety, oppression, affliction, misery and persecution, and at the peril of my life, have been compelled everywhere to live in fear and seclusion."[7]

Today, just under one million people call themselves Mennonites or are affiliated with groups that can trace their lineage back to the Dutch Anabaptists and Anabaptist groups. The emphasis on biblical authority and the need for a pattern of worship like that of the New Testament church has benefited many Protestant groups. The contribution of Menno Simons and those like him have endured for centuries. For them, biblical faith was not a casual or part-time thing, it was the very fabric of their lives. Their love for God made them willing to endure scorn, threats, arrest, torture, and death.

Menno Simons shaped the church by making the church relevant, important, and personal. He elevated the Bible to the highest level in a time when not even priests read the Book. It was the Bible that took Simons from comfortable priest to fugitive for the faith.

Simons wrote three books: *Christian Baptism* (1539), *Foundation of Christian Doctrine* (1540), and *The True Christian Faith* (1541), but his greatest work was written on the hearts of those to whom he ministered.

Twenty-five years after he left the priesthood, Simons died. It was January 31, 1561. Those who sought to arrest him never succeeded. Simons died at his home and was buried in his garden.

29

JOHN CALVIN

Predestined Reformer

(1509–1564)

> All things being at God's disposal, and the decision of salvation or death belonging to him, he orders all things by his counsel and decree in such a manner, that some men are born devoted from the womb to certain death, that his name may be glorified in their destruction.
>
> John Calvin, *Institutes of the Christian Religion*

He may be the most polarizing man in church history. He is loved by many and despised by others. Hailed by some theologians and dismissed by others. Some consider him to be one of the most significant thinkers and Reformers in history while others think he undermined the world's view of God.

Saint or devil? Over five hundred years later people are still arguing about this shy, sickly Frenchman named John Calvin.

Education of a World Changer

Calvin was born in Noyon, a small town sixty miles from Paris. His father was a lawyer who worked for the church. His mother died just a few years after Calvin's birth, the cause unknown. His father, Gérard Cauvin (Calvin is a shortened, Latinized version of Cauvin), valued education and sent Calvin, only fourteen at the time, to Paris so he could study with the finest academic minds. There John developed a writing style that would forever influence French prose. He also developed a keen sense of logic. Both talents would serve him during his life and ministry.

Initially, Calvin's father planned for his son to work in the church, but that changed with a falling-out between his father and the Catholic Church. Calvin was forced to switch from theology to something his father believed would earn Calvin more money: law. Calvin studied law at the University of Orleans and Bourges, but his heart remained drawn to theology and the classics. He wanted to spend his life in study and teaching. Such a career suited his shy, antisocial leanings, but it was not what his father wanted. But in 1531, Calvin's father died after a two-year battle with testicular cancer, freeing Calvin to pursue his academic dreams. He returned to Paris to study, looking forward to a scholar's career.

Not all of Calvin's education came from books and professors, however. Some things he learned through life experiences. He made friends with Nicholas Cop, who had recently been appointed rector at the University of Paris. In general, Reformers like Martin Luther were disdained at the college, but Cop, in his inaugural speech, aligned himself with those who believed the Catholic Church needed reform and renewal. Charges of heresy were brought against him and within two days he was forced to flee. John Calvin chose to flee with Cop, and because of their friendship many assumed Calvin had written or at least contributed to Cop's speech. Calvin eventually landed in Basel, Switzerland. There the young scholar first gave his greatest gift to the church.

The Institutes

In March 1536, Calvin released the first edition of *Institutes of the Christian Religion*. The work is considered one of the greatest and clearest descriptions of Protestant thought ever conceived. Calvin would continue the work through his adult life, expanding it over time. The first edition brought fame to the twenty-seven-year-old theologian, and that fame drew the attention of a man who would alter the great Reformer's life.

Calvin wanted to go to Strasbourg, but war in the area forced him to detour to Geneva. His plan was to spend one night there, but William Farel, a Reformer in the city, heard the author of the *Institutes* was in town and sought him out. After a discussion, Farel insisted Calvin join him in his Reformation efforts. At first Calvin wanted nothing to do with it. He simply desired a quiet place to study, which was for him, heaven. Farel refused to let the matter rest, accusing Calvin of chasing his own interests instead of those of God. He promised God's punishment on Calvin and the threat worked. Farel's strong words and tone terrified Calvin. He said it was as if God had reached from heaven and touched him. Geneva became his new home.

Church and City

Geneva was a city in turmoil and known for its lax morality. In an interesting combination of work, Calvin—perhaps because of his law degree and his theological aptitude—was given a position in the city: Professor of Sacred Scripture. In this role, and the role he would later play in the city, he blended church and city, at least in function and administration.

Calvin drew up a confession of faith, a set of doctrines, that everyone who wanted to be a citizen of Geneva had to agree to. He also worked on an education program for the population and delved into the operations of the city government. He had no desire to be a city manager, but he did long to set up a city for God. He even established rules for excommunication.

It is easy to understand how some people would object to this. One dispute centered on who was responsible for excommunicating those who gambled, skipped church, drank too much, or went dancing. It was a tense dispute, one that Calvin and Farel's opponents won. This defeat forced them to leave Geneva within three days.

After his forced exit from Geneva, Calvin finally made his way to Strasbourg, and for three years did what he had always wanted to do: study and write. He also served as pastor to a church of French refugees. He even found a wife, the widow Idelette de Bure, who remained with him until her death in 1549. He never remarried.

Yet Geneva wasn't finished with John Calvin. His supporters regained power in the city and pleaded with him to return to take up his Reforming work again. He did so from a sense of duty to God. His three-year forced sabbatical was over.

The next few years would see great progress in the church and in the city, with many of his ideas put in place, but opposition still remained and he came close to being forced out of town several times. John Knox, the Scottish Protestant Reformer, visited Geneva and called it, "The most perfect school of Christ that ever was on earth since the days of the Apostles."[1]

Black Spot

In 1553 an event happened in Geneva that many consider a smudge on Calvin's reputation, a stain that is difficult to overlook. A Spanish physician held a doctrine the Roman Catholic Church considered heretical. Protestants felt the same. Michael Servetus was a polymath, capable of working in many fields. He wrote on theological matters that challenged traditional doctrine, especially the Trinity and infant baptism. Having been declared a heretic, he fled Spain and came to Geneva, where he was recognized and arrested. He had as much to fear from the Protestants as the Catholics.

Calvin wrote to his friend William Farel in August of 1553 recounting some of the early events:

> After he [Servetus] had been recognized, I thought he should be detained. My friend Nicolas summoned him on a capital charge, offering himself as a security according to the *lex talionis* (punishment resembles offense). On the following day he adduced against him forty written charges. He at first sought to evade them. Accordingly we were summoned. He impudently reviled me, just as if he regarded me as obnoxious to him. I answered him as he deserved . . . of the man's effrontery I will say nothing; but such was his madness that he did not hesitate to say that devils possessed divinity; yea, that many gods

were in individual devils, inasmuch as a deity had been substantially communicated to those equally with wood and stone. I hope that sentence of death will at least be passed on him; but I desired that the severity of the punishment be mitigated.[2]

Calvin felt beheading was kinder than burning at the stake. The others ignored his suggestion. Still, Calvin believed Servetus' doctrinal crimes deserved death. It is difficult to overlook the irony of Calvin's consent to Servetus' execution since he fled Paris to escape a similar manhunt. There is, however, more background to the issue.

Today, church and state are often kept apart. One does not control the other. In Calvin's time things were different. Church and state were inseparable, a blend of heavenly and earthly kingdoms. To attack one was to attack the other. Church leaders believed it was the responsibility of the state to protect and enforce church doctrine. This was especially true in Geneva where Calvin helped set up the city as a near-theocracy (a God-led government). When Servetus came to town, it was the theological equivalent of an invading army. At stake was not just belief but the operation of the city and the churches within.

Calvin had had dealings with Michael Servetus in the past. The latter had taken a copy of Calvin's *Institutes* and wrote challenging notes on nearly every page. In response Calvin said every page had Servetus' vomit on it. So there were certainly also personal issues at stake.

To Calvin and those around him, Servetus presented a real danger to church, city, country, and person.

T.U.L.I.P.

Some of Calvin's doctrine split the Reformers in Geneva, primarily his view of predestination. Although the idea was not unique to Calvin, as others including Martin Luther held to a form of predestination, the doctrine is most clearly defined by, and therefore associated with, him.

Predestination, in Calvin's doctrinal view, is the belief that God has, from the beginning of time, elected (selected) some people to be saved, and by doing so leaves those not elected to be forever outside

God's love and grace. This doctrine walks in lockstep with other key beliefs. Over the years a memory device has been used to help students remember these elements. Each doctrine is defined by a letter that spells *tulip*.

T: Total Depravity

The belief that sin from Adam's fall in the Garden of Eden affects all people, leaving everyone spiritually dead and therefore unable to do anything to help in his or her salvation.

U: Unconditional Election

Since all humans are spiritually dead and unable to do anything about it, God must do something about it and he has, in eternity past, selected some to receive salvation. This is "unconditional," meaning that a person's election is not based on their response. It is solely God's doing.

L: Limited Atonement

Jesus died on the cross so the elect—not everyone or anyone—and the elect alone could be saved. In other words, Christ's death and the salvation that comes from the sacrifice applies to the elect alone. Jesus died for the elect, not all humanity.

I: Irresistible Grace

Those whom God chose and Christ died for will come to faith. God has willed it and every one of the elect will be saved. There can be no change.

P: Perseverance of Saints

None of the elect will be lost. Their salvation is eternally secure. God through the Holy Spirit will cause the saints (the elect) to persevere.

These elements are at the heart of several denominations, including Presbyterians, some Baptists (but not all), Congregational churches, and Reformed churches. Others, however, are uncomfortable with Calvin's conclusions (see chapter on Arminius) and find in the Bible passages that suggest the opposite of the above. Instead of "total depravity," they believe that all humans inherit a sin nature but still have free will to accept or reject Christ. They deny "unconditional election," believing instead that God loves everyone and each person has the opportunity to accept salvation should they choose. "Limited atonement" doesn't work for the non-Calvinist who believes that Christ died for the world, not just the elect. They also reject the idea that grace is irresistible, believing that people have free will and can resist God. Perseverance of the saints is accepted by some non-Calvinist groups and rejected by others, primarily Church of Christ and Pentecostal churches.

Impact

Agree with Calvin or not, there is no denying that he has shaped the church and theology as much as Luther or Augustine. His ideas have also shaped governments and philosophy. His *Institutes* is a tour de force in theological writing and his writing style influenced French composition.

The young man who wanted to be a classical scholar became one of the most influential people in church history.

30

JOHN FOXE

A History Book That Made History

(1516–1587)

> What force of princes, kings, monarchs, governors, and rulers of this world, with their subjects, publicly and privately, with all their strength and cunning, have bent themselves against this Church! And, thirdly, how the said Church, all this notwithstanding, hath yet endured and holden its own!
>
> John Foxe, *Book of Martyrs*

Some books educate. Some entertain. Some address needs. Some inspire. Every once in a while a book comes along that changes the world. Not just the present world of the writer but the world of millions of readers to come. John Foxe, a Puritan minister, wrote a history book that became history. It was a book that would expand over time, as additional stories of horror and death were added. In its pages are accounts of death by burning at the stake, inhumane and lengthy torture, and scalding oil. Woodcuts, crude by today's standards, were vivid enough to leave indelible images on the brains of sixteenth-century English citizens and others.

Five centuries later, John Foxe's epic work is still read, chilling the blood while filling the heart with the courage of those willing to die for their beliefs.

English Politics and Faith

England in Foxe's day was divided by religious loyalty. On the one hand were those whose minds and hearts were centered in Rome with the pope and the Catholic Church; on the other hand were those known as Protestants, who felt the Roman Church had left its moorings to become something God never intended.

Whenever and wherever a line is drawn in the sand, people are divided. England was split over religious commitments. This divide extended to its kings and queens. It was a time of intolerance and punishment for those on the wrong side.

Henry VIII died in 1547, leaving the throne to his ten-year-old son Edward. Edward VI was too young to lead the country, and administrative duties fell to a group of royal advisors. These advisors were sympathetic to the Protestants and the court charted a Protestant-friendly course.

Edward was not a healthy child and endured physical problems into his teenage years. Many medical historians think he may have had a mass in his lung or severe pneumonia, tuberculosis, bronchopneumonia, septicemia, or perhaps a combination of disorders. At times he would rally, but ultimately the disease won. Edward VI died at the age of sixteen, and with him died the protection the Protestants had enjoyed.

Edward and his advisors arranged for his cousin Jane to be declared queen, bypassing his older half sister Mary. But Jane ruled as queen for only nine days before allegiances switched to Mary, who would rule for four years. Jane was executed at the age of sixteen.

Mary had an agenda: she wanted to return England's religious identity to the Roman Catholic Church and was willing to take brutal action to make that return a reality. Under her reign, three hundred Protestants died a martyr's death. These acts led to the nickname that has followed Mary through the centuries: "Bloody Mary." Foxe documented these killings, and the brutality seen by

Englanders of the day forever changed their view of the Roman Church.

Foxe's father died when Foxe was a youth, and his relationship with his stepfather was cold. He excelled at Oxford, earning a master's degree and a teaching fellowship—which he lost when he associated himself with the Protestants. His choice cost him his fellowship at the university, and his family disowned him. He turned to tutoring, but finding steady work was difficult. For a time he tutored the orphaned children of the Earl of Surrey. While Edward VI was alive, he could do his work in the open, but when Mary took the throne things changed. Many Protestants lived in fear until Mary's death in 1558. Foxe was one of those who fled the country to escape Mary's persecution. To feed his family, he worked in a print shop.

Original Intent

Foxe had already begun to write about those who had paid the ultimate price for their faith, starting with the apostles. His goal was to show how their courage and faith came to change England. As Mary took power and began executing Protestants by the score, Foxe updated his work, chronicling the horrible ways these people were killed—many of whom he called friends.

The book, originally called *Acts and Monuments of Matters Happening to the Church*, was first written in Latin and ran over two hundred pages. It would grow to over twenty-five hundred pages and be printed in English. The book, better known as *Foxe's Book of Martyrs*, went through four editions during his lifetime (1563, 1570, 1576, and 1583).

Foxe's book would become extremely popular, and for a time was displayed in churches, colleges, and other places where it could be read. Unlike today, where books abound, most commoners of the time had very little to read—if they were literate at all. Those who couldn't read could view the woodcut images showing the death of Protestants and the instruments of torture used against them. Until Foxe, many had the Bible as their only book.

Unending Work

The impact of the work was partly due to Mary's persecution. The execution of people of faith was not a distant historical aberration to Foxe's readers—they were eyewitnesses to these executions. Mary may have wanted to turn England back to the Roman Church, but in the end she turned an entire country against Roman Catholicism. Her zeal destroyed her goal.

Foxe would write many other books, but none so well-known as his history of martyrs. He continued his hard work of preaching, teaching, and writing, but did so at the cost of his health. At times his friends, if they came across the worn Foxe walking down the street, couldn't recognize him.

Enduring Work

John Foxe, a man with keen eyes, angular features, a mind hungry for learning, and a heart that yearned for God, changed the church and the world by writing a book of history—a book of sacrifice. In the process, he energized the Protestant movement and encouraged others to persevere by showing them the steadfastness of those who came before.

John Foxe made history by writing about history.

31

JACOB ARMINIUS

The Anti-Calvin

(1560–1609)

Religious dissension is the worst kind of disagreement, for it strikes the very altar itself. It engulfs everyone; each must take sides or else make a third-party of himself.

Jacob Arminius, "On Reconciling Religious Dissensions Among Christians"

There is an old joke that says, "There are two types of people in the world: those who divide the world into two types and those who don't." Church history is full of examples of people choosing sides over some issue, and from these disagreements a new denomination is birthed.

One of the great divides came in the sixteenth century, and although many others were involved, the lightning struck two men more than anyone else: John Calvin and Jacob Arminius. In the battle, Arminius and his followers took the bigger beating.

The Dutchman

Today we know him by his Latinized name, Jacob Arminius, a name he adopted in college. He was born Jacob Hermansen in Ouderwater, near Utrecht, in the Netherlands. He never knew his father, who died sometime around his birth, leaving his mother to care for Arminius and his siblings. Family friends took responsibility for Arminius' education and support.

He attended several colleges, including Marburg University in Germany. While there, Spanish invaders massacred Dutch civilians in his hometown. Jacob rushed home to find that his mother and some of his siblings had been killed. Carl Bangs, in his book *Arminius: A Study in the Dutch Reformation*, described it this way:

> [The Spanish cannons attacked and] breaches were made in the town walls, however, and although they were repaired in the night, the artillery of the attacking army kept up its work of destruction faster than repairs could be maintained. The Spanish troops then entered the city itself and a new phase of the attack began.[1]

It is not a nice story. First the defending soldiers on the walls were shot or stabbed to death. Those who fled into the town were pursued and killed. Then the massacre spread to noncombatants. Mothers were killed in front of their children and children in front of their mothers. Girls and women were raped in view of fathers and husbands, and then all were killed. No place, no person, was exempt from the pillaging invaders. When nuns in the cloisters were discovered, they pleaded that they were faithful Roman Catholics. "So much the better for your souls," said the soldiers as they raped and murdered them.[2]

The Spanish had previously been forced from the city when the inhabitants became Protestants. The Spanish took the city back in brutal fashion. No doubt Arminius heard horrible tales from the survivors. We can only guess the impact this had on the young man's mind and emotions.

After a time he returned to his studies, and when the new University of Leiden was opened in 1576, Arminius enrolled. He was one of the university's first students.

In 1588, after having traveled in Italy and eventually returning home, he was ordained and began ministering in Amsterdam. He married Lijsbet Reael, a merchant's daughter, in 1590.

The Turnaround

Calvinism, a system of belief that relied heavily on predestination—the idea that God ordained before time who would and would not be saved—had swept the area. Arminius had studied under Calvin's son-in-law Theodore Beza in Geneva. He even debated those who disagreed with Calvin. One such opponent was the Dutch writer, philosopher, and theologian Dirck Volckertszoon Coornhert. Arminius did his best to outflank the theologian but failed. Feeling Coornhert had made better arguments, Arminius began to challenge his own commitment to the principles of Calvin, leading to a reversal in his thinking.

Arminius came to believe that Calvinism led to an understanding of God as harsh and evil. Predestination in the High Calvinist view meant God had selected some people to salvation and some to eternal punishment. God appeared as a tyrant, and mere humans as automatons with no choice in matters of personal salvation.

He took these views with him, quietly, from Geneva to his church work in Amsterdam. His studies in the New Testament book of Romans sealed his belief that the Calvinist position was wrong and improperly reflected Scripture. He began preaching that message, frustrating other ministers in the area. He was soon accused of heresy, although no proof of such guilt was ever offered.

The die was cast. The debate was on.

Arminius was no troublemaker. He just had a deep desire that God be properly represented by his servants. Calvinism, in his opinion, was tarnishing the Creator's image. The division bothered him. In his 1606 sermon, "On Reconciling Religious Dissensions Among Christians," he said, "Religious dissension is the worst kind of disagreement, for it strikes the very altar itself. It engulfs everyone; each must take sides or else make a third-party of himself."

The goal was not to overthrow Calvinism in total but to moderate it; not to make it more palatable but to make it align with Scripture. Of course, Calvinists felt their principles were already aligned with the Bible. Still, Arminius felt the doctrines of predestination and irresistible grace had gone too far and needed to be addressed. He petitioned the government of the Netherlands to step in and arrange a synod to deal with the issue.

The synod was called, but by the time it met Arminius had been in the grave for nine years.

Differing Views

The issues that divided the followers of Calvin from the followers of Arminius are deep and complicated, requiring robust theological study to understand fully, but the basics are clear enough, and summarized as follows:

Calvin: In the eternal past, God predestined (determined ahead of time) who will be saved and who will not.

Arminius: No, God elected (chose) those whom he *knew* would believe of their own free will.

Calvin: Free will and God's foreknowledge have nothing to do with it. God has chosen some; others he has condemned.

Arminius: Wrong. We have all been given enough grace to decide to believe or not. That's free will. Election is conditional on the one being saved.

Calvin: That's where you're wrong. Depravity extends to every part of a person, including the will. No one can make the decision by themselves. It takes God's call on their lives, a call he decided on before the foundations of the world.

Arminius: Of course we all have inherited a corrupted nature from Adam and the fall, but God has removed that guilt and condemnation so we can accept God's love and grace.

Calvin: Corrupt *nature*? It's more than that. Adam's sin is passed to us all. We are all born in sin. This is why Christ died for the elect.

Arminius: Not just the elect. Jesus died for all humankind, and that means anyone and everyone is redeemable should they choose to commit to Christ.

Calvin: That would mean the death of our Lord was unsuccessful, because surely not everyone will believe.

Arminius: Never! Jesus' sacrifice is effective for all who choose to believe.

Calvin: So we're back to free will again.

The arguments are much deeper than this fabricated dialogue indicates, but it does reveal the crux of the debate: predestination and free will. Calvin taught that those whom God chose will surely believe; Arminius taught that it's up to the individual to choose God.

There was also the issue of what has become known as the "security of the believer." Calvin believed that the elect would not only believe because God chose them but that God would cause them to persevere to the end of their lives. In other words, the elect could not lose their salvation. Arminius said that Scripture taught the opposite: a person could surrender their salvation by choosing to reject the salvation they once had.

Irresistible force meets immovable object; oil meets water. The two sides would not budge. Once they locked horns, the battle would continue until one side won out.

Except it didn't quite go that way.

Synod of Dort

Arminius left his church to become professor of theology at Leiden University, where he served from 1603 until his death in 1609. During this time the debate over predestination heated up, prompting Arminius to make his appeal to the government to intervene with a synod composed of representatives from both sides. As already mentioned, the synod met years after Arminius died. The gathering lasted from November 13, 1618 until May 9, 1619, and it didn't go well for the followers of Arminius. Some historians have described the conclave as a "kangaroo court" because the body was slanted to the Calvinist side. Of the eighty-four members, nearly sixty were Dutch Calvinist. The "Remonstrants" (named after *Remonstrance*, a document drawn up in 1610 listing the views of the anti-Calvinists) were outnumbered. To make matters worse, the president of the synod and the first secretary were strict Calvinists. The Five Articles of the *Remonstrance* were rejected and the Five Canons of Calvinism were adopted, as were the Belgic Confession and the Heidelberg Catechism, two Calvinistic documents.

Simon Episcopius, the successor to Arminius at Leiden, and a dozen other Arminian leaders were summoned to the synod as defendants.

Over two hundred Arminian pastors lost their churches. Arminians who would not agree to keep silent were forced to leave their homes and country. Hugo Grotius, part of the Arminian contingent, was sentenced to life in prison but managed to escape after two years. This persecution continued until 1625, when Arminians were allowed to return and rebuild their churches and lives.

Arminianism Today

The views of Jacob Arminius did not die with him. His followers continued to teach and preach the free will of persons, conditional grace, and the ability for a person to walk away from his or her salvation. Arminian theology spread throughout the world, with Arminius' thinking exerting great influence on John Wesley, a branch of the Anglican church, and other groups in England and, later, in the New World.

Today there are denominations that align closely with Arminius, including the Nazarene church. Some Baptist denominations lean toward Calvin; others lean the direction of Arminius. Certain Baptist groups believe in eternal security of the believer, so are in agreement with Calvin on that point, but reject the limitations he put on human free will in the salvation process.

The quiet orphan of the Netherlands did not set out to be one side of what may be one of the greatest, most divisive doctrinal debates in history. He endeavored to preach and teach the truth as he saw it in the Bible. It sounds simple today, but in Jacob Arminius' day it was a dangerous thing to do.

32

FRANCIS BACON
What's a Man Like Him Doing in a Book like This?

(1561–1626)

> There are two books laid before us to study, to prevent our falling into error; first, the volume of Scriptures, which revealed the will of God; then the volume of the Creatures, which expresses His power.
>
> Sir Francis Bacon, *Essay on Learning*

At first it might seem odd to see the name Sir Francis Bacon listed among those who shaped the church. After all, he was not a churchman, a priest, or a theologian but rather a government official—a government official whose career started off rocky, rose to great heights, and then was stripped away, leaving him nothing. Yet this prolific writer (who has been associated by some as the writer of plays attributed to Shakespeare) is known more for his contribution to science than to government service.

A Man of Government

Francis Bacon (not to be confused with Roger Bacon the Franciscan monk, who lived nearly 350 years before) was born into a distinguished family. His father, Sir Nicholas Bacon, was Lord Keeper of the Seal, and his mother, Lady Anne Cook Bacon, was the highly educated daughter of Anthony Cook, the tutor of Edward VI. His early education was conducted at home, and he later went to Trinity College in Cambridge along with his older brother.

His father secured a position for him to serve the ambassador to France, Sir Amis Paulet. That came to an end when his father died in 1579. Bacon was left with very little inheritance. He continued his studies and charted a life of his own in politics, something at which he excelled. In a span of seven years he practiced law, became a member of Parliament, and went on to teach law.

However, work in government was as tricky in the seventeenth century as it is today. His rapid rise hit the doldrums under the reign of Elizabeth I, who was not as fond of Sir Francis as others had been. Fortunately for him the queen respected his mentor, the Earl of Essex. And once James I took the throne, Sir Francis' career took off again. He served in several roles and ultimately rose to Lord Chancellor.

A Man of Science

Sir Francis proved to have an active, inquisitive, and restless mind. Science became one of his great interests, and like others in his day he felt the need for change in the way science approached its work. Much of science at the time was done deductively; that is, general principles were observed and through logic refined to more detailed ideas. Start with the general, then move to the specific. It was a very old way of doing things. Such thinking has its place, but it often leads to error.

The flipside of the thinking coin is called inductive reasoning: moving from the specific to the general. Science makes observations, conducts experiments, then draws conclusions. Today we call it "the scientific method," and while Sir Francis Bacon was not the first to propose such thinking, he championed its cause better than any other. Today, the scientific method is taught in schools around the world. It would undergo refinement over the years, but Sir Francis brought this practice to the forefront of current thinking. Systematic science has helped us understand archaeology, history, language, and other areas of the Bible and its people.

A Man of Faith

Sir Francis was a devout member of the Anglican church and often wrote about spiritual matters in his essays (he introduced the essay form of writing to England). He believed that God had given humankind two guiding lights: the Bible and nature. "There are two books laid before us to study, to prevent our falling into error; first, the volume of Scriptures, which reveal the will of God; then the volume of the Creatures, which express His power."[1]

He believed that knowledge and faith went together. In his treatise *Of Atheism*, he wrote, "A little philosophy inclines man's mind to atheism, but depth in philosophy brings men's minds about to religion."[2]

From the Top to the Bottom Again

Sir Francis' career ended abruptly when he was accused of participating in acts of corruption. He maintained that he was a just judge; nonetheless, he confessed to "the abuse of the times." That was 1620. Stripped of his positions, Sir Francis turned to his writing, his scientific studies, and experiments. After working in cold and snowy conditions while experimenting with food preservation, he became deathly ill. In 1626, Sir Francis Bacon died of pneumonia, leaving a legacy of public service, scientific philosophy, and the faith attached to every area of his life.

33

GALILEO GALILEI

Balancing Science and Spirituality

(1564–1642)

> I'm inclined to think that the authority of Holy Scripture is intended to convince men of those truths which are necessary for their salvation, which, being far above man's understanding, cannot be made credible by any learning, or any other means than revelation by the Holy Spirit.
>
> Galileo Galilei, *Letter to Benedetto Castelli*

In July of 1971, an interesting experiment was done on the moon by Apollo 15 astronaut David Scott. The moon has no atmosphere to provide air resistance to a very light object, so the objects can fall unhindered. To prove the results of an experiment conducted over three hundred years before, Scott dropped a hammer and a falcon feather (the landing module was dubbed *Falcon*) and both landed on the lunar surface at the same time. Galileo Galilei would have been thrilled.

If everything we read in the media is to be believed, then science and faith are incompatible. A thinking man or woman must choose between intelligence and superstition. There is no doubt that in the late twentieth and early twenty-first centuries we have seen an increase in this tension. But many of the greatest scientists in history have been devout individuals, including Blaise Pascal, Nicolaus Copernicus, Louis Pasteur, and Gregor Mendel. Perhaps one of the most accomplished men of faith and science is Galileo Galilei, the Italian mathematician, physicist, astronomer, inventor, and accomplished musician.

Born in Pisa, Italy, in 1564 to a musician father—who played the lute—he was the oldest of six children. Only four of his siblings lived through infancy. The family had financial problems that were left to Galileo after his father's death in 1591, including the need for dowries for his sisters. His brothers-in-law sought legal help to get the money they felt they deserved. Michelangelo, Galileo's young brother, often needed financial help. It seemed everyone had a hand in Galileo's pocket.

Galileo's education began in a monastery near Florence. He then attended the University of Pisa to study medicine. After a number of years of study, the future scientist dropped out of school but continued to study on his own. He supported himself by tutoring. He also applied himself to some challenging mathematical problems, and his skill was noticed and rewarded with a teaching position at Pisa. He chaired the Department of Mathematics.

A Thinking Man Takes on the Thinkers

Galileo argued for an experimental approach to science with results explained with mathematics. This was a new approach.

Scientists speak of the Law of Falling Bodies. Galileo's contribution to this comes from one of his most famous experiments—an experiment that made enemies. The thinkers of his day followed principles laid down by Aristotle eighteen centuries before. Based on those principles, scientists of the day believed heavier objects fell faster than lighter ones. It was a conclusion reached by Aristotelian logic. But Galileo wasn't so sure. He experimented with balls of different mass and discovered they fell at the same rate. According to Galileo's biographer Vincenzo Viviani, the mathematician proved his point by dropping balls of differing weights from the Tower of Pisa. They hit the ground at the same time.

This was more than a simple experiment. It was an attack on the accepted reasoning of the time. It meant Aristotle was wrong, and if the ancient Greek was wrong about that, what other errors might be in his teaching? Those who had been taught the principles of Aristotle all their lives were being shown the error of their thinking, and not many people respond with kindness to such correction. Many of his fellow teachers in Pisa turned against him, forcing Galileo to look elsewhere for work. Thanks to some friends, he found and took a teaching position in Padua, a more intellectually open environment.

Telescoping a Future

While at Padua he heard of the telescope (more of a spyglass) having been invented in the Netherlands. Unable to acquire one, he made his own, grinding the lenses himself. His version was superior to the earlier devices. While the early telescopes could magnify distant objects threefold, Galileo's scopes had a magnification of up to twenty times. This moved the telescope from novelty to serious scientific instrument.

While best known for the advancement of the telescope and being the first to turn it skyward, Galileo invented other items including the geometric compass, the isochronous pendulum, the pendulum clock, and an early thermometer.

A Thinking Man Takes on an Old Idea

Ptolemy was a Greek astronomer who lived thirteen hundred years before Galileo. He taught that the earth was the center of the solar system, a belief that fit nicely with the Catholic Church. There was a certain logic to it. Appearance is a powerful influence. Situated as we are on this planet, it seems that everything in the heavens rotates around us. Even in the twenty-first century we still speak of "sunrise" and "sunset." Why? Because that's what we see. Deeper investigation has proven beyond any doubt that the earth spins on its axis, making it appear that the sun rises and sets. Yet even knowing that doesn't keep us from using the "language of appearance." It is easy to understand how Ptolemy and those who followed him could believe in an earth-centric solar system.

Nicolaus Copernicus, who lived a generation before, advocated a heliocentric system—a "sun-centered" system. However, by Galileo's time, the Ptolemy model had been engraved into the thinking of theologians, many of whom could not see the benefit of knowledge gained by observation and experimentation.

Galileo, who was initially more mathematician than astronomer, had to confront the old ideas. His telescope had shown him that the moon was covered in mountains and craters, that Venus—like the moon—showed phases that meant it orbited the sun, and that moons circled Jupiter.

Johannes Kepler, a German astronomer and contemporary of Galileo, urged the Italian to go public with his findings and his belief in the Copernican structure of the solar system. It meant going against long-held beliefs, but Galileo was accustomed to rocking the scientific boat. He published *The Starry Messenger* (*Sidereus Nuncius*), a pamphlet outlining his discoveries.

Not everyone was impressed.

The Price of Truth

Galileo was accused of heresy, with much of the anger coming not from the church but from his fellow scientists who resented his emphasis on an experimental, mathematical approach to science. At the instigation of Pope Paul V in 1616, an inquisition was formed to investigate charges of heresy. He defended himself and his views— "The intention of the Holy Spirit is to teach us how one goes to heaven, not how the heavens go"[1]—but the investigators ruled against him. He was forbidden from teaching that the earth orbited the sun.

Then Barberini became Pope Urban VIII. Galileo considered him a friend and approached him about a release from the gag order that had been forced on him. Urban couldn't see his way clear to do so. It would mean saying the inquisitors and the previous pope had been wrong. He was also under great pressure from court intrigue and infighting. But Galileo didn't walk away empty-handed. He was allowed to write a book about the matter as long as he presented both theories of the solar system equally and did not push one over the other. Galileo wrote *Dialogue Concerning Two Chief World Systems*, finishing in 1632. It was translated into Latin shortly thereafter.

Although he had full permission to write the book, he made a miscalculation: he named the character defending the earth-centric position Simplicio ("simpleminded"). Some believe he drew the name from Simplicius of Cilicia, a sixth-century defender of Aristotle, but Pope Urban believed his friend Galileo was characterizing him. Urban saw himself in Simplicio and didn't like it. Galileo's critics were certain he was mocking the pope and his followers. Although the book was written with full support of the pope and was a bestseller, it brought nothing but grief for Galileo.

In 1633, Galileo endured another inquisition. Sometimes these investigations into Galileo's heresy are portrayed as grueling sessions, including torture. While torture did occur in some inquisitions, Galileo was left unharmed—at least physically. They sentenced him to life in prison but lifted the sentence and allowed the scientist to live under house arrest. He was seventy years old. That year, *Dialogue Concerning the Two Chief World Systems* was added to the Roman Catholic List of Prohibited Books.

A Spiritual Man

It would be understandable if Galileo turned against the church, yet he never did. He was a faithful believer who felt science revealed God's work. He also believed the Bible was a special revelation giving the reader knowledge he could obtain no other way. "I'm inclined to think that the authority of Holy Scripture is intended to convince men of those truths which are necessary for their salvation, which, being far above man's understanding, cannot be made credible by any learning, or any other means than revelation by the Holy Spirit."[2]

For Galileo, science was one way man learned about God and his design of the universe. "For the Bible is not chained in every expression to conditions as strict as those which govern all physical effects; nor is God any less excellently revealed in Nature's actions than in the sacred statements of the Bible."[3]

Final Days

Galileo spent his last days writing his final book: *Discourses and Mathematical Demonstrations Relating to Two New Sciences*. It was a compendium of his earlier work. Not long after, he lost his sight to glaucoma.

In 1981, the Catholic Church formed a commission to look into Galileo's trials and the judgments against him. Eleven years later Pope John Paul II said errors had been made in the treatment of the scientist. The church made efforts to unwind the decisions made so many centuries before. As of today, Galileo is respected by the church and the scientific community. He has been praised by the likes of Stephen Hawking and Albert Einstein.

He shaped the church by showing that science can enrich faith, and that observation and testing can lead to new truth or strengthen well-known truth. His life is a testament that a scientific mind can be a spiritual mind.

34

BROTHER LAWRENCE

A Heavenly View from the Kitchen

(1611–1691)

> The greater perfection a soul aspires after, the more dependent it is upon Divine Grace.
>
> Brother Lawrence, *The Practice and Presence of God*

O ur reflections of the people who shaped the church might cause us to think that all the mighty influencers were people of great bravery, high scholarship, persuasive words, powerful position, and giant intellects. We would be wrong to think so. There's a different kind of spiritual genius, one that comes without fanfare or notice in one's life. In seventeenth-century France, a young man born in poverty had a deep, soul-shaking insight that would change him forever. His life would not be lived upon the public stage but in the hot environs of a Paris monastery amid tedious, wearying kitchen work. He was a simple man with a simple idea that has touched the lives of millions.

The Wisdom of the Tree

Born to peasant parents, Nicholas Herman arrived with nothing to offer. Surviving was his only goal, and at the age of eighteen he did what many young men did both then and now: he joined the military, knowing it was a means to regular meals and a meager wage. He remained in the army for eighteen unexceptional years, until an injury forced him from the service. But he left the army with more than he expected.

One winter's day, he came upon a tree, its leaves having dropped as was normal for the season. As Herman studied the tree, insight struck. Here was a tree that had no leaves, no buds, and was nothing more than trunk, limbs, and branches. But soon, as winter turned to spring, the sun would grow warm, the rains would come, and the apparently dead tree would come to life once more. He was like the tree: barren, with little to show for his life, but the future—God's future for him—would be different. Just as God had planned abundance for the waiting tree, his grace and providence could bring Herman life, fullness, and joy. That moment he fell in love with God.

A New Life

While working as a valet and doing other odd jobs in his post-army days, Herman encountered the life of Carmelite monks. The monastic life they lived was demanding and difficult, but it appealed to him. He entered the monastery as a lay monk—an adherent who was not part of the clergy. He lacked the education to be anything more.

Here, in the heart of Paris, he worked in the kitchen, cooking meals and cleaning. At times it was lonely, but loneliness was something Herman—now Brother Lawrence—needed. He developed a simple philosophy: a man could worship God while busy with the most menial of tasks. Status had no value. Only heartfelt worship did.

For Brother Lawrence there was no separation of work and prayer. Worship could be done in the kitchen as well as the chapel.

> The time of business does not differ with me from the time of prayer; and in the noise and clatter of my kitchen, while several persons are at the same time calling for different things, I possess God in as great tranquility as if I were on my knees at the blessed sacrament.[1]

There is an old saying that a person can be so earthly minded as to be no heavenly good, and so heavenly minded as to be no earthly good. But Brother Lawrence learned to be both heavenly and earthly minded.

A Reputation Wider Than His Kitchen

We would know nothing about Brother Lawrence and his simple but powerful lifestyle had it not been for Abbe de Beaufort, investigator for the French cardinal Louis Antoine de Noailles. The cardinal had heard of Lawrence's piety and wanted to know more. Beaufort visited Lawrence in the Carmelite monastery and conducted four interviews. From those interviews, a few letters, and some writings found after Brother Lawrence's death, we learn of the man who took humility to its heights.

His simple statements carry a spiritual weight:

I drove away from my mind everything capable of spoiling the sense of the presence of God.[2]

I make it my business to persevere in His holy presence.[3]

My soul has had an habitual, silent, secret conversation with God.[4]

Let us think often that our only business in this life is to please God. Perhaps all besides is but folly and vanity.[5]

There is not in the world a kind of life more sweet and delightful than that of a continual conversation with God.[6]

The Practice of the Presence of God is more than the title for the book composed of Brother Lawrence's collected papers and quotes. It is a way of life. A quiet, unassuming lay monk who spent his life in obscurity cooking and cleaning lived a life that still inspires today. Sometimes the church is shaped by a person who wants nothing more than a daily conversation with God.

35

BLAISE PASCAL

The Fiery Mind

(1623–1662)

Reason's last step is the recognition that there are an infinite number of things which are beyond it.

Blaise Pascal, *Pensées*

It is fair to say that the "new age of reason" has launched an assault on people of faith. There is a renewed freedom to ridicule people of religious conviction, portraying them as ignorant, uneducated, and antiscientific. Those without a sense of history might think this is new, that rationalism is the new kid on the block and faith-based thinking is being moved to a retirement home where it belongs. But history says otherwise.

Many great people of faith have spent their lives in scientific pursuits. The blending of science and faith found a perfect match in a seventeenth-century Frenchman: Blaise Pascal. Pascal was one of the brightest minds in the history of scientific accomplishment. He also possessed a brilliant spiritual mind. He, Isaac Newton, and many other brilliant figures did not see faith and scientific inquiry as diametrically opposed.

Pascal was a child prodigy with a lightning-fast mind, a dedication to science, and a hunger for God. His life exemplifies the struggle of the individual to better know God and find peace in this world.

An Early Start

Blaise Pascal was born in 1623 to a father who was a lawyer and skilled mathematician. His was not an easy life. At the age of three Pascal's mother, Antoinette Begon, died, leaving his father to rear Pascal and his two sisters. His father, Étienne, moved the family from Clermont-Ferrand to Paris to provide a better cultural experience for his children. There he homeschooled them. On occasion he would take young Pascal with him to the Academy of Science, where his son developed a love for science.

By age ten, Pascal was mastering mathematics and conducting experiments in the physical sciences. Étienne Pascal had become a tax collector and struggled under the weight of calculations his job required. At nineteen, to lessen the burden on his father, young Pascal invented the first calculator, a mechanical device whose principles would be used for many decades.

He was one of those people whose interest and imagination bounced from one area of study to another. In the course of his short life, he not only invented the first calculator but also tested the theories of great scientists like Galileo and Torricelli (who discovered the principles of the barometer). He formulated laws of hydraulics and hydrostatics; wrote papers on the vacuum in nature; calculated the density of air, invented the syringe, the hydraulic lift, and the hydraulic press; founded the theory of probabilities; and developed a form of integral calculus. It is also said that Pascal invented the first wristwatch, and he is credited with mapping the first Paris bus route.

His studies and accomplishments, however, did not satisfy his soul. He had a keen interest in spiritual matters. Christianity in the seventeenth century was undergoing change. There was the Piety Movement in Germany, and the teaching of Wesley was making its way through England, but France remained staunchly Roman Catholic.

Still, changes were brewing within the Roman Catholic Church in France. To many, the church was becoming far too centered on free will and the belief that works were necessary for salvation. A reformation group formed to challenge what they saw as a doctrinal problem: a reliance on good works that cheapened the redeeming work of Christ. The Jansenists, named after their founder Cornelius Jansen (1585–1638), were in some ways a Protestant movement within the Roman Church. Jansenism called on the church to embrace the principles of Augustine, bishop of Hippo, specifically predestination and the inability of individuals to save themselves through good works.

Pascal first encountered the teachings of Jansen when two physicians came to the aid of his father, who had fallen on hard, icy ground, dislocating his hip. The doctors, both Jansenists, cared for Blaise Pascal's father and answered the young man's many questions about suffering. What they said made sense, and he and his family converted to the sect. His sister Jacqueline would later enter a Jansenist convent at Port-Royal, south of Versailles.

Vision

On November 23, 1654, Pascal had a strange, life-changing experience. That night, beginning about 10:30 and lasting for two hours, Blaise Pascal had a vision of the cross. In some ways it broke him; in others it empowered him. He wrote an emotional response on parchment and sewed it to the interior of his coat, where he carried it for the rest of his short life. After his death at the age of thirty-nine, a servant found the parchment while cleaning out a few of Pascal's things. Pascal had written:

> The year of grace, 1654
> Monday, November 23rd . . . from about half past ten in the
>   evening until about half past twelve . . .
> God of Abraham, God of Isaac, God of Jacob,
> not of the philosophers and scholars.
> Certainty, certainty, feeling, joy, peace.
> God of Jesus Christ . . .

195

I have separated myself from Him, I have fled from Him,
Renounced Him, crucified Him.
May I never be separated from . . .
Renunciation, total and sweet.[1]

This was his conversion experience, heartrending but joyful.

Before his death he wrote eighteen *Provincial Letters*, which were widely read in France. The letters were an attempt to expose the weaknesses in Jesuit thinking and their emphasis on good works. He wrote with eloquence and at times sarcasm. His skill with prose makes him one of the most admired French writers of all time. The pope condemned the letters, but they were still widely read.

Pascal then turned his attention to what he hoped would be a book defending Christianity, a book offering evidences for faith. Pascal lived in the Age of Enlightenment, when tossing off old beliefs was fashionable and considered a sign of intelligence. France was becoming more secular and many were beginning to see Christianity as something that had outlived its usefulness. Pascal could not accept that premise or conclusion. He remained committed to defending the faith.

He would never finish his book. For most of his life Pascal had suffered from a variety of ailments, and in the summer of 1662 he became gravely ill. He died on August 19 without seeing his fortieth birthday. The cause of his death is unknown but an autopsy showed problems with some of his internal organs and his brain. Stomach cancer has been suggested as the cause of death and a brain lesion as the cause of his many headaches. Regardless of the cause, science and faith lost a champion when he died.

Eight years later, friends gathered his notes and had them published. *Pensées (Thoughts)* is a collection of notes Pascal meant to include in his next book. In it he describes what has become known as "Pascal's Wager" or "Pascal's Gambit." It can be paraphrased like this:

1. God exists or he doesn't.
2. A game is being played in which you make a choice about God's existence.

3. You wager your life on this decision.

4. If you wager that God does exist and you're right, you win.

5. If you wager that God exists and you are wrong, you lose nothing because service to God is a joy.

6. If you wager there is no God and you're wrong, you lose everything.[2]

Pascal's point is simple: you can't lose betting *on* God, but you can lose much betting *against* him.

Pascal's genius played in many fields: math, physics, invention, writing, and faith. He saw more than his share of troubles in the world and lived at a time when being a person of faith often brought more ridicule than praise, but he remained unmoved by irrational rationalists. To Pascal, science was no enemy of God. Faithful living, he believed, could change the world.

Pascal shaped the church through his emphasis on faith without sacrificing reason. He was a man who saw the individual's need for salvation, a need he couldn't accomplish on his own. He needed God.

36

JOHN BUNYAN

Gifted Tinker

(1628–1688)

And some said, Let them live; some, Let them die. Some said, John, print it; others said, Not so. Some said, It might do good; others said, No.

John Bunyan, *Pilgrim's Progress*, "The Author's Apology for His Book"

The most famous and influential book in English is the Bible; the second is John Bunyan's *Pilgrim's Progress*. The book was first released in 1676 and became so popular that nearly every house in his country had a copy. Wherever there was a Bible, it seemed, there was a copy of *Pilgrim's Progress*. Not bad for a tinker turned preacher, a convict turned author.

Penniless

John Bunyan was born in November 1628 to a tinker's family. A tinker traveled from house to house fixing metal pots for a living. Thomas and Margaret Bunyan of Elstow, Bedfordshire, England, eked out a living this way for themselves and their children. As was done in those days, the son followed in the father's footsteps and Bunyan became an itinerant tinker, plying his trade the same way his father had, traveling from place to place fixing pots and pans for those who could not afford new ones.

During the English Civil War, he served in the parliamentary army before returning and taking up his father's trade. Around the age of twenty, he married a woman as poor as he. She was an orphan with a dowry of just two books: *Plain Man's Pathway to Heaven* by Arthur Dent and Lewis Bayly's *Practice of Piety*, both Christian books. These books would play a role in his spiritual formation.

The name of his wife is lost to us. We do know he had a blind daughter named Mary. Some speculate she might have shared the name with her mother.

Bunyan was not a practicing Christian. In fact, he considered himself a great sinner, prone to swearing and disreputable behavior. His wife tried to reform him but had little luck. Yet a spark of spirituality burned within him.

Two Books + Three Poor Women + One Pastor = Conversion

Bunyan behaved well enough to be considered a fine Christian by his neighbors, but he knew better. "For though as yet I was nothing but a poor painted hypocrite, yet I loved to be talked of as one that was truly godly."[1]

The books that came as part of his wife's meager dowry had raised an interest in spiritual matters, but had still not instigated true change in him. But in his early twenties, Bunyan began attending a church in Bedford. The church was an independent congregation. There he encountered a pastor who taught the Bible with intensity, and soon Bunyan was poring over the Holy Book.

Bunyan admitted that he was trying to work out his own righteousness but failing. He was acquiring head knowledge but had yet to connect to Christ in a personal way. While plying his tinker's trade in Bedford, he "came where there were three or four poor women sitting at a door, in the sun, talking about the things of God; and being now willing to hear their discourse, I drew near to hear what they said."[2] Bunyan had become someone who talked religion but did not understand faith. He listened to the impoverished women speak of God and faith and came to a moment of self-discovery. "They were far above [his understanding], out of reach. Their talk was about a new birth, the work of God in their hearts, as how they were convinced of their miserable state by nature. They talked how God had visited their souls with his love in the Lord Jesus."[3] He would spend more time with people like this, and gradually came to understand his soul's need.

A third catalyst in Bunyan's path to faith came from John Gifford, the minister of the church in Bedford who invited him to his home, where he spoke to others about faith. Bunyan accepted the invitation, and soon after joined the church. A rapid spiritual transformation began taking place. Within four years he was drawing large crowds to hear his preaching. Bunyan now had head and heart in the church.

Go to Church or Go to Jail

For two decades the Separatists—those churches that chose to be apart from the Church of England—worked with little fear, but that changed suddenly. Charles II came to the throne and allowed the Clarendon Code to be reenacted. The code was designed to keep anyone who was not in fellowship with the Anglican church from holding a political position. It also required adherence to the Anglican church. Nonconformists like Bunyan were forbidden to preach. Later, it became illegal for a Nonconformist minister to come within five miles of incorporated towns.

Those who did not comply with the code could be jailed. Bunyan chose the Bedford jail over submission to the code. It would be his home for twelve years. To be freed, all he had to do was promise to stop preaching. Bunyan couldn't do it. He would sit in jail until "moss shall grow on mine eyebrows, rather than thus to violate my faith and principles."[4]

His incarceration was not as brutal as some imagine. He was allowed visitors, he was allowed to go home from time to time, and on occasion he was even allowed to preach to crowds who gathered outside the prison. But these occasional liberties shouldn't take away from the sacrifice Bunyan made. While his family could visit him, the separation was grueling. His incarceration made supporting his family nearly impossible and the family had to rely on the kindness of others. Making this all the more poignant was the fact that Bunyan had four children. Concern for his family tormented him, yet he remained true to his cause.

Turning a Jail Cell into an Office

Bunyan remained in jail for twelve years. During that time he wrote nine books. He was released for a time in 1666, but the authorities soon brought him back to his cell. From 1667–1672 he worked on *Pilgrim's Progress*, the timeless classic that would make him a household name and cement his legacy. One of the greatest English classics was not written by some intellectual in a famous university but rather by a creative genius in a jail cell who had, at best, a grammar school education.

When not working on his writing, he served as prison chaplain to other inmates, made musical instruments from items in his cell, and wove shoelaces to help support his family.

The Declaration of Religious Indulgence, issued in 1672, eased the restrictions on non-Anglicans. Bunyan was freed and accepted the post as pastor of the Bedford church. Later, he was forced to return to prison again but this time the stay was much shorter—six months. After his second release, *Pilgrim's Progress* went to press. The book became a bestseller, and crossed the lines of social class. In one year the book sold over one hundred thousand copies, and to date has never been out of print.

Pilgrim's Progress

Pilgrim's Progress is an allegory, a story that carries additional meaning or a lesson. Bunyan wrapped spiritual truths around his characters, the places they visit, and the people they meet. The protagonist is Christian, who represents "the everyman" on a journey from his City of Destruction (the world) to Celestial City (heaven). His journey is made difficult because of the great burden on his back. He seeks help along the way and receives it, but he also faces temptations and trials.

The story parallels Bunyan's struggle with faith. His was not an instant conversion but one that went through several steps and involved interaction with others. Like Christian, he felt the burden of his sin and wanted to be released of it, and to be assured of entrance into a better world.

Anyone familiar with the gospel message and the basics of Christian belief will see the meaning behind the story. Bunyan makes no effort to hide the truth in some clever way. The names of the characters (Christian, Obstinate, Pliable, Companion, etc.) and the places they visit (Vanity Fair, House Beautiful, Wicket Gate, etc.) are easy to recognize as illustrations of biblical concepts.

Fame and Faith

Pilgrim's Progress made Bunyan famous. Although none of his other books rose to similar acclaim, each was still well-received on its own merit. Despite the change in his fortunes, Bunyan remained on the job as a pastor. He had spent twelve years in prison because he refused to give up his calling to preach, and he had no desire to surrender it now that he was free.

Bunyan may have been slow to come to faith, but once he arrived he never left. He remained the pastor he had become, forged from his own pilgrim's journey. Out of his hardships came a book that opened many eyes to the challenges and benefits of the spiritual journey.

His commitment to service may have cost him his life. In August of 1688, the fifty-nine-year-old Bunyan—now nicknamed "Bishop Bunyan"—rode through a summer rainstorm in hopes of healing a rift between a father and son. He became ill soon after and died.

Pilgrim's Progress has withstood changes in language, cultures, technology, social shifts, and more to become one of the most revered religious books written for the average person. It still touches lives today. Bunyan showed by deed and word how deep a commitment a person can make to his or her calling.

37

ISAAC WATTS

Singing His Songs

(1674–1748)

> Joy to the world! the Lord is come;
> Let earth receive her King.
> Let ev'ry heart prepare Him room,
> And heav'n and nature sing.
>
> Isaac Watts, "Joy to the World"

He wasn't much to look at: five feet tall, rail thin, and pale, with a head that looked too large for his body; but oh, what was in that head. Isaac Watts was a multitalented man, a prodigy in several fields, but he will always be remembered as the man who helped introduce hymns to the English church.

Music is an integral part of the contemporary church. Regardless of denomination or church size, music is one of the first acts of worship and as much a part of the service as the sermon. This has not always been the case.

In Isaac Watts' day, singing in church was uncommon. Old Testament psalms might be sung, but there was nothing "contemporary" about the music. Lutherans in Germany had been singing in church for decades, largely due to Martin Luther's love of music (he wrote many hymns). English churches, however, frowned on the practice.

A Prodigy

Watts was the first of nine children in his family, born on July 17, 1674, in Southampton, England, to a father who spent a stretch or two in jail for not conforming to the Church of England. His mother told him tales of sitting on the jailhouse steps caring for her children.

Watts was a child who learned quickly. He could truthfully be called a prodigy. He began learning Latin around the age of four, Greek at nine, French at eleven, and Hebrew at thirteen. He also had a gift for rhyme.

As a teenager he, like his father, shunned the Church of England, which meant he could not attend Oxford or Cambridge, even though there were friends and neighbors willing to pay his way. Instead, he went to a Nonconformist academy in London. He spent the first years after his graduation as a tutor.

In 1702 he became pastor of Mark Lane Independent Chapel in London. He had not been in the pulpit long before he developed an illness that plagued him the rest of his life. The nature of the illness is unknown, although he refers to "Gaundise" (jaundice) and "Cholic" (colic). The disorder lasted for years and took a toll on body, mind, and emotions. Each year he had to pass more responsibility to his assistant pastor, until Watts finally resigned. Sir Thomas Abney, mayor of London, took him into his home and there he stayed for thirty-six years, remaining with the family even after Sir Thomas' death in 1721.

Something New for Churches

Watts was disenchanted with the singing of Psalms in church. The singing lacked enthusiasm and Christian content—it was biblical content to be sure, but not Christian. The Psalms were a beautiful representation of worship and praise, but were restricted to Old Testament revelation. Worshipers couldn't sing about the cross, the resurrection, the ascension, the Trinity, or the nativity. Watts wanted to give worshipers an avenue to do that, but English churches had adopted the restraint of Calvin. Anything new was suspect.

Isaac Watts compiled *Hymns and Spiritual Songs*, which he published in 1707. In its pages are familiar hymns such as "Joy to the World," "O God, Our Help in Ages Past," "When I Survey the Wondrous Cross," and many more. He also wrote *Psalms of David Imitated in the Language of the New Testament* (1719), in which he transformed David's poetry as if the great king had written in Watts's time. He had a love for children and published the first hymnal for young people, *Divine Songs for Children* (1715).

Some referred to his hymns as, "Watts' whims." While his songs made inroads with the independent churches in England, it wasn't until 1861—over a century later—that his work made it into a Church of England hymnbook.

Although he met resistance in England, his work was well-received in America. Benjamin Franklin published Watts' paraphrases of David's psalms. Revolutionary Americans loved the hymns. Fellow Englishman John Wesley used the word "genius" to describe Watts.

How many hymns did Watts write? The exact number is still debated, but with confidence we can say that he wrote anywhere from six hundred to eight hundred hymns over the course of his lifetime, a truly amazing accomplishment.

More Than Hymns

There was more to Watts than spiritual songs. He also penned thirty theological treatises; essays on philosophy, psychology, and astronomy; a textbook on logic; and three volumes of sermons.

Watts may not have been a physically imposing or dashing man, but his creativity, perseverance, and dedication to church music lives long after him. Modern hymnals still carry his hymns and many worshipers could not imagine church without the occasional hymn from Isaac Watts.

38

GEORGE FRIDERIC HANDEL
Music to Make the Soul Soar

(1685–1759)

I should be sorry if I only entertained them. I wished to make them better.

George Frideric Handel, in response to a compliment from an audience member

Every Christmas, the music of George Frideric Handel fills concert halls and churches around the world. There's some irony in that. Handel never meant for his now famous *Messiah* to be associated with Christmas. He intended it for the Lenten season—the days preceding Easter. Still, over 270 years after it was written, the *Messiah* is still loved and performed around Christmas.

It wasn't that way in the beginning.

Against Dad's Wishes

Born in the German town of Halle, Handel grew up with a mother who nurtured his love of music. But his surgeon-barber father, who was in his sixties when Handel was born, forbid his son to study it. He had chosen law as the career his son would pursue; music was just a distraction. Tradition says Handel would sneak into a room and play the clavichord—a keyboard instrument popular in the time—whenever his father was gone. Handel's father relented when his son turned nine, allowing the boy to take lessons in organ. His father died when Handel was eleven. By the time he was twelve, Handel was capable of substituting for the church organist and had written his first musical composition. The future composer did take a stab at studying law but soon abandoned it in favor of music.

Handel continued his musical studies in Germany and Italy, then moved to England, where he would spend the rest of his life.

Changing Tastes

Handel's first musical love was opera, but such large musical presentations had lost popularity in England. Handel began to lose money on his productions, yet stubbornly continued to write opera music. He often played to nearly empty halls, joking that the acoustics were better with fewer people in the seats. Finances were often a problem for the maestro, and became so severe he feared debtor's prison. Handel had to make adjustments. His humor was being tempered by financial need.

In 1737 his opera company went bankrupt and, likely due to the stress this caused, he suffered a mild stroke. Handel then turned to writing oratorios. Unlike opera with its costumes, drama, and acting, oratorios were less dramatic, had no costumes, and were usually based on biblical persons or events.

One such oratorio, *Esther*, offended many church leaders, who felt such sacred material shouldn't be performed in theaters. Still, Handel pressed on, and when the royal family attended, things turned around and the work obtained some success despite its opposition.

Advertising posters for *Israel in Egypt* were torn down, and some people disrupted performances. All of this puzzled and angered Handel. After all, he was a Christian man, devout, and well-versed in Scripture—better than most bishops, according to him. He continued his work in the face of criticism, but financial problems continued to hamper his career.

Down and Depressed

Despair was a familiar feeling for Handel; the roller-coaster ride that was his life had left him depressed and broke. Financial problems and constant criticism by the English church and by detractors who called him "that German nincompoop" haunted him. In those dark days, his friend Charles Jennens came to visit. Jennens was a wealthy landowner and patron of the arts. He was also a librettist—a person who writes the text for operas or librettos. A devout member of the Anglican church, he had written a text he wanted set to music. The material was taken directly from the Bible and meant to show God's work of redemption. Much of the material came from the Old Testament. He needed Handel to compose the music around the work. Over time Jennens and Handel would work on five oratorios, including the *Messiah*.

Handel received a second visit, this time from a charitable group wanting to use the oratorio to raise money to free men confined to debtor's prison. Handel would receive a commission for composing the work.

The work consumed Handel, who locked himself away and worked night and day, scarcely eating. His production of the *Messiah* is the stuff of legend. He produced Part I in six days, Part II in nine, and Part III in another six. It took only two days to finish the orchestration. In those twenty-four days, he produced 260 pages of material. A traditional story has Handel saying to a servant after finishing the Hallelujah Chorus, "I did think I did see all heaven before me, and the great God himself."[1]

Messiah premiered on April 13, 1742 in Dublin, where it was well-received and highly praised. Over seven hundred people attended. To make it possible to seat more, women were asked not to wear hoops in their dresses and men not to wear their swords. This allowed for the seating of about a hundred additional people. (Women stopped wearing hoops to concerts after this.) The first performance raised enough money to free over 140 people from debtor's prison. It seemed as if Handel's fate had turned.

It hadn't.

London was a different matter. It took a year before *Messiah* would play in a major city, and when it did, it was panned by critics. To settle some of the controversy, Handel changed the title, which some thought was blasphemous, to *A New Sacred Oratorio*. King George II attended and stood at the singing of the Hallelujah Chorus. Of course, when the king stands, everyone stands. Historians debate why he did this. Some suggest the king, who had hearing problems, thought the national anthem was being played; others suggest he just needed to stretch his legs; still others say it was a spiritual statement. Whatever the initial reason, audiences around the world have been standing during the chorus ever since.

But it didn't take long before Handel was playing to empty houses again, and he was on the brink of poverty once more. He would conduct thirty performances and only one of those was in a church—Bristol Cathedral.

Handel faced health issues, including strokes. Later in life he was hindered by cataracts. Despite surgeries to correct the problem, he eventually went blind. He died the day before Easter, April 14, 1759, and was buried in Westminster Abbey.

The Impact

Handel followed his musical dreams and experienced fame and disgrace. Still, his work continues to inspire. He was a man whose faith and art were inseparable. Although he also wrote secular work, it is his Bible-inspired composition that lives on after him, proving that art is a viable means of spiritual expression. There are those whose only exposure to the redemptive work of Christ is what they've heard in *Messiah*.

39

JONATHAN EDWARDS
The Quiet Man

(1703–1758)

> The God that holds you over the pit of hell, much as one holds a spider, or some loathsome insect over the fire, abhors you, and is dreadfully provoked: his wrath towards you burns like fire; he looks upon you as worthy of nothing else, but to be cast into the fire; he is of purer eyes than to bear to have you in his sight; you are ten thousand times more abominable in his eyes, than the most hateful venomous serpent is in ours.
>
> Jonathan Edwards, "Sinners in the Hands of an Angry God"

The man standing in the pulpit wore his black ministerial robes, puritan-style white clerical collar, and lace drop "preaching" bands. His face was narrow and his light hair was receding. He displayed a dignified, serious manner as he read the manuscript of his sermon—twenty-five pages when later typeset and published. Most of the city of Enfield, Connecticut, that July in 1741 had come out to hear him. He kept his eyes fixed on the words of his sermon. He stayed behind the pulpit as if he had grown roots. From time to time, he paused to let the congregation settle, many of whom were weeping, groaning, moaning, and agonizing over their sin.

Jonathan Edwards, pastor of the Church of Christ in Northampton, had come to deliver a message, a message designed to call the descendants of settlers who had fled England to establish religious communities back to faith. The offspring of those settlers had wandered, something that concerned the faithful church leaders. At the time Edwards took the Enfield pulpit, the Great Awakening—a widespread spiritual revival—had been spreading for twenty years (1720–1740).

Edwards' sermon is considered the most famous in American history. Spiritual revival continued to roll through the colonies, and Edwards was one of the men who stoked the fires.

"Sinners in the Hands of an Angry God" is chilling even when just read from the page. Edward described the plight of the sinner with such firmness and directness that listeners were shaken to the marrow. Yet he didn't rant, he didn't prance around, he didn't use theatrics, didn't point fingers—he just read with conviction and it was enough. Although often portrayed as a hellfire and brimstone preacher, Edwards was anything but. He was always calm, scholarly, and dignified in his manner. Still, he pulled no punches. He told the congregation that God was under no obligation to save anyone; that he had no binding agreement to keep anyone from hell. He described their plight as standing on a decaying floor with the fires of hell below, as God bending the bow and pointing an arrow of judgment at the heart, as God holding a person over fiery hell like someone holding a spider over an open flame.

The sermon starts slow and is based on seven words from Deuteronomy 32:35: "Their foot shall slide in due time" (KJV). The first part of the sermon is almost academic in tone. Then Edwards makes it personal, and everything changes. His direct but emotionless reading drove men to tears.

Precocious Preacher to Be

Often those who deliver such sermons are considered intellectual weaklings who rely on emotionalism rather than content. Such a description could never be applied to Edwards. He was an intellectual's intellectual. He started his studies at Yale at age thirteen and graduated four years later. He then continued his studies, earning a master's degree in theology. He also favored philosophy and, later in life, found the writings of physicist Isaac Newton fascinating. Many historians have dubbed Edwards as America's greatest theologian. His written works are tours de force of theological thinking.

As a young man he wrestled with his spirituality and came to an understanding of faith. He created for himself a list of seventy resolutions that he reviewed weekly throughout his life.

> Resolution #5: Resolved, never lose one moment of time; but improve it the most profitable way I possibly can.
> Resolution #6: Resolved, to live with all my might, while I do live.
> Resolution #10: Resolved, when I feel pain, to think of the pains of martyrdom, and of hell.[1]

He was a man of great personal discipline. He rose every morning at 4:00 and spent thirteen hours a day in study (and somehow still made time for his family, which included eleven children).

Ministry

Edwards' grandfather was Solomon Stoddard, an influential pastor in Northampton, Massachusetts. After his theological training, Edwards, in 1727, joined him as associate pastor. Stoddard died in 1729, leaving Edwards as the sole minister of the congregation of two hundred families.

More and more people in New England were moving away from the church or living a diluted faith. This grieved Edwards and he prayed for a "harvest," meaning a spiritual revival. His prayers were answered in 1734, when revival swept through his church. "The Spirit of God began extraordinarily to set in. The town seemed to be full of the presence of God. It never was so full of love, so full of joy, and yet so full of distress, as it was then."[2]

Like many leaders in the Great Awakening, Edwards delivered guest sermons at other churches. Of course, there were critics who accused him of pandering to emotion and fear. Edwards was not comfortable with public outbursts of emotion, but he acknowledged such responses were part of the Holy Spirit's work in the congregation. Academic that he was, he wrote a book on the subject: *A Treatise Concerning Religious Affections.*

Despite all the good he did and his dedication to the Northampton church, they came to a parting of ways. Edwards wanted to limit communion to those who had had a salvation experience. This was a different practice from that of his grandfather Solomon Stoddard. The church was unwilling to change, and Edwards had to vacate the pulpit. This, however, was not the end of his ministry. For several years he served as a missionary pastor to Native Americans and continued his writing, including a treatise called *Freedom of Will,* which dealt with divine sovereignty.

In 1758, he became president of Princeton University (College of New Jersey). His tenure was cut short when he died after receiving a smallpox vaccination. He was only fifty-five.

The Great Awakening was not the work of a single individual, but Jonathan Edwards was one of the driving forces behind its success. Although best remembered for his sermon "Sinners in the Hands of an Angry God," he should also be remembered for his contributions to faith in America and his keen theological mind.

JOHN WESLEY

Man Standing on a Tombstone

(1703–1791)

> I look at all the world as my parish; thus far I mean, that, in whatever part of it I am, I judge it meet, right, and my bounded duty to declare unto all that are willing to hear, the glad tidings of salvation.
>
> John Wesley, journal entry, June 11, 1739

It wasn't something seen every day. A man preaching in a graveyard and standing on a tombstone—and not just any tombstone: his father's headstone. The man was a good-looking, Oxford-trained Anglican priest, with hair that parted in the middle and hung to his shoulders. Nearby stood the church at Epworth. John Wesley knew it well. He had grown up in that church and his father, upon whose tombstone he stood, had served as rector there for four decades. That was then. Now, John Wesley, a fully ordained Anglican minister, was forbidden to speak in the church his father had helped build and where he had served as his father's assistant.

Church building or no, Wesley was going to preach and the crowds, the largest the town had ever seen, came at six in the evening to hear the traveling preacher. There, at the east end of the church, Wesley raised his hands and said, "For the kingdom of God is not meat and drink; but righteousness, and peace, and joy in the Holy Ghost" (Rom. 14:17 KJV).[1]

Wesley always found a place and a way to preach. He was unstoppable.

A Good Beginning

John Wesley was child number fifteen of the nineteen his mother, Susanna, would bring into the world, nine of whom died. The household was familiar with death. When Susanna died in 1742, only eight of her children were still living. Still, she was more than the hand that rocked the cradle; she was the one who formed the minds of her children. She made time each week to teach religious principles—one-on-one. Two of her children would change the world of the church: John and Charles Wesley left a still-visible stamp on history.

Although a strict disciplinarian, she was loved by her children. John Wesley turned to her for advice until the day she died. It was from Susanna much of John's discipline came, a discipline that would result in his being called a "methodist."

John's father was an Anglican minister and served the church much of his life. Still it was their home, more so than his father's church, that provided a foundation of faith for John, a faith he would struggle with but remain true to for nearly nine decades.

When John was six, his parents left him alone in the rectory, and it caught fire. When he appeared in a second-story window, he was rescued by two men, one standing on the shoulders of the other. The boy began calling himself the "brand plucked from the burning."

When he was seventeen, John went to Oxford University and studied at Christ Church and Lincoln College. When he was twenty-three, he was elected a fellow of Lincoln College, which granted him a standing in the academic world and provided a source of income. After his ordination in the Anglican church, he returned home and served as an associate to his father.

He later returned to the college, where his younger brother Charles was attending. Charles and others had started a close-knit group that became known as the Holy Club. The title had come from their critics but it was much better than "Bible moths," which they were also called. Another name was thrown at them: "methodist." It was a moniker that would follow them all their lives and become the name of future followers of their ministry.

Sick at Sea

John Wesley was dedicated and disciplined, wanting his life to reflect that of first-century Christians. He rose early every morning, studied the Bible constantly, and did his best to be a good minister, focusing on a disciplined lifestyle he hoped would bring him peace and spiritual fulfillment.

Except it wasn't working.

He admitted to those in the Holy Club that he struggled with feeling worthy or holy. When Dr. John Burton requested that John and Charles travel to the colonies to take the message of God to the natives and minister to the church in Georgia under General James Oglethorpe, both men jumped at the chance. John would preach to the Native Americans and serve as chaplain to the colony. Charles would work as a secretary to the general. It was a mission trip that fit John's idea of Christian service.

It turned out to be a disaster for both men, especially John.

They boarded the *Simmonds* in October, full of dreams and enthusiasms. They faced a difficult crossing, and during one especially vicious storm John became convinced he and everyone on the ship were going to die at sea. Waves washed over the decks, and the ship pitched and rolled like a cork on the ocean. John and others panicked, certain all was lost—all except a group of Moravian Christians, a sect of Protestants who held to the supremacy of the Bible in matters of faith and who emphasized piety and unity. While others lost their heads, the Moravians calmly spent the storm in prayer and hymn singing.

When the storm abated, John asked them if they had been afraid. No, they said. They trusted Jesus in all things, life and death. This shamed John, who thought of himself as devout a believer as could be.

His work in Georgia went poorly. He distrusted the Native Americans, and the colonists in the church chaffed under his attempts to instill his rigid, methodical brand of Christianity. An example of this rigidity was John's stance that women not be allowed to wear fancy dress or jewelry.

Ministry challenges were grueling enough, but matters of the heart made things worse. John had fallen for Sophie Hopkey, the young niece of Savannah's chief magistrate. He longed for marriage and proposed. She declined and, as if to make the point clear, married one of John's rivals. John could be vindictive and he proved it by refusing to allow her to take communion. This was more than a religious restriction. It was public humiliation and implied sinfulness on Sophie's part. Her new husband sued on her behalf, stating that the act defamed his innocent wife. The court case lasted six months.

John had had enough. He left Georgia for England, defeated, jilted, and uncertain of his calling.

> I went to America to convert the Indians, but oh, who shall convert me? Who, what is he that will deliver me from this evil heart of unbelief? I have a fair summer religion. I can talk well; nay, and believe myself, while no danger is near: but let death look me in the face, and my spirit is troubled . . . I have a sin of fear, that when I've spun my last thread, I shall perish on the shore.[2]

Warmed in England

It was a defeated man who returned to England in 1738. People could be hard on John Wesley, but none could be more critical about him than himself. He questioned his ability and his faith. Something was missing and he didn't know how to find it. In his search he sought out a young Moravian preacher named Peter Böhler, who made it clear to John that he needed a spiritual birth. He had the head knowledge, but that had not changed his heart. Wesley lacked a personal experience with the God he served.

Wesley was a product of his upbringing in a strict Anglican home and had trouble believing that salvation could come in a moment. To him it was a process of discipline and service.

On May 24, 1738, he—with great reluctance—fulfilled an agreement to join a small group of people listening to the preface of Martin

Luther's *Epistle to the Romans*. He went to Aldersgate Street out of a sense of duty. He later wrote:

> About a quarter before nine, while he was describing the change which God works in the heart through faith in Christ, I felt my heart strangely warmed. I felt I did trust in Christ, Christ alone for salvation: and an assurance was given me, that he had taken away my sins, even mine, and saved me from the law of sin and death.[3]

The man who walked away from Aldersgate that May day was different than the one who had arrived only a short time before. The warming in his heart would blaze for the next fifty years.

Eye-Opener in Bristol

In his college days, John had made friends with a man who would become one of the greatest preachers in history, a man who set the fires of revival burning in England, Scotland, Ireland, and the American colonies; a man whose voice could be heard, it was said, a mile away; a man who drew the friendship of men such as Benjamin Franklin. His zeal exceeded that of anyone else John knew.

Whitefield preached with emotion and the skill of a great actor. His enthusiasm drew great crowds, but also drew the ire of church officials. Soon he found the doors of churches closed to him, so he took his message outdoors. John Wesley found this repugnant. Sermons were meant to be delivered within the walls of a church, not under the sky. Still, when Whitefield recruited the former leader of the Holy Club to come help, John went even though he was uncomfortable with the whole idea. "Having been all my life so tenacious of every point related to decency and order I should have thought the saving of souls almost a sin if it had not been done in church."[4]

John knew he could never match Whitefield's oratorical skill—no one could—but when he saw the impact the message had on the hundreds who gathered, John was forced to change his mind about preaching outdoors.

Where there had been anxiety and uncertainty, Wesley left energized. As a man who had as a child dubbed himself the "brand plucked from the burning," Wesley became the brand determined to keep others from the fire. John Wesley found himself and his place in God's plans.

A Worldwide Parish

Wesley began to see church work differently than what he had grown up with. One could wait for people to come to the church to hear the gospel—but there were many, like the miners in Bristol, who wouldn't or couldn't go to church—or the preacher could go to the people. Whitefield was doing the latter. Wesley would too. He no longer felt bound to the parish but to the world. He began to think of the people around him as his parish—no matter where he might be at the time.

He preached in prisons, on ships, and in Cornwall, where he spoke to thirty thousand people at once. Critics lumped him with other controversial evangelicals and church doors closed in his face. Still he preached, and when his father's former church refused to let him help even with prayer or reading the Scriptures, he met with crowds in the church cemetery, using his father's tombstone as a podium.

Wesley began traveling and preaching wherever he could, and the constancy of his travel began to cost him. In 1751 he had married Mary Vazeille, a widow, who had helped nurse him back to health after he was injured falling on ice. She tried to travel with him but it proved too much. After two years her health broke, and so did their marriage. She left him. When she died in 1781, Wesley wasn't told and therefore didn't attend her funeral.

Still he traveled. By his count, he averaged 4,500 miles a year.[5] If this is an average, it means he traveled over 250,000 miles in the course of his ministry—greater than the average distance between the earth and the moon.

John Wesley was more than a dedicated preacher. He was an organizational genius. He would assign converts to "societies," fellowship classes, and prayer bands. Over time the societies were organized into units. This applied to both sides of the Atlantic. The Methodists, as they were called, became a denomination almost against Wesley's wishes. He saw the Methodists as a church within a church, a subset of the Anglican church. When accused of being a Methodist, he would protest and reply he had been an Anglican all his life and would die as such. And he did.

Wesley continued preaching long past when most men would have retired, continuing his work well into his eighties. He died in London at the age of eighty-seven, and he left behind seventy-nine thousand followers in England, forty thousand in America, and 233 books. Today seventy-five million people across the world are considered Methodists.

It took many years of struggle and searching for John Wesley to determine his role in the church, but once he did he was never the same.

And neither was the church.

41

CHARLES WESLEY

The Other Wesley

(1707–1788)

God buries his workmen, but carries on his work.

Charles Wesley, as quoted in *Cyclopedia of Biblical,*
Theological, and Ecclesiastical Literature

If you've been in church during the Christmas season, then you've likely sung some of his hymns. If you've been in church on Easter, the same holds true. In fact, no matter what time of year you attend a church service, there is a good chance that the words of Charles Wesley will have filled the worship area.

Shaped by a Godly Mother

Charles was born on December 18, 1707, in Epworth in Lincolnshire, England, to Samuel and Susannah Wesley. He was child number eighteen of the nineteen Susannah would bear. For a time it was uncertain if Charles would make it. He was born prematurely and appeared close to death, silent for his first few weeks of life. However, Charles rallied from this difficult start to life, and ended up living for over eighty years.

When he was old enough, he began his homeschooling, spending six hours a day learning from his mother. When Charles continued his education at Westminster School, he excelled. He also studied at Oxford and received a master's degree. While at Oxford, he helped found the Holy Club, an informal group concerned with the school's lack of spiritual vitality. The small band adopted a strict routine of rising early, Bible study, and prison ministry. This regimen earned them the name "methodists."

Ministry Abroad

Charles followed his father into the ministry and developed a missionary's heart. He and his brother John sailed for America to minister to the Native Americans. The trip was, in their eyes, an abysmal failure. Charles worked as secretary for Georgia governor General Oglethorpe. Charles endured slander and illness, and someone even took a shot at him. Oglethorpe showed him no respect. He and his brother left Georgia a year later, disheartened and uncertain of their own spiritual character.

Charles took up reading Martin Luther's commentary on Galatians. One verse struck him: "I have been crucified with Christ; and it is no longer I who live, but Christ lives in me; and the life which I now live in the flesh I live by faith in the Son of God, who loved me and gave Himself up for me" (Gal. 2:20). He wrote in his journal, "I labored, waited, and prayed to 'feel who loved me and gave Himself for me.'"[1]

Peter Böhler (who had such a positive influence on John), while learning English from Charles, challenged him to reassess his spiritual standing, which he did. As his brother would do just a few days later, Charles had a conversion experience. Charles had the training and the family faith instilled inside him, but longed for something personal, not something handed down. He found it—and it forever changed his life.

John Wesley's Lesser-Known Brother?

Charles Wesley has been called the "forgotten Wesley." But he deserves better than to be left standing in John Wesley's shadow. Both men were tireless ministers who stretched what was acceptable practice for ministers in England. While John Wesley is considered the organizational genius behind what would become the Methodist church, it was Charles who brought the heart and the art. Just two days after he found "peace with God," he began composing a hymn celebrating the change in his spiritual condition. He would continue writing hymns for the duration of his life.

Often history is tempted to paint Charles Wesley as just a writer of hymns, but that is an injustice. He was a theologian on par with any in his day. He was also an evangelistic preacher. Having been challenged by George Whitefield to be "more vile" (in the eyes of the established clergy) and preach outside of the church, Charles agreed that those most needing a message from God would be found outside the walls of the local congregation.

Charles kept count of the numbers he preached to from 1739 through 1743, which he reported as exceeding 149,000. So active was he in travel and preaching that his brother John complained he never knew when Charles was leaving or where he was going.

It was on one such preaching trip that Charles met Sarah "Sally" Gwynne. He was in his early forties; she just twenty-two. Despite their age difference and, more importantly to her family, financial difference, they married six months later. She would give birth eight times, but only three of their children lived to adulthood.

Health and family duties gradually curtailed his travels, and after a time, he limited himself to preaching in Bristol and London, but continued to write hymns.

Hymn Machine

Saying that Charles Wesley wrote some hymns is an understatement of historic proportions. He was a hymn-writing machine. He penned ten lines of poetry a day for over fifty years, compiling nearly nine thousand hymns contained in fifty-six volumes.

223

These are more than just songs with spiritual themes. Charles was a trained theologian with a preacher's heart. His hymns were loaded with doctrine. In "Hark the Herald Angels Sing" the singers intone, "Hark the herald angels sing, Glory to the newborn King! Peace on Earth and mercy mild, God and sinners reconciled." Simple, beautiful lines that include the meaning of Christmas: the reconciliation of God and people.

Charles' hymns were short doctrinal messages that stayed with the worshiper much longer than, arguably, a sermon might.

Today, we still sing many of his hymns, such as "Oh, for a Thousand Tongues to Sing," "Love Divine, All Loves Excelling," "Christ the Lord Is Risen Today," and others. Charles Wesley continues, through his hymns, to minister to the church.

42

GEORGE WHITEFIELD

The Voice

(1714–1770)

If your souls were not immortal, and you in danger of losing them, I would not thus speak unto you; but the love of your souls constrains me to speak: methinks this would constrain me to speak unto you forever.

George Whitefield, "Christ the Only Rest for the Weary and Heavy Laden"

He didn't look like a commanding orator: medium height, round face, and a few qualities some considered effeminate. Appearing in his Anglican minister's dress with its lace clerical collar, this Englishman faced skeptical expressions on both sides of the Atlantic. When he began to speak, however, raucous crowds fell silent, and every eye was on the pudgy man as he moved and delivered message after message with such power. Men wept. Women sang. Children sat in rapt attention, taking in every word.

George Whitefield was an enigma who set in motion the Great Awakening in America, introducing the concept of mass evangelism. Some consider him the greatest preacher to have taken the pulpit. Jonathan Edwards delivered his "Sinners in the Hands of an Angry God" from a stationary position behind the pulpit, but Whitefield pranced about, gestured, and projected so forcefully he could be heard a mile away.

He was the founder of Methodism, although he would turn leadership of the fledgling denomination over to John Wesley. He brought the need for a personal "rebirth" for salvation to the forefront. He pleaded with his audience, speaking directly and pulling no punches, but did so with such loving conviction the people left feeling blessed, not blasted.

He was a workhorse of the gospel. Before he died in 1770, he had preached eighteen thousand times, made seven trips to the American colonies, preached in several countries in Europe, and had tremendous results in Scotland. Estimates for the number of people who heard him preach reach as high as ten million.

A Rocky Start

Whitefield was born in Gloucester, England, to innkeeper parents. His father died when he was two, cause unknown. In school, he found an interest in the theater and enjoyed performing. What he didn't know at the time was that his theatrical talents would propel him to the forefront of preaching history.

Coming from humble means, Whitefield worked his way through Pembroke College, Oxford, as a servant to wealthier students. While there he joined a group called the Holy Club, largely led by John and Charles Wesley. He had an interest in the Bible as a child, but he had no religious conviction. Before settling in with the Holy Club, he was led astray by other students. "In short, I soon made a great proficiency in the school of the Devil."[1]

His salvation experience came over time. It was more process than immediate decision. The influence of the Wesley brothers and the other "methodists" helped him along his way. He felt unworthy of salvation and struggled to adjust his life through discipline to be acceptable to God. He fasted for days and deprived himself of everything that gave him pleasure, yet this made him feel all the more unworthy.

As part of the "method" of the Holy Club, members would visit prisons. Whitefield did this dutifully, and became known to the prisoners and their families. One day a woman came to him seeking help. Her husband was in prison and caring for her hungry children was pushing her to a nervous breakdown. Watching them dying from hunger pressed her to the brink of suicide. She was close to leaping to her doom from a bridge when a passerby intervened. She sought out Whitefield, who gave her some immediate help then asked her to meet with him and her husband at the prison. During that meeting the husband and wife had a spiritual experience that changed their lives. They received what Whitefield longed for but had yet to experience.

It was during a seven-week battle with illness that he received his heart's desire. He had been denying himself food and fighting an internal spiritual battle so long that he could no longer climb stairs. Someone reminded him that Jesus on the cross, when close to the end of his suffering, had cried, "I thirst!" From his bed, Whitefield did the same.

> Soon after this, I found and felt in myself that I was delivered from the burden that has so heavily oppressed me. The spirit of mourning was taken from me, and I knew what it was truly to rejoice in God my Savior; and, for some time, could not avoid singing psalms wherever I was.[2]

Whitefield began referring to such changes as "the new birth." The need for others to come to Christ thus became the center of his life.

Love and Hate in England

He was ordained in 1736 at Glouchester and soon began preaching the new birth message. He was young, and few felt a twenty-one-year-old could bring much of a sermon. They were soon proven wrong. The people loved him. Many of the clergy did not. Some were jealous; others didn't like his direct, simple style. The preaching pattern of the day was to focus on some aspect of doctrine and deliver a scholarly message on the topic. Whitefield called on people to make a decision for Christ. Doctrine was important to him, but his preaching focused on the need of individuals to accept the offer of salvation in Christ. Soon, church doors began to close to him.

Whitefield had a global vision, and like the Wesleys wished to take his message to the colonies in America. The Wesleys' experience had nearly broken them. They came back feeling every bit the failure. Whitefield's experience would be different.

In James Oglethorpe's Georgia, the mission lasted four months and every day more and more people came to hear Whitefield. When he returned to England, his fame had grown and so had the distrust of the clergy, who refused to relinquish their pulpits to him. With only a few churches who would let him speak, Whitefield made a decision that would forever change his approach: if he could not preach *in* the churches, then he'd preach *outside* them.

On a hill near Bristol, Whitefield gathered the families of coal miners. About two hundred attended. A few weeks later, the crowd had grown to twenty thousand. "I believe I never was more acceptable to my Master than when I was standing to teach those hearers in the open fields," he wrote.[3]

Preaching outdoors was suspect to many in the church at that time, but Whitefield didn't care. Neither did the thousands who came to hear him.

Back in America

In 1739, the evangelist returned to America. Wherever he set up to preach, the people came. This would be the story of his ministry. As he traveled, preaching from colony to colony, folk would hear of his arrival and come from miles away by horse, by buggy, or on foot. No building in the New World could hold the crowds. While in England he preached outdoors because the churches were closed to him, in America he did the same because the crowds were too large for the churches.

So popular were his meetings that store owners closed up shop while he preached. At times, the congregation would exceed the population of the town he was preaching in. He was described by many at that time as the best English-speaking orator the world had ever seen. Some said he could bring listeners to tears merely by the way he said "Mesopotamia." The famous actor David Garrick is often quoted as saying, "I would give a hundred guineas, if I could say 'Oh' like Mr. Whitefield."

The crowds kept coming and Whitefield kept preaching.

The Ben Franklin Connection

One observer wrote:

> The multitudes of all sects and denominations that attended his sermons were enormous and it was a matter of speculation to me, who was one of the number, to observe the extraordinary influence of his oratory on his hearers, and how much they admired and respected him, notwithstanding his common abuse of them, by assuring them they were naturally half beasts and half devils.[4]

This observer was Benjamin Franklin. He had joined the throngs in Philadelphia. Franklin and Whitefield, although very different people, became friends and exchanged letters until Whitefield's death. Franklin, a deist, had different views of God than Whitefield, yet he still respected the man.

He recounted a little experiment he conducted while Whitefield preached. Whitefield stood at the top of the steps at the Philadelphia courthouse on Market Street:

> [Whitefield] had a loud and clear voice, and articulated his words and sentences so perfectly, that he might be heard and understood at a great distance, especially as audiences, however numerous, observ'd the most exact silence. He preached one evening from the top of the Court-house steps, which are in the middle of Market-street, and on the west side of Second-street, which crosses it at right angles. Both streets were fill'd with his hearers to a considerable distance. Being among the hindmost in Market-street, I had the curiosity to learn how far he could be heard, by retiring backwards down the street towards the river; and I found his voice distinct till I came near Front-street, when some noise in that street obscur'd it.[5]

Franklin calculated how many people could hear Whitefield, and his math lead him to theorize the number as thirty thousand. The newspapers had been reporting crowds of twenty-five thousand, which Franklin had originally doubted until his own experiment confirmed the newspaper's numbers.

Franklin also told of attending one sermon in which Whitefield was going to take up a collection. He said he had a handful of copper money, three or four silver dollars, and five pistoles (a European coin) in gold. He determined that he would leave with the same amount of money he arrived with, but the sermon wore Franklin down. In the end, he emptied his pockets.[6]

Franklin was impressed enough by the man (although not moved to accept his teaching) that he arranged to publish Whitefield's sermons and journals. Certainly he saw the potential profit in such a partnership. The demand for Whitefield's content in ink and paper indeed proved tremendously popular, as evidenced by the multiple print runs that were required.[7]

Trials

Whitefield's ministerial success came at a price. As with any great endeavor, problems and resistance arose. While thousands hung on his every word, a few pelted him with stones, dirt clods, vegetables, and even small dead animals. Despite this unpleasantness, he considered it an honor. Similar things had also happened to John Wesley. Success is always met with opposition.

There was also a physical toll. Whitefield was often ill, and traveling across the ocean and through the American colonies and British and Scottish cities taxed his body. He struggled with asthmalike "colds." Health was an ongoing problem, and he would die while just in his midfifties.

There also came a break with the Wesleys. Whitefield was a Calvinist, and although he believed in predestination, he preached like a "whosoever" Arminian. Still, John Wesley could not abide the doctrine of Calvin. The rift between them grew, endangering the growing Methodist movement. For a time, Whitefield led a Calvinist branch of the group but ultimately released control to John Wesley. He did this over the objection of friends, but he could not tolerate the discord. He cared nothing about who was the head of what or whose name would live on longer. He wished to be a slave to Christ and master over no one.

George Whitefield died in Newburyport, Massachusetts, on Sunday, September 30, 1770, the morning after an evening of preaching. He was fifty-five, working to his dying day as if he were still a young man. He once said that he'd rather wear out than rust out. Others would continue to stoke the fires of the Great Awakening, but none could do it with the same fervor or captivating voice of George Whitefield.

43

JOHN NEWTON
Slave Ship, Pulpit, Pen

(1725–1807)

My memory is nearly gone, but I remember two things: that I am a
great sinner and that Christ is a great Savior.

John Newton, spoken shortly before he died, recorded
by William Jay in his autobiography

For the first three decades of his life, John Newton worked hard
at being self-serving, causing trouble and, not to put too fine
a point on it, debauchery. He was the kind of man people would
cross the street to avoid. He excelled at unpleasantness. It seemed
that life conspired against him and he was more than willing to
return the favor.

Born to a Christian mother and seafaring father, Newton heard
the stories of the Bible at his mother's knee, but that education
and influence were cut short. His mother died of tuberculosis when
Newton was seven. The formative influence in Newton's life switched
from his kindly mother to his roughneck father, a commander on a
merchant ship. At age eleven, Newton began his life at sea, sailing

with his father until he was seventeen. Later he worked onshore in the merchant's office until he was fired for bad behavior.

When he was nineteen, the British navy decided he needed to return to a life on the ocean and, against his will, inducted him into service aboard HMS *Harwick*, a man-of-war ship. His father had enough influence to have his son installed as a midshipman—a low-ranking officer. This was a much better situation than others forced into service had to endure, but it was still too much for the young man. He deserted, something the navy wouldn't tolerate. He was found, shackled, and flogged. Somehow he talked his way out of the navy by suggesting he be discharged to a slave ship, and they allowed it. As it turned out, this was no favor.

Newton served under Captain Amos Clow, a harsh and cruel man. Clow owned a lemon plantation on a West African island. Newton was forced to live there in horrible conditions until his clothing wore to rags and he had to beg for food. In many ways, he was a slave to Clow's African mistress.

In 1746, he was transferred aboard the *Greyhound*, a slave ship from Liverpool, which proved to have better living conditions. He now had clothing and food. Newton sailed the waters between Africa and ports of call where slaves could be sold. He rose through the ranks, and at the age of twenty-two he became a slave ship's master. His cruelty and wickedness even put off his crew. Once, while drunk, Newton fell overboard. His crew rescued him—by harpooning him in the leg and drawing him back to the ship. The scar stayed with him throughout his life and served as a reminder of how low he had sunk.

In 1748, on a return trip to his home port, his ship was caught in the teeth of a vicious storm. He had been reading Thomas à Kempis' book *The Imitation of Christ*, one of several classics that Newton had recently taken to in an attempt at self-education, and had been pondering a passage that dealt with the "uncertain continuance of life." The storm must have been fierce, because the seasoned sailor was shaken. On the pitching ship, Newton committed his life to Christ. It was a beginning, but in some ways his conversion took time, at least when it came to his work on a slave ship.

He continued his slave work but with a more humane bent. Part of his goal was to lessen the cruelty experienced by the slaves—still, they were slaves and would be sold. Slave trading gradually grew abhorrent to Newton, leading him to taking a job on land officially tracking tides in Liverpool.

Newton may have left the slave trade behind, but it didn't leave him. It ate at him, troubling his mind and soul. More and more he felt called to ministry and studied to prepare himself for life that exchanged the ship's wheel for a pulpit. In 1764, at the age of thirty-nine, he was ordained as an Anglican priest and took a church in Olney. Although anyone would have been hard-pressed to see it during Newton's wild years, the new priest had an artistic side as a gifted lyricist. He held Bible studies on Thursday nights and liked to have his parishioners sing hymns. Unable to find enough hymns suitable for the people who attended, he began composing lyrics and setting them to common tunes. He did this almost weekly.

During that time William Cowper joined the church. Cowper was a man troubled with mental problems that left him depressed and suicidal. Although he found comfort in the church, he fought his mental demons all his life. Like Newton, he was gifted with words. He is best known for the opening lines to the hymn "Light Shining Out of Darkness":

> God moves in a mysterious way,
> His wonders to perform;
> He plants his footsteps in the sea,
> And rides upon the storm.

These words no doubt resonated with John Newton, who found faith in the midst of a storm. Together they wrote scores of hymns. In 1779, they compiled what became known as the *Olney Hymns*. The hymnal contained 280 of his hymns and sixty-eight of Cowper's. Many of these hymns are sung today and are loved by millions, and included what may be the best-known hymn of all: "Amazing Grace."

"Amazing Grace" reflects the new heart in Newton:

> Amazing Grace, how sweet the sound,
> that saved a wretch like me.
> I once was lost but now am found,
> Was blind, but now, I see.

'Twas Grace that taught my heart to fear,
and Grace, my fears relieved.
How precious did that Grace appear,
the hour I first believed.

The treatment of slaves at the hands of their captors and owners haunted Newton. What he had seen and done troubled him. In 1787, he wrote *Thoughts on the African Slave Trade*, in which he hoped "this stain of our National character will soon be wiped out." He further wrote, "If I attempt, after what has been done, to throw my mite into the public stock of information, it is less from an apprehension that my interference is necessary, than from a conviction, that silence, at such a time, and on such an occasion, would, in me, be criminal."[1] Forty years after his conversion, he was still haunted by his contribution to the enslavement of his fellow man. Perhaps this is why, despite the urging of friends, he refused to slow down in his last years. "I cannot stop. What? The old African Blasphemer stop while he can still speak?"[2]

Newton died at the age of eighty-two, a changed man from his days of sailing ships with holds packed tight with humans who would be bought and sold by other humans. Newton had been changed from a man who made his living in trading human flesh to one who lived to save the souls of men.

Centuries later, John Newton stands as an example of the change faith can make in a single life, and how that life can change others. He became proof of the transforming message of faith and the need to stand for the protection of those who have no voice.

In the heart of the slave trader rested the soul of a poet, one whose words have been sung for over two centuries. He remains proof of God's amazing grace.

44

WILLIAM WILBERFORCE
Faith-Motivated Politician

(1759–1833)

Never, never will we desist till we have wiped away this scandal from the Christian name, released ourselves from the load of guilt, under which we at present labour, and extinguished every trace of this bloody traffic, of which our posterity, looking back to the history of these enlightened times, will scarce believe that it has been suffered to exist so long a disgrace and dishonor to this country.

William Wilberforce, speech before the House
of Commons, April 18, 1791

Two years earlier, May 12, 1789, Wilberforce finished a similar speech to the House of Commons with these words:

As soon as ever I had arrived thus far in my investigation of the slave trade, I confess to you sir, so enormous, so dreadful, so irremediable did its wickedness appear that my own mind was completely made up for the abolition. A trade founded in iniquity, and carried on as this was, must be abolished, let the policy be what it might—let the consequences be what they would, I from this time determined that I would never rest till I had effected its abolition.[1]

There is perhaps no greater, no more vile a stain on the pages of history as slavery. England had long been in the slave trade when a young politician from a wealthy family arrived on the political scene. In 1770 alone, approximately one hundred thousand slaves were transported out of West Africa. Half of those were carried in chains on British ships. The slave trade had been conducted for so many years, and slaves used in the West Indies for so long, that many believed ending the practice would destroy the economy of England and other nations. Powerful people had grown rich trading humans for money. "The impossibility of doing without slaves in the West Indies," one proponent of the practice wrote, "will always prevent this traffic being dropped. The necessity, the absolute necessity, then, of carrying it on, must, since there is no other, be its excuse."[2]

During this time, the official Church of England was largely silent. It had become the church for the upper crust. Methodism and other non-Anglican churches appealed to the lower class, and very few "movers and shakers" missed them.

The slave trade had become critically important to the economic health of England. There were some however who, driven by their faith, could no longer abide the practice. One such person was William Wilberforce, who made abolition his life's aim.

The Young Gentleman from Hull

William Wilberforce was born to a wealthy and influential family on High Street of Hull. Such things, however, could not make Wilberforce physically strong. He was small and sick and suffered from poor eyesight.

His father died when he was nine, and Wilberforce was sent to live with an uncle and aunt. After attending several schools, he entered St. John's College in Cambridge. Independently wealthy, he lacked a compelling reason to excel in studies, but he did excel in the party life. Nonetheless, he went on to earn bachelor's and master's degrees.

When he was twenty-five his life changed. He had been reading Philip Doddridge's *Rise and Progress of Religion in the Soul*, and his faith stirred in him again.

During his college days he made friends with William Pitt, who would one day become prime minister. Politics would be Wilberforce's life—and this would mean life to a great many others.

William Wilberforce made it to the House of Commons in 1780.

The Clapham Sect

Wilberforce was not the only person of faith concerned about England's direction. A short distance from London was the town of Clapham, a hamlet for the wealthy. He regularly met with a group of influential people there who shared his concerns. These included the Reverend John Venn and Henry Thornton, a wealthy banker. With Wilberforce leading, they would meet for prayer, Bible study, and discussion of pressing political issues. This gathering proved vital to Wilberforce's eventual successful abolition of the slave trade. It also served as a catalyst for his involvement in other social causes and his commitment to giving 25 percent of his income to the poor.

The Nightingale of the House of Commons

Oratory was Wilberforce's strong suit. Even a cold reading of his speeches can send chills through a reader. He made his first speech before the House of Commons on the slave trade in 1789, but while well-written and powerfully delivered, it lacked arguments necessary to convince his fellow leaders. A series of resolutions against the slave practice met a similar fate. Often they were simply outmaneuvered in Parliament.

Together with the Clapham Sect, Wilberforce did an in-depth study of the problem. Two years after his first antislavery speech, he introduced a bill to cease the importing of slaves to the West Indies. He told Parliament, "Never, never, will we desist till we have wiped away this scandal from the Christian name, released ourselves from the load of guilt, and extinguished every trace of this bloody traffic."[3]

The bill failed.

Wilberforce and his supporters took the message to the people, educating them through literature, lectures, billboards, and more.

The goal was to drive public opinion, and by doing so gain the attention of the public leaders.

Victory finally came in February 1807. The tide had turned and the House of Commons, which before had offered only a polite listening to Wilberforce, now heard others preaching the same message and doing so with such intensity that the members came to their feet. When the measure passed, Wilberforce could do nothing but sit and weep.

It was only a partial win. The law halted only the trafficking of slaves. Those already slaves were still bound. More work had to be done. What was needed was emancipation. Wilberforce continued his battle as long as he could, but age and health required the mantle be passed to another: Thomas Fowell Buxton. Success was achieved on July 25, 1833. Four days later Wilberforce died.

Soon after, slaves in the West Indies rose before dawn, gathered on hills, and watched the sun come up on their freedom. It was an expensive success. Slave owners were compensated for their losses—one hundred million dollars in total. Ultimately, the cost was worth it as Wilberforce and his collaborators helped free seven hundred thousand slaves.

Propelled by a Cause

A onetime party animal in college became the voice for hundreds of thousands of slaves. He battled health problems that sometimes kept him bedridden, but he continued with sheer determination. He was targeted by slave traders and others who made money in the sale of human beings. He carried on. Defeat followed defeat, still he pressed forward. The engine of his life was vital Christianity. He had no patience with comfortable Christians.

William Wilberforce showed that faith-driven purpose can alter the very destiny of a man, a country, and the world.

45

WILLIAM CAREY
From Mending Shoes to Mending Souls

(1761–1834)

Expect great things from God; attempt great things for God.

William Carey, *The Baptist Magazine*

It is difficult to imagine this happening in a meeting of ministers, but it did: when William Carey stood before a group of Baptists to call for mission work in foreign lands, he was told to shut up and sit down. God would save the heathen if he wanted to and the Almighty didn't need Carey's help.

Carey sat, but he didn't shut up. This balding former cobbler could not ignore the plight of the unreached, and would follow his words with action, even as it cost him dearly.

The Cobbler

William Carey called himself a plodder.[1] His only genius was his ability to keep moving forward, one trudging step after another. His life bears out his statement. Plodding is the ability to keep moving forward when everything is trying to push you back. Carey was a master at it.

He was born into poverty in the village of Paulerspury in Northamptonshire, England. His father was a weaver who also taught school to make ends meet. Born with a keen mind but little opportunity, Carey made the best of his situation. He enjoyed reading and writing, and consumed books like *Robinson Crusoe* and *Gulliver's Travels*. When Carey was a teenager, his father arranged an apprenticeship with the cobbler Clarke Nichols in Piddington, a village near his home. There he met John Warr, another apprentice. Warr was a dissenter—he attended a church not part of the Anglican system. Carey attended church with Warr, and at the age of seventeen had a conversion experience.

During his days as an apprentice cobbler, Carey taught himself Greek and showed skill at self-education. He might have been financially poor but he was rich in intelligence. His greatest achievements were linked to his aptitude for languages.

When his master Clarke Nichols died, Carey went to work for shoemaker Thomas Old. Carey married Old's sister-in-law Dorothy Plackett in 1781. Dorothy had no education and could barely sign her name. In time Thomas Old died, and Carey took over the business. He continued his self-education, teaching himself Hebrew, Dutch, Italian, and French.

Soles and Souls

Soon Carey began preaching in churches. During one period, he walked eight miles every Sunday to a neighboring town to fill the pulpit of a local church. He continued his cobbling work and his self-education, taught school when he could, and pastored.

William Carey had never been robust, and often suffered from ill health, but he continued on, dealing with poverty, the death of a child, and his wife's resulting mental illness.

In the midst of this turmoil, Carey's mind became more and more fixed on the need to take the gospel to the world. He found little support for this, however, as any focus on world missions was repeatedly shot down by one gathering of ministers after another.

In 1792, he wrote and published *An Enquiry into the Obligation of Christians to Use Means of the Conversion of the Heathen.* In the treatise he argued for a world missions effort. A few weeks later he received an invitation to speak at the minister's association, which he accepted. There he uttered the line most associated with him: "Expect great things *from* God; attempt great things *for* God."

The message was received politely but without enthusiasm. Nonetheless, a mission society was formed in part because of Carey's message. Dr. John Thomas volunteered to go to India as a missionary if someone would go with him. Carey—a man prone to illness with a pregnant wife and three young sons—said he'd go.

Only Carey and his oldest son boarded an English ship. His wife refused to leave England. The ship set sail, but was soon forced to return to port shortly after it left. After some searching, he and Dr. Thomas booked passage to India on a Dutch ship. This time, Carey was able to convince his wife to accompany him, but only if his wife's sister was allowed to go as well. By the time the ship sailed, Dorothy had given birth.

India

In November 1793, they arrived in Calcutta and set up work. Sadly, their health and financial troubles followed them. The Careys moved to Midnapore to manage an indigo plant. Carey worked in the dye business for six years while he learned Bengali, the language of the region. During this time he began translating the New Testament into the local language.

There were other problems and tragedies. Dr. Thomas was running up debt. Some suspect his motivation for going to India was to escape creditors, and Thomas would later abandon the mission. Despite Carey's efforts, there were no converts. Then came the deepest loss: their youngest son, Peter, died of dysentery in 1796.

Still, Carey plodded on.

The Careys moved to Serampore in January of 1800 to join a group of Danish missionaries. It was there, after seven years of service, that he saw his first Hindu convert and baptism. He also became a professor of Sanskrit and Bengali at Fort Williams College, a school for civil servants. He formed a church, and in 1801 finished his Bengali translation of the New Testament.

Dorothy

The strain on Carey's wife was enormous. She had never traveled more than a few miles from home before she found herself in the strange land of India. She never adjusted and her emotional and mental state declined, made worse by the loss of two children. At times she would accuse Carey of infidelity and even threatened his life. Carey had no means of helping her, and at times had to lock her in a room for her own safety.

Dorothy died in 1807. Carey wrote that she died of a fever that had plagued her for some time. He also noted that her sound mind had never returned.

The next year, Carey married a Danish woman in his church. Charlotte Rhumohr was bright and articulate, in many ways the opposite of Dorothy. Their marriage lasted until her death thirteen years later.

Lasting Impact

When William Carey's life is discussed, the conversation often focuses on the "lack of success" he endured for so many years. He worked from late 1793 until 1800 before baptizing a single convert: Krishna Pal. While this shows Carey's ability to "plod on" during what must have seemed an extended period of failure, there are other numbers that show great success in related efforts.

When Carey died in 1834, he left behind a remarkable body of work, including forty-four translations of the Bible. He (and the other missionaries who came to work with him) also started 126 schools, twenty-six churches, and mission stations in India, Burma, and Bhutan. He also was one of the first to see the need for an indigenous Indian church, one made up and led by Indians.

He also helped make social changes such as ending *suttee*, the Hindu practice of a widow throwing herself on her husband's flaming funeral pyre. He began the Agricultural and Horticultural Society of India in 1820, organized the first printing operation and paper mill in India, and made English translations of Indian epic literature.

Carey is often called the father of modern missions. He was certainly not the first modern missionary, but his determination provided an example for many to come. The poor, undereducated cobbler laid the groundwork for what would become a thriving Christian church in India.

He died in Serampore, India, on June 9, 1834. His grave marker reads: "A wretched, poor, and helpless worm. On Thy kind arms I fall."

46

CHARLES FINNEY

The Father of American Revivalism

(1792–1875)

I have a retainer from the Lord Jesus Christ to plead his cause, and cannot plead yours.

Charles Finney, to one of his law clients

Almost everyone knows the name Billy Graham. But before Billy Graham, before Billy Sunday, and even before Dwight L. Moody, there was Charles Finney, lawyer turned minister turned evangelist.

Many church groups used to have an annual revival. A professional evangelist would come to the church and preach; the people would encourage family and friends to attend. Often these events were preceded by weeks of prayer, advertising, the distribution of flyers, potluck dinners, and more. It was more than a church service; it was an event.

The preacher would travel to the church and deliver a series of messages, usually nightly over the course of a week or two. At times the events were emotional. People who would not normally step across the church threshold would make an exception to hear a "special speaker" and musicians. In some denominations, revivals were held like clockwork.

In some cases, these events spread from one church to involve other churches in the neighborhood. It was the one time of the year when Methodists and Baptists would rub elbows. Revivals often evolved into citywide crusades.

Many of the techniques used to make such gatherings successful were first developed by Charles Finney.

The Conversion in the Woods

Charles Finney was born to farming parents. He was their seventh child. Although born in Warren, Connecticut, he grew up in New York state. As a young adult he took a teaching post in New Jersey, but his mother became ill and he moved back to Adams, New York. There he undertook the study of law.

The six-foot-two, popular, winsome, good-humored Finney struggled with his spiritual life. On an October day in 1821, he marched into the woods outside of town determined to come to grips with God, saying, "I will give my heart to God, or never come down from there." Hours later he returned to his office a changed man with a different set of goals. "The Holy Spirit . . . seemed to go through me, body and soul. It seemed to come in liquid waves of love."[1]

Sometime soon after, a potential client came to his office, but Finney refused to represent him. "I have a retainer from the Lord Jesus Christ to plead his cause and cannot plead yours," he said.[2] Finney had become more concerned with the law of God than the law of man. He began to prepare for ministry in the Presbyterian Church, and was ordained in 1824.

Having been hired by the Female Missionary Society of Western District, Finney began preaching in settlements in upstate New York. He preached in Jefferson and St. Lawrence counties, then in cities such as Troy, Rome, Auburn, and Utica.

Finney's style was different than most revivalists. He preached like a lawyer, building a case on behalf of Christ. He also instituted "new measures," new ways of promoting and conducting his meetings. These measures included prayer gatherings in which individuals prayed aloud for people by name, preaching multiple nights, and involving townspeople in promotion and follow-up. He also used an "anxious bench," a pew where congregants could come forward to receive prayer and instruction. Many of the "new measures" had been around for some time, but Finney made better, more purposeful use of them.

His reputation spread, and he moved from preaching in small towns to preaching in cities like New York, Boston, Philadelphia, and Rochester. Although his fame spread, fame was not his goal. He was a soul-winner and would often call for public commitments to Christ, challenging worshipers who wanted to claim Christ as their Savior to stand or to come to the "anxious bench." Oftentimes, in response, worshipers would stand suddenly, while others would fall to the floor, moaning and groaning. In some churches this was unsettling, and members didn't know how to respond. However, over time this behavior was more readily accepted, and some of those same church members experienced these moves of the Spirit themselves.

Still, these emotional outbursts brought criticism from other spiritual leaders who feared Finney was leading thousands to the brink of fanaticism. In the end he demonstrated his sincerity.

Finney also preached a message encouraging people to change their hearts, as anyone could be saved—an idea that didn't sit well with those Presbyterians who believed in predestination. Although a Presbyterian himself, Finney believed anyone could repent and that everyone should.

The community became involved in his revivals. Store owners closed during the services and posted notices encouraging their customers to attend. It is said that when Finney preached, the crime rate dropped.

His techniques would be shared in his 1835 book, *Lectures on Revival*. The book altered the way revival and crusade meetings were conducted and influenced William Booth, founder of the Salvation Army, and George Williams, founder of the YMCA.

Tuberculosis eventually forced Finney to curtail his many travels, but the disease didn't keep him from pursuing the path he believed God had laid before him.

He also wrote *Lectures on Systematic Theology*, and taught an "Arminianized Calvinism," which had a more open view about free will and the ability of an individual to choose salvation. This was not received well among his fellow Presbyterians. For a time, Finney served a Presbyterian church as pastor but left when his frustration over the doctrine became too burdensome for him. He moved to the Broadway Tabernacle, a large church built by his followers. Soon after, he left the church to accept a teaching position at Oberlin College.

Oberlin College and the Social Gospel

He ministered at the Oberlin Congregational Church and taught theology at Oberlin College. In 1851, he became the president of the college. It was more than an honor. Finney had been at the forefront of the social gospel movement. He believed that being a Christian required involvement in the community addressing social issues. He was a force in the antislavery movement, and the college served as one of the stops on the underground railroad helping escaped slaves to freedom.

The list of organizations he founded or helped form is staggering: the American Board of Commissioners for Foreign Missions, 1810; the American Bible Society, 1816; the American Sunday School Union, 1817; the American Tract Society, 1826; the American Home Mission Society, 1826; and the American Temperance Society, 1826.

His college was the first to grant a bachelor's degree to a black woman, Mary Jane Patterson. During his revival days, he encouraged women to pray aloud in mixed company.

To Finney, the church wasn't the church unless it was an active force for change and righteousness. Although slowed by illness, Finney continued his work until his death in 1875 at age eighty-two. Finney's influence on the church revival movement is unrivaled and has forever shaped the church.

WILLIAM GLADSTONE
"The Great Christian Man"

(1809–1898)

I have known ninety-five of the world's great men in my time, and of these eighty-seven were followers of the Bible. The Bible is stamped with a Specialty of Origin, and an immeasurable distance separates it from all competitors.

William Gladstone, *Halley's Bible Handbook*

William Ewart Gladstone is a man of such great achievement that it is nearly impossible to write an abbreviated chapter on his life. Biographer and statesman Roy Jenkins took well over six hundred pages to write a one-volume biography called *Gladstone*.

Born to a well-to-do family in Liverpool, Gladstone attended school at Eaton and Christ Church, Oxford, and entered Parliament soon after graduation (1832). He would spend sixty years in government, serving in various positions including four terms as prime minister, something unique in British history. Some referred to Gladstone as "G.O.M.," the Grand Old Man. His long-term opponents said that "G.O.M." stood for God's Only Mistake.

Most of those who write about Gladstone write about his ups and downs in government, about how Queen Victoria disliked him, about how another powerful prime minister—Benjamin Disraeli—became and remained his rival, but there is another side to the great Gladstone.

Man of Faith

William Gladstone was a man of faith and active in the Church of England. "Most men at the head of great movements are Christian men. During my many years in the cabinet I was brought in contact with some sixty masterminds, and not more than perhaps three or four of whom were in sympathy with the skeptical movement of the day."[1]

His was not the pseudo-faith of many politicians who were "believers" because voters expected them to be. Gladstone attended church regularly and took communion weekly. His diaries show he felt a sense of his own sinfulness and spiritual need. His support helped the Church of England with its growth overseas. He was known to speak with prostitutes in an effort to convince them of the error of their ways.

A story is told of a young boy he befriended who came to his home and No. 10 Downing Street to speak to the prime minister. "Mr. Gladstone, my brother is dying, will you come and show him the way to heaven?" Gladstone was working on a speech he was to deliver to Parliament that day and had yet to complete it. Nevertheless, he went to the dying boy and did as the brother had asked. The boy made a profession of faith, and when Gladstone returned to his office and to his speech, he wrote at the bottom of one page, "Today, I am the happiest man in London."

Politics an Act of Service

Gladstone saw politics as a blessing. "My political and public life is the best part of my life: it is the part in which I am conscious of the greatest effort to do and avoid as the Lord Christ would have me do and avoid."[2] He felt blessed to be in public service. To him, public service was Christian duty.

"Christianity established . . . the duty of relieving the poor, the sick, the afflicted,"[3] he said. Where many men in the public sector keep a fence between their faith and their political decisions, Gladstone blended both into an inseparable way of thinking.

More Than a Politician

"William Ewart Gladstone was, perhaps with no one other than Tennyson, Newman, Dickens, Carlyle, and Darwin, one of the stars of the nineteenth-century British life," said Roy Jenkins in his biography *Gladstone*.[4] Gladstone was a man of many skills. He read over twenty thousand books in his lifetime. Not content to be just a reader, he was also a writer who penned both articles and books, and in his later years wrote books defending Christianity including *The Impregnable Rock of Holy Scripture*.

He was a classical scholar and did not shy away from the theological debates of the day. His topics ranged from *On Books and the Housing of Them*, to poetry, economics, and church history. His was not a mind wasted.

The life of William Ewart Gladstone proves that faith and public life are left and right hands of the same cause. He serves as an example that Christians can, and some should, enter the rough-and-tumble world of politics to bolster policy with faith-driven hopes.

The Grand Old Man, with his balding head and large sideburns, retired from public life in 1894. Four years later he died of cancer and was buried in Westminster Abbey. Lord Salisbury said it best. He called Gladstone, "A great Christian man."

48

FANNY CROSBY

Inspiration by Word and Life

(1820–1915)

> It seemed intended by the blessed Providence of God that I should
> be blind all my life, and I thank Him for that dispensation.
>
> Fanny Crosby, *Fanny Crosby's Life Story*

The words above come from the first lines in the first chapter of Francis Jane, better known as Fanny, Crosby's book, *Fanny Crosby's Life Story*.[1] They are shocking words. Could a person blind since infancy be thankful for the loss of her sight?

Fanny often stated that she saw her blindness as a blessing. In one of her first poems, written at the early age of eight, she wrote:

Oh, what a happy soul I am,
Although I cannot see!
I resolve that in this world
Content I will be.
How many blessings I enjoy
That other people don't,
To weep and sigh because I'm blind.
I cannot, and I won't!

252

Unnecessary Tragedy

"I was born with a pair of as good eyes as any baby ever owned," she also wrote in that first paragraph. Crosby was born in 1820 in Putnam County, New York. Just six weeks later she developed an eye inflammation and a doctor was called. The doctor prescribed hot mustard poultices, which the family believed damaged her eyes beyond repair. There is some disagreement about both the cause of blindness and the malpractice that may have led to it. Some have written that the local doctor was out of town, and instead a quack administered the advice and fled when he learned of the damage he had caused. Crosby simply refers to him as a doctor who was so grieved he left town. Some think the blindness was congenital, but because of her young age went unnoticed. She and her family, however, attributed the cause to the doctor who treated her. Quack, malpractice, or congenital disorder, it didn't matter to her condition. Other doctors confirmed the damage was permanent. Nothing could be done.

This was a perfect opportunity for Crosby to harbor hate and resentment, but she held no such animosity toward the man potentially responsible for her permanent loss of vision. She stated that if she had met him years later, she would thank him. Thank him! Crosby had the rare ability to find blessing in what others called misfortune. To her, blindness freed her from distraction, allowing her to focus on what mattered.

A second tragedy struck the family just a few months later when John Crosby, Fanny's father, died, which forced her mother to find work as a maid. Crosby makes no mention of what caused his death.

An Unbelievable Mind

Crosby was a prodigy, highly intelligent, articulate, self-confident, and in love with words and music. She developed an amazing memory. While she was young, her godly grandmother and others would read the Bible to her, much of which she committed to memory. She had a goal of memorizing five chapters a week and could, as a child, recite the first five books of the Bible, the Gospels, Proverbs, Song of Solomon, and many of the Psalms. This memory she described as being like a desk with drawers. Later she would write:

> After any particular hymn is done, I let it lie for a few days in the writing-desk of my mind, so to speak, until I have leisure to prune it, to read it through with the eyes of my memory, and in other ways mold it into as presentable a shape as possible. I often cut, trim, and change it.[2]

She could recall hundreds, perhaps thousands of poems. Her mind was a storehouse.

School

In 1835, when she was fifteen, she enrolled in the New York Institute for the Blind, where she would remain a student for eight years and two more as a graduate student. The school proved pivotal for her in several ways. There she learned to play several instruments and to sing. Her future husband had also been a student there. She became a teacher at the institution and served in that capacity for over a decade.

Perhaps one of the most influential events—and certainly the strangest—occurred when the school invited a phrenologist to visit. Phrenology was a popular study at the time. Practitioners of the "science" studied the shape and bumps of the skull in a belief that they could ascertain, among other things, a person's skills. Today the practice is dismissed by science, but it was a popular belief during Crosby's school days. When Dr. George Combe, the phrenologist, reached young Crosby, he laid his hands on her head to feel its size, shape, and contours. She later said she trembled and felt the impulse to run.

Dr. Combe said, "Why here is a poet! Give her every advantage that she can have; let her hear the best books and converse with the best writers; and she will make her mark in the world." The school took him at his word. She was encouraged to write poetry and received great instruction in the art. Phrenology might be quackery, but that day, the phrenologist's diagnosis opened a significant door for the greatest American hymn writer. Crosby wrote: "I was indebted to Phrenology, and the good Dr. Combe."[3]

A Fountain of Production

Fanny would pen one thousand secular poems and eight thousand hymns. The bulk of her work, and the work that consumed her throughout her adult life, was the penning of praise set to music. Crosby was so prolific that she had to write under pen names—approximately two hundred of them.

She was under contract to send three hymns a week to her publisher, and had days when she produced twice that many. She was usually paid one to two dollars per hymn produced.

William Doane, for whom Crosby had written hymns, showed up at her home in dire need of a hymn. He had composed the music but needed the lyrics. "Fanny, I have just forty minutes to catch the cars for Cincinnati; during that time you must write me a hymn, and give me a few minutes to catch the train."[4] He hummed the melody. Fifteen minutes later he left with the words to, "Safe in the Arms of Jesus."

Fanny Crosby was capable of writing more complicated hymns and music, but she preferred something closer to the heart that could be used in evangelism—in other words, simple to learn and easy to sing. Her material reflected an orthodox Christian view but also a faith born of experience. Worshipers still sing her words a century after her death.

A list of her works show five autobiographies, four books of poetry, seven cantatas, and five popular (secular) songs. Her professional writing spanned over fifty years.

Her hymns are familiar to anyone who has spent much time in church:

"All the Way My Savior Leads Me"
"Blessed Assurance"
"He Hideth My Soul"
"More Like Jesus"
"I am Thine O Lord"
"Near the Cross"

"Pass Me Not, O Gentle Savior"
"Praise Him! Praise Him! Jesus, Our Blessed Redeemer"
"To God Be the Glory"

The list goes on. Just the mention of a title will, for some, release a flood of lyrics.

Although blind all her life, she often spoke in her hymns of seeing Jesus face-to-face. She believed that when she died, the first person she would see with heavenly eyes would be her Savior. Until then, she would write of his light even though her world was forever dark.

Two Contributions to the Church

Fanny Crosby contributed much to the church, helping worshipers express emotions and thoughts that would not otherwise find release. The excellence of her poetry and music is enduring and of such encouraging quality they have ministered to millions of people. She will always be remembered for her contributions to the heart and soul of the church.

She also contributed the example of her life. Eight thousand hymns is almost too much to fathom and places her as one of the greatest hymn writers alongside Isaac Watts and Charles Wesley. Her example of inner strength, determination, and ability to face the difficulties of blindness with humor, modesty, and faith is an example and an encouragement to anyone facing life's challenges.

All of this from a blind girl who refused to feel sorry for herself or accept limitations and had an unending desire to write for God.

When she died in 1915, just shy of her ninety-fifth birthday, she had been working on a hymn. Her last written words were, "You will reach the river brink, some sweet day, by and by."

49

FYODOR DOSTOYEVSKY

Troubled Genius

(1821–1881)

> If someone proved to me that Christ is outside the truth and that
> in reality the truth were outside of Christ, then I should prefer to
> remain with Christ rather than with the truth.
>
> Fyodor Dostoyevsky, *Letter to Mme. Fonvizina*

Novelists write from their pain. To Dostoyevsky, that was more than a writer's aphorism.

Russian writer Fyodor Dostoyevsky, son of a dominating and cruel physician, is one of the best-known novelists in history, but his path to fame was brutal. Like many who show artistic genius, he was uncomfortable in this world. A man of deep faith, he was also conflicted and raised the questions voiced by the skeptical characters in his work. Most of his life was difficult, and his problems were compounded by illness and financial stress.

Damaged Goods

As often happens between fathers and sons, there was a difference of opinion about young Dostoyevsky's future. Dostoyevsky longed to write, but his father wanted him to be a military engineer. For a time his father won out. Dostoyevsky completed his military training in 1843, but resigned his commission. Writing was his calling, not engineering. In 1846, his first novel, *Poor Folk*, was released and quickly became successful. Dostoyevsky's dream had taken flight.

However, soon after he and others were arrested for participating in a discussion group considering the writings of utopian socialist Charles Fourier. He and the others were told they would be executed. His captors lined him and other prisoners in front of a firing squad. The twenty-nine-year-old waited for the impact of the bullets, believing he was about to breathe his last.

The bullets never came. It was a mock firing squad assembled as part of the punishment. The czar had granted a "reprieve," but sentenced the men to four years of imprisonment in Siberia and after that a five-year service in the army. The experience was mind-shattering. Indeed, at least one of the men lost his mind. It was during the hardship of the Siberian work camp that Dostoyevsky's health began to fail. Never a strong man, he grew weaker and suffered his first bouts with epilepsy, a disorder he would live with for the remainder of his life. If there was a silver lining in his disorder, it was that he was released from the half-decade of military service that was to follow the Siberian punishment.

During his time in Siberia, he was allowed only one book to read: the Bible. He returned to his life a much more diligent Russian Orthodox believer. (It was his opinion that Christ could only be found in the Russian Orthodox Church.)

Once free he took up the pen again, this time drawing on his prison experience. *The House of the Dead* was released in 1861.

His prison experience had changed Dostoyevsky, as it would any man. On the positive side, he dove deeper into the themes that marked his writing: suffering, the failings of humanism and rationalism, and salvation in Christ. Some of the more overt Christian passages were weeded out by censors.

Dostoyevsky soon faced new hardships. First he suffered from financial woes. His wife had died, as had his brother, and he was left with a family to support. At times he borrowed money from friends. This problem was further exacerbated by a gambling addiction. He gambled away what money he had, and even what had been loaned to him.

· He could also be cruel to those around him. How much of this had to do with the ordeal he endured at the mock execution, the years spent in Siberia, the loss of his wife and brother, and his epilepsy can't be said.

Later Works

The great author encountered Fyodor Stellovsky, an unscrupulous publisher who offered him a dangerous deal. In financial desperation, Dostoyevsky took it. Authors and publishers use "deadline" to refer to the date when a project is due. It is not uncommon for a writer to miss a deadline by a few days or weeks, but in this case more was at stake than a publishing schedule. If Dostoyevsky failed to provide the contracted novel on time, the publisher could claim rights to *all* of Dostoyevsky's work for nine years without compensating the author. The publisher knew of the author's penchant for starting late, and was wagering he would not meet the November 1, 1866 deadline.

Dostoyevsky indeed started late, leaving himself only a month to write *The Gambler*. He would have been doomed had he not hired an eighteen-year-old stenographer named Anna Snitkina. Night and day they worked, Dostoyevsky dictating and Anna writing his words. Together they made the deadline, and the author knew the young woman had saved his work and his career.

He married her.

His best work followed, including *Crime and Punishment* (1866), a work based on the commandment "Thou shalt not kill," and *The Brothers Karamazov* (1880), which includes a Christ-figure and an agnostic.

Not long after *The Brothers Karamazov*, Dostoyevsky died at the age of fifty-nine. Life had been unkind to him, and he made it worse with his gambling. Out of that misery, which included the loss of a child, Sonya, Dostoyevsky managed to leave an indelible mark on literature and show that Christianity affects all, even those who deny its teaching.

The church benefits, not by Dostoyevsky's lifestyle, not by his philosophy, but by his commitment to showing people of faith struggling against a harsh world, and by weaving elements of faith in the characters he created. He was no theologian, no preacher, and no social minister, but he was a man who fought demons inside and out, and who, in the end, leaned on his faith to survive.

50

WILLIAM BOOTH

A General in Salvation's Army

(1829–1912)

> While women weep, as they do now, I'll fight; while little children
> go hungry, I'll fight; while men go to prison, in and out, in and out,
> as they do now, I'll fight—while there is a drunkard left, while there
> is a poor lost girl upon the streets, while there remains one dark
> soul without the light of God—I'll fight! I'll fight to the very end!
>
> William Booth, final speech to the Salvation Army, May 9, 1912

Those born in poverty often go to extremes to get out. William Booth went to extremes to stay in.

This is not to say that Booth enjoyed poverty. Growing up in Nottingham, England, in a poor home and doing his best to help the family finances by being a pawnbroker's apprentice, Booth knew poverty firsthand. He was surrounded by it.

Changing Times

Late nineteenth-century England was in the midst of dramatic change. Like much of the Western world, its society was transitioning from an agricultural to an industrial age. Jobs could only be found in the city, not on the farm, and many moved into London hoping to improve their lot. But those that could not find work found poverty instead. The inner-city population began to swell, especially in the East End. Poverty expanded rapidly. Children went hungry; people died in the streets.

The government was at a loss to help, mired in red tape. Sadly, so was the Church of England, which was operating as if the world hadn't changed. The Church of England was ill-prepared to deal with the issues at hand, needing more parishes and more clergy to handle the load, both of which required an act of Parliament. The Methodists, although they contributed good work to the cause, were primarily a middle-class church, and their reach into impoverished communities was minimal. The poor were falling through the cracks. William Booth would later write a book, *In Darkest England and the Way Out* (1890), in which he drew parallels between the Africa described by David Livingston and England. The book states that in a single year 2,157 people were found dead, 2,297 had committed suicide, 30,000 were practicing prostitution, 160,000 had been convicted of drunkenness, and over 900,000 were designated paupers. Bleak.

It was in this environment that Booth decided to conduct his ministry.

The Beginning

Booth's parents were not religious, but at age fifteen, a year after his father died, he was taken to a Wesleyan chapel where he made a commitment to Christ. In his diary he wrote, "God shall have all there is of William Booth." Those were more than the dreamy words of a teenager. Booth would spend his life in ministry. In a second event, he attended a revival service featuring an American preacher. He saw what a well-crafted approach to preaching could do, became a student of the practices of revivalist Charles Finney, and put that knowledge to use.

His first work was in street preaching. He and some friends took the gospel message to the people rather than waiting for the people to come to church. He used instruments and popular styles of music to gain interest. This brought him criticism. For a time, Booth served as pastor of a Methodist church, but it was a poor fit. He returned to work in East London. In 1855, he met and married Catherine Mumford, a powerhouse in her own right. Much of Booth's success in ministry is due to her support, diligence, and preaching.

The thin-framed man with long, untrimmed beard formed his own mission society to reach the "heathen masses." After a time it stalled, so he made changes. In 1878, he changed the name of the group to the Salvation Army, a name it still uses today. He organized the group as if it were a military unit. He became General Booth and assigned ranks to various positions. Later he added uniforms, brass bands, and other military images and terms. He started a magazine called *The War Cry*.

The work was hard and at times dangerous. The success of the Salvation Army hurt some businesses, especially those providing alcohol. Many who came to faith through the organization's ministry gave up drinking, and the group was successful enough that saloons and breweries were feeling the pinch. "Soldiers" were attacked and ministry buildings damaged.

There was also a great toll on Booth, who preached close to sixty thousand sermons and traveled an estimated five million miles during his long service.

The Salvation Army grew quickly, spreading to other countries and reaching the United States, Canada, and other nations within the first decade. Today it serves 124 countries and has grown to nearly sixteen thousand "corps," with seventeen-thousand-plus "active officers." It operates homeless hostels, children's homes, elderly care homes, mother and baby homes, and other ministries to lessen the pain of others and present the gospel. It also runs twenty-one hospitals and over two hundred health clinics.

Booth believed that a man with a full stomach was more likely to listen to the gospel. His organization dealt with (and still deals with) physical need as a means of building relationships and addressing spiritual needs.

William Booth died in 1912 at the age of eighty-three. Forty thousand people attended his funeral, including Queen Mary. Approximately 150,000 people filed past his casket. The man born near poverty stayed near poverty, and through his organization changed the lives of millions.

51

HUDSON TAYLOR

Man on a Mission

(1832–1905)

All God's giants have been weak men who did things for God because they reckoned on his being with them.

Hudson Taylor, "Hold God's Faithfulness," *China's Millions*

Most young boys dream of being policemen, firemen, or famous athletes. Not so for young James Hudson Taylor of Barnsley, Yorkshire, England, who by the age of five was talking about being a missionary to the "heathen" in China. No doubt much of this came from the influence of his parents, James and Amelia Taylor. James was a pharmacist and preacher in the Methodist church. Both were devout and often had other religious leaders and preachers from the area in their home. There, young Hudson heard stories of missionaries in distant lands, especially China. These stories captured his imagination.

Despite his early interest in mission work, Taylor's conversion didn't come until he was seventeen, when, alone at home, he wrestled with his future and his God. In the end he found peace regarding both. Taylor longed to go to China as a missionary. He would spend half a century doing that work.

Single-Minded Goal

China consumed Taylor. He read whatever books about the country he could lay hands on, and did his best to learn Mandarin. He wanted to do more than just show up in a foreign country with a Bible in one hand and a wad of tracts in the other. He moved to Kinston upon Hull and worked as a medical assistant to Dr. Robert Hardey. A year later, in 1852, he entered the Royal London Hospital in the Whitechapel district of London to study medicine.

At twenty-one, he left school without completing his studies and, under the sponsorship of the Chinese Evangelization Society, made his way to China. The trip took five months and nearly ended in disaster. In March of 1854, Taylor, a fresh-faced young man with wavy, dark hair, stepped from the deck to the solid ground of Shanghai.

He was a stranger in a strange land. No one knew he was coming. He didn't know the language well and two of the people he planned to contact were no longer available. One had died; the other had sailed home. But with the help of the British consulate, he was able to locate Dr. Walter Medhurst, who was in China as a minister from the London Missionary Society. Taylor had a place to stay until he could get on his feet.

He made close to twenty preaching tours around Shanghai, handing out tracts. Although he provided some medical care and supplies, he was still unwelcome, and often called the "black devil" because of the dark coat he wore. Taylor was an outsider who spoke differently and looked and dressed in a way that made him stand out. So, true to Taylor's independent nature, he addressed this problem by starting to dress like the Chinese men he met, going so far as to grow the traditional queue, a Chinese pigtail. This sounds fine and noble today, but in Taylor's time it was shocking. Other missionaries criticized the decision. Taylor did it anyway.

I am fully satisfied that the native dress is an absolute prerequisite. Quietly settling among the people, obtaining free, familiar, and unrestrained communication with them, conciliating their prejudices, attracting their esteem and confidence, and so living as to be examples to them of what Chinese Christians should be, require the adoption not merely of this costume but also of their habits. . . . The foreign appearance of chapels and indeed the foreign air given to everything connected with religion have very largely hindered the rapid dissemination of the truth among the Chinese. But why need such a foreign aspect be given to Christianity? The word of God does not require it. . . . It is not their denationalization but their Christianization that we seek.[1]

Breaking Away

Taylor relocated to Ningbo in 1857 and started a small church. He also resigned from the Chinese Evangelization Society. The troubled mission organization was failing on several counts and could not pay their missionaries. The organization would disband a few years later. Taylor's independent spirit reared its head again, and he decided to work as an independent missionary and let God provide for his needs.

In 1858, he married Maria Dyer, the daughter of a missionary. She worked in a local girls' school. During this time, Taylor put his medical experience to work by running the operations of the Ningbo hospital.

Taylor's health declined until, in 1861, he had to return to England for recovery. He had spent six years in China. He would then stay in his homeland for close to six years, but although he was absent from China in body, his heart still remained in the country he loved. He continued to work on a Bible translation and wrote *China: Its Spiritual Need and Claims*. Still he was conflicted.

Besides his physical concerns, Taylor was troubled with depression, something that afflicts many people, even the most spiritual. Their first child had died in China, he had been treated rudely, was nearly killed during the Chinese Civil War, had lost all his medical supplies in a fire, and was robbed of all he had while traveling across country.

More misery yet awaited him. His wife, Maria, would die at the young age of thirty-three, and four of his eight children would die before the age of ten.

During his recovery time in England, he struggled in heart and soul. It was not an easy battle.

Insight on the Beach

Taylor received an invitation to continue his recovery at a friend's home in Brighton. He spent the time in thought and reflection. While strolling the sands and praying, things came clear: "There the Lord conquered my unbelief, and I surrendered myself to God for this service. I told him that all responsibility as to the issues and consequences must rest with him; that as his servant it was mine to obey and follow him."[2]

This encounter with God was freeing. Taylor would go back into China focused on his work, and let God provide the support. Here he made some interesting decisions. He formed the China Inland Mission (CIM), but it would operate differently than the mission organization that first sent him to China. He would ask for no financial support. His missionaries would not be promised salaries, but he would share with all equally. They could not appeal for funds. And the missionaries in his organization would dress like the Chinese.

A year later, Taylor and his family sailed back to China. With them were sixteen missionaries from London.

Stress and Success

Taylor worked nonstop. While in England he had studied to be a midwife, a useful skill in nineteenth-century China. Although not a doctor, he used his medical training as part of his outreach. At times, he saw more than two hundred patients a day. He expected the same commitment to work from his missionaries, some of whom resented the pressure. For some, the strain proved too much and they left CIM for other mission organizations. Nonetheless, the organization grew. By November of 1887 there were scores of missionaries working under his direction. He also allowed unmarried women to serve as missionaries—something unheard of in his day.

Recruiting missionaries was a priority, and Taylor traveled widely to teach about the work being done, drawing in new workers. He traveled to the United States and Canada, but the work and travel wore on him. By 1900 he had a physical breakdown.

Taylor died in 1905 in China at the age of seventy-three. At the time of his death, his vision for mission work in China had grown from one man stepping off a ship to 205 mission stations, nearly 850 missionaries, and over 125,000 Chinese converts. The China Inland Mission continues Taylor's work and dream today as the Overseas Missionary Fellowship International.

CHARLES SPURGEON

Prince of Preachers

(1834–1892)

The truest lengthening of life is to live while we live, wasting no
time but using every hour for the highest ends. So be it this day.

Charles Spurgeon, *Faith's Checkbook*

I t must be a mistake."
Those were Charles Haddon Spurgeon's words when he read
the letter. The British Baptist preacher had received an invitation
from a Reformed Baptist church: New Park Street Chapel in Southwark, London. It was not unusual for one church to invite the pastor of another to speak, but New Park Street had a distinguished
history, although it had fallen on hard times. The real surprise was
Spurgeon's age. He was just twenty. Still, word of his unique and
gripping preaching style had spread from his church in Waterbeach
near Cambridge to London. It was there that Spurgeon made history as one of the most successful pastors to stand behind a pulpit.

Salvation in a Snowstorm

Charles Haddon Spurgeon was born into a family of clergy in Kelvedon, Essex, in 1834. His father and grandfather were Nonconformist pastors (not part of the Anglican church). It was assumed that he would follow in their footsteps, and perhaps he intended to at first. In January 1850 he was attempting to make his way to a particular church. He was serious about attending. Not even the snowstorm that came up could deter him. While it didn't stop him, it did divert him down a side street, where he came upon a Primitive Methodist church. This branch of methodism was known for loud singing.[1]

Spurgeon entered and found only a handful of people in attendance. The storm had not only kept parishioners homebound but the pastor as well. One of the laymen rose to speak and Spurgeon was less than impressed. The text of the impromptu sermon was, "Look unto me, and be ye saved, all the ends of the earth." The text was from Isaiah 45:22 (KJV) and the man hammered on the word "look" for much of his short sermon. Spurgeon considered the speaker uneducated and out of his depth, but there was no questioning the man's sincerity. After ten minutes of preaching, the speaker turned his eyes on fifteen-year-old Spurgeon.

"Young man, you look miserable."

Spurgeon was not used to seeing anyone in the pulpit speak directly to a congregant, especially a stranger. The crowd was so small that Spurgeon stood out. "It was a good blow, struck right home," Spurgeon later admitted.[2]

The speaker wasn't done. "You will always be miserable—miserable in life, and miserable in death, if you don't obey my text; but if you obey now, this moment, you will be saved."

Spurgeon was never the same. He began to question his previously held doctrine, especially the infant baptism practiced by the prevalent Anglican church as well as the Nonconformist church he grew up in. Feeling the Baptist belief in "believer's baptism" had greater biblical support, he left behind his Nonconformist membership and joined a Baptist church. There he was baptized. He remained a Baptist from then on.

Salvation had come to Spurgeon, and he was determined to take it to others. The Methodist layman's preaching was so unrefined Spurgeon first thought the man was stupid, but it was his direct approach that made the difference in Spurgeon's life. Ironically, Spurgeon's preaching would be criticized frequently, even while people came by the thousands to hear him.

A Sensation in the Pulpit

Spurgeon had minimal education, never earning a degree from a university. At best he was a self-taught man, but that is no reason to discount him. He amassed a library of twelve thousand books, and anyone who reads his writing will see a man with a keen mind and a gift for communication.

His speaking prowess was noticed early on. He began his preaching ministry as a pastor of a small Baptist church in Waterbeach, Cambridgeshire. The church soon filled to hear the boy preacher—he was still a teenager—and word spread.

In April 1854, he received a letter asking him to preach at the New Park Street Chapel in Southwark, London. The church, although slimmer in attendance than what it experienced in its glory days, was still a significant church and the largest Baptist congregation in the area. Spurgeon thought a mistake had been made. What would such a church want with a twenty-year-old preacher-boy?

Regardless, he went and preached to a handful of people. Only about eighty came to the service. Still, the church felt he was the man to fill their pulpit. They issued a "call" for him to become pastor for the next six months. He agreed. The six-month period was extended time and time again—for forty years. Spurgeon would remain the pastor at New Park for the rest of his life.

Larger and larger crowds arrived to hear Spurgeon preach. Soon, the church moved the services to Exeter Hall, which seated 4,500, and it still wasn't enough. Spurgeon had become the pastor of what we would now label a megachurch.

A new church was constructed that could seat 5,600, with standing room for an additional thousand. Often that was too little. The church changed its name to the Metropolitan Tabernacle, and Spurgeon preached in that building for the next three decades.

Spurgeon focused on his listeners, believing he had a message from God and he was the conduit of that message. He wanted to get to the thousands of people in his church the way the unnamed lay preacher got to him that snowy day in the Methodist church. He was loud, moved around the platform, and acted out biblical stories. It was offensive to the refined clergy and some in the media. Some called him the "pulpit buffoon" and accused him of being vulgar. The *Ipswich Express* reported Spurgeon's sermons as "redolent of bad taste, vulgar, and theatrical."[3]

Spurgeon had a response: "I am perhaps vulgar, but it is not intentional, save that I must and will make the people listen. My firm conviction is that we have had quite enough polite preachers, and many require a change. God has owned me among the most degraded of off-casts. Let others serve their class; these are mine, and to them I must keep."[4]

Other criticism came from the media, but Spurgeon kept going and the crowds kept coming.

Tragedy at Church and Criticism

It is easy to think great men and women are free from challenges, but as we have seen throughout this book, difficulties are what usually make them great. Spurgeon's life had tragedy and challenge. As the church grew, they again moved into larger facilities. They rented the Surrey Music Hall, which seated twelve thousand people. One day, the place was packed for the service when several people—for unknown reasons—shouted, "Fire!" A panic ensued, leaving seven dead and nearly thirty seriously injured.

Spurgeon was also plagued by periods of depression. In some ways, it helped him minister to others. Perhaps only those who have wrestled with depression can know how taxing it is to mind, body, and soul.

Some of his opinions stoked the fires of criticism, not from the press but from other ministers and denominations. He managed to offend Calvinists even though he was one of their number. To him, some were too Calvinistic, others were not Calvinistic enough. He also upset the Anglicans and even accused his Baptist brethren of downgrading the gospel in the modern era. He had to withdraw from the denomination's organization. Controversy dogged him through the last years of his ministry and may have contributed to his declining health.

Other Works

Spurgeon was more than a preacher; he was also a prolific writer, composing 140 books of sermons, devotions, and commentaries. Starting in 1855, his weekly sermons were printed, and many of these have been reprinted in collections that are still read. He started a monthly magazine, *The Sword and the Trowel*. He also produced a book of advice to young preachers, *Lectures to My Students*.

In addition to his work with the church, Spurgeon established the Stockwell Orphanage after challenging his church in a Monday night prayer meeting to begin a new work. The resulting orphanage took care of thousands of children over the course of its existence.

In 1856, he opened the Pastor's College to train ministers. It continues today under the name Spurgeon's College. He also created a Bible distribution organization.

Death

Spurgeon died at age fifty-seven while in France. They brought him back to London, where sixty thousand people filed past his body as it lay in state. On the day of his funeral, one hundred thousand people lined the streets to watch the hearse pass. A trail of people followed in a procession that stretched two miles.

At times controversial, at times outspoken, Spurgeon was loved by his people and the citizens of England. Today he remains the "Prince of Preachers," an example to thousands of ministers who would follow. Through his writings he continues to move souls.

DWIGHT L. MOODY

Not So Mr. Average

(1837–1899)

> I know perfectly well that, wherever I go and preach, there are many better preachers . . . all that I can say about it is that the Lord uses me.
>
> Dwight L. Moody, *The Life of Dwight L. Moody*

It's a long way from being one of nine children of a widowed mother to being one of the greatest lay preachers in history. Moody was not a clergyman. He never attended seminary and was never ordained. He had very little education. Reading his original writing can be painful. It is filled with misuses and misspellings. What he lacked in formal education, however, he made up for with commitment, zeal, and humility.

Seller of Shoes

Unlike many of the great evangelists, Moody was born into a less than orthodox home. His family were Unitarians, a group that rejected traditional Christian beliefs and emphasized the rational over the spiritual. The family did not read the Bible. Moody grew up wanting to make something of himself in business, although he only had a fifth-grade education. When he was seventeen, he left Northfield, Massachusetts, for Boston and began looking for work. Unable to find anything better, he settled for employment in his uncle's shoe store. His uncle, Sam Holton, made Moody promise that he would attend church and Sunday school. Moody did.

At the time, Moody was more concerned with making money, probably due to the poverty he left behind. When his father died, he left his family in debt and creditors took everything. And two months after she buried her husband, Betsey Moody gave birth to twins. Life was hard and no doubt made Moody think wealth was the answer. He set a goal to save one hundred thousand dollars, a substantial sum even now, but much more so in the nineteenth century.

It was Sunday school at Mount Vernon Congregational Church that changed Moody. His teacher was Edward Kimball, a Christian committed to his students. Moody had been on his mind. More accurately, he was burdened for the young man. On April 21, 1855, Kimball made his way to the shoe store where Moody worked—and walked past it. A few moments later, he pushed his doubts aside, mustered his courage, and entered the store to talk to Moody about his salvation. He found young Moody shelving shoes; he also found a willing listener. That day, Moody gave his life to Christ. He was eighteen years old.

He became active in the church, but it took four years before he became a member. The church required a certain ability to explain what Christ did for the world and for an individual that, for some time, Moody didn't possess. Still, he persisted, and was eventually granted membership.

Chicago

In 1856, Moody decided to leave Boston, and made his way to Chicago to find his fame and fortune. Boston had been an uncomfortable fit for young Moody but he found Chicago more to his liking. He returned to the business he knew: shoes. Some think he could have been an empire builder despite his lack of education. That would have been fine with Moody, had something not stirred in his soul. His faith was changing his vision. He became convinced that he should be more concerned with souls than shoes, and spiritual matters over business.

He found a mission on North Wells Street and asked if he could teach a Sunday school class. Churches are always looking for volunteers, but this particular fellowship had more teachers than students. If he wanted to teach, they told him, then he'd have to create his own class. That was fine with him.

He established a mission in one of the slum areas of Chicago. He approached families, drawing the children with candy and pony rides and drawing the adults, who were poor German and Scandinavian immigrants, with English lessons and prayer meetings. Soon he had his class—and more. In 1861 he began working in full-time ministry, dividing his responsibilities between his Sunday school and the YMCA. He had been involved with the latter for some time and would become influential in its success.

Sunday school was good to him in another way: he met and married Emma C. Revell, one of the Sunday school teachers. Together they would have three children.

What had begun as a Sunday school turned into the Independent Church, which laid the foundation for what would become the great Moody Memorial Church. He later became the president of the Young Men's Christian Association, which had come over from England, and served in the position for four years.

"Enough, Lord!"

The Great Chicago Fire of 1871 changed the city, and changed Dwight L. Moody. The blaze began Sunday evening (Moody had been preaching when the congregation heard the fire bells) and blazed into Tuesday, October 10. It consumed over three square miles of the city and left Moody's home, his church, and the YMCA in ashes. Everything was lost. It also destroyed the businesses of many of his supporters. Despite the widespread devastation of the fire and the financial challenges in its aftermath, Moody remained hopeful and enthusiastic, setting out on fund-raising expeditions to other cities.

It was while Moody was on one such trip to New York that, while walking down Wall Street, he was suddenly awash in the presence and power of God. It flooded him with such intensity that he would never be the same.

> I could not appeal. I was crying all the time that God would fill me with His Spirit. Well, one day, in the city of New York—oh, what a day!—I cannot describe it, I seldom refer to it; it is almost too sacred an experience to name. Paul had an experience of which he never spoke for fourteen years. I can only say that God revealed Himself to me, and I had such an experience of His love that I had to ask Him to stay His hand. I went to preaching again. The sermons were not different; I did not present any new truths, and yet hundreds were converted. I would not now be placed back where I was before that blessed experience if you should give me all the world—it would be as the small dust of the balance.[1]

Moody had left Chicago the leader of a successful church and president of the city's YMCA, and came back a preacher with an expanded vision.

England and the United States

The Chicago fire could destroy buildings, but not the faith of Moody and his church. While the church began to rebuild, Moody set his eyes on the world. Moody would add "traveling evangelist" to his list of accomplishments.

Moody believed people could be reached through music, and that meant finding a musically talented man who would be willing to travel abroad with him. At a YMCA meeting he heard Ira Sankey sing, and immediately knew he had found his music man. All that remained was convincing Sankey of the fact. It took months, but Sankey finally agreed and left his government job to join Moody.

Moody and Sankey received an invitation to preach in England from a pair of Anglican ministers. However, both pastors died while Moody and Sankey were in transit, leaving them without sponsors for the trip. Despite this, Moody went on to preach in several cities to small congregations. Their situation changed in the city of

Newcastle, where the services were well-received and many converts were made. For two years they preached overseas then returned to Chicago, now internationally renowned.

Moody never considered himself a great preacher. "I know perfectly well that, wherever I go and preach, there are many better preachers known and heard than I am; all I can say about it is that the Lord uses me."[2]

While he took many cues from Charles Finney, he made adjustments better suited to the age of industry: a simple nondenominational sermon, lots of music, spiritual counseling, and a robust organization. Many of his techniques laid the groundwork for other evangelists to follow, including Billy Graham.

Doing More

The work of evangelizing an entire generation would require more than one man or even a dozen. People were needed to go into the field with the gospel message, but they needed training. The man who had, at most, a grammar-school education became an administering educator. "If this world is going to be reached, I am convinced that it must be done by men and women of average talent. After all, there are comparatively few people in this world who have great talent."[3]

To this end Moody created the Northfield Seminary for Young Women in 1879. Two years later he opened the Mount Hermon School for Boys. In 1886 he began the Chicago Evangelization Society, which later became Moody Bible Institute, an organization that continues to train people for ministerial work.

Moody was an evangelistic entrepreneur, starting these and other organizations that still carry on the work begun over a century ago.

Passing

Dwight Moody died on November 16, 1899 at the age of sixty-two. He thought often of that future day and several times spoke of the next life:

Someday you will read in the papers that D. L. Moody, of East North-field, is dead. Don't you believe a word of it! At that moment I shall be more alive than I am now. I shall have gone up higher, that is all; out of this old clay tenement into a house that is immortal—a body that death cannot touch; that sin cannot taint; a body fashioned like unto His glorious body.

I was born of the flesh in 1837. I was born of the Spirit in 1856. That which is born of the flesh may die. That which is born of the Spirit will live forever.[4]

Moody changed the face of evangelism and showed that the work of ministry doesn't reside just with the ordained.

54

BILLY SUNDAY

Blue-Collar Preacher and the Sawdust Trail

(1862–1935)

> I'm against sin. I'll kick it as long as I have a foot. I'll fight it as long as I have a fist. I'll butt it as long as I have a head. I'll bite it as long as I have a tooth. And when I'm old and fistless and footless and toothless, I'll gum it till I go home to glory and it goes home to perdition.
>
> Billy Sunday, frequently quoted in his sermons

For much of his life, William Ashley "Billy" Sunday was the least likely person anyone would expect to find behind a pulpit. In many ways he was the epitome of the very things he would later preach against. He was a professional baseball player who frequented saloons and enjoyed the fame the sport brought him. No one saw the turnabout that was to come in 1886.

A Tough Beginning

Billy Sunday was the son of a Union soldier who died of pneumonia the same year Billy was born. He never met his father. Life after the

Civil War was exceptionally difficult for those who had lost their fathers and husbands. Much of Billy's childhood was spent in a log cabin being cared for by his widowed mother who was so impoverished that for a period of time she had to surrender her children to the Soldiers Orphans Home.

Although those days were difficult, Billy found relief playing sports. He had a knack for baseball and his success on amateur teams landed him an invitation to play for the Chicago White Stockings. From 1883 through 1891, he played for various teams, including the Pittsburgh Pirates and the Philadelphia Athletics.

From Fame to Faith

His life changed one Sunday in 1886 as he and some of his fellow players emerged from a saloon to find a band of people playing instruments and preaching the gospel. He listened for a time and the message touched him. "Boys," he said, "I'm through! Going to turn to Jesus. We come to the parting of our ways."[1] And he entered the Pacific Garden Mission and later emerged a believer.

Billy Sunday's conversion was real, and he remained faithful to it to the day he died. As time passed he felt a greater and greater calling to preach. He began working with the YMCA, and they soon convinced him to leave baseball to preach at their services, something he agreed to at great financial sacrifice. For a time he worked with other evangelists, but then began conducting services of his own with great success.

Sunday was not formally trained. At best he had a high school education, and therefore for many years he preached as a lay evangelist. It wasn't until 1903 that the Presbyterian Church ordained him, over fifteen years after he began public evangelism.

A Tornado for the Everyman

What Billy Sunday lacked in refinement he made up for in enthusiasm. He did not possess the cultured tone and appearance of that day's clergy. His preaching was at times "salty," direct, funny, and filled with antics. He was a tornado on the platform, throwing his body into his presentation. At times he would use objects around him such as a chair, which he would swing around during his message. Billy Sunday was as athletic behind (and around) the pulpit as he had been on the baseball field.

His messages were peppered with one-liners that made the truth memorable and quotable:

When the English language gets in my way, I walk over it.

I tell you that the curse of God Almighty is on the saloon.

And if you think that anybody is going to frighten me, you don't know me yet.

They tell me a revival is only temporary; so is a bath, but it does you good.

I believe that a long step toward public morality will have been taken when sins are called by their right names.

Going to church doesn't make you a Christian any more than going into a garage makes you an automobile.

Despite his uninhibited approach to preaching, he was no carnival act. His mind was set on drawing people out of a life of sin and into the arms of Christ. He saw the value in people and often swam against the tide of social trends. He became involved in social causes including women's rights and child labor, and involved African Americans in his crusades even when preaching in the deep South. He also fought against "Mr. Booze," and his preaching helped usher in Prohibition.

There was never a doubt where Billy Sunday stood.

At the end of each sermon, Sunday would invite people to follow Christ and walk the "sawdust trail," an aisle to the front of the "tabernacle." Today this is often referred to as an altar call or public invitation. Many churches practice this every Sunday. The evangelist wanted his hearers to step out in their new faith. Walking the aisle meant a public commitment and demonstrated the person's desire to be a follower of Christ.

There Are Always Critics

As in every case of success, there were critics who denounced him for his style, his lack of follow-up with converts, and the "love offerings" he received (which he often gave to charitable causes). Criticism came with the work, but it didn't slow Sunday down. He continued to preach to large crowds. In a span of a few weeks in 1917, Sunday preached over 120 sermons in New York City. No one preached to more Americans until Billy Graham came on the scene. Some estimate Sunday reached over three hundred thousand converts (some put the number closer to one million) and preached to tens of millions.

Until the End

Billy Sunday, with the help of his wife, Helen Amelia Thompson, who did much of the behind-the-scenes work, continued his ministry until shortly before his death. His popularity waned after World War I, but he continued to preach. He faced financial strain and the death of two of his four children. Still, he continued on.

Billy Sunday was a blue-collar everyman, plainspoken, honest, and driven, who reminded the church once again of the need for effective evangelism, social awareness, and dealing with the problem of sin. He also blazed a trail for other evangelists, such as Billy Graham, to take crusade-style preaching to the masses.

55

OSWALD CHAMBERS
His Utmost

(1874–1917)

> Jesus Christ is always unyielding to my claim to my right to myself.
> The one essential element in all our Lord's teaching about disciple-
> ship is abandon, no calculation, no trace of self-interest.
>
> Oswald Chambers, *Disciples Indeed*

In March of 2003, *Newsweek* published an article about a powerful man who spent a part of each morning in private reading. Rising at dawn, he would set aside scores of documents, reports, and articles demanding his attention and instead pick up a book first published in 1927: *My Utmost for His Highest*. This powerful man was President George W. Bush.

In Christian circles, *My Utmost for His Highest* is well-known. Some contend that it is the most recognized book apart from the Bible. Millions of copies have been sold over the eight decades the work has been in print.

The odd thing is the content was never meant to be a book, and the author never saw the manuscript.

Born in Aberdeen, Scotland, on July 24, 1874, Oswald Chambers began his short, meaningful life. His father was a Baptist preacher, but young Chambers had his mind set on a more creative occupation. Gifted in the fine arts, Chambers pursued art and music at London's Royal Academy of Art, but he did so with spiritual intent. Chambers saw his Christian ministry as portraying God's truth through art.

It was not to be.

While continuing his studies at the University of Edinburg, Chambers began to question his purpose. Faith was central to his thinking, and he had made a profession of faith while in his middle teens. The great Baptist preacher Charles Spurgeon was instrumental in his salvation. Chambers' faith was too large for the confines of his plans. It appeared God had a different course in mind.

"Four Years of Hell on Earth"

Some assume that the great men and women of the church come to faith easily and live their days in full knowledge of what God wants for them and from them. That is seldom true. Chambers' life shows that a good deal of spiritual wrestling is involved. During those months of searching, Chambers decided he had been called to preach. That decision led him to Dunoon College in Scotland for Bible training. We might expect those were days of joy, now that Chambers had found his purpose, but we'd be wrong. Chambers called that period of life "four years of hell on earth."

The source of his turmoil was a profound awareness of his depravity and the feeling that his faith lacked power. Always an excellent student, he excelled in his work, but his soul languished. Difficult as it is to understand, this spiritual storm became the catalyst that made him the powerful man he would become. In desperation, he prayed, dependent on the biblical promise that God would give his Spirit to anyone who asked.

He received what he sought. In an instant, the unending storm of emotion settled, replaced by peaceful joy. "Glory be to God," Chambers said after the event, "the last aching abyss of the human heart is filled to overflowing with the love of God."[1] He would later call this event his baptism in the Spirit. There are various meanings to that phrase, but for Chambers it meant he had been fully accepted by Christ.

From Classroom to World

It wasn't long before Chambers was on the preaching circuit. The thin man with high cheekbones, a full head of hair, an aquiline nose, and piercing eyes became a sought-after speaker. He became a traveling preacher for the Pentecostal League of Prayer, an organization founded in 1891 by British barrister Reader Harris. The Pentecostal League of Prayer emphasized prayer, infilling of the Holy Spirit, holiness, and revival in the churches.

But Chambers wasn't satisfied with preaching messages and then leaving for the next church. He believed the spiritual mediocrity prevalent in his day was rooted in lazy thinking. In 1911, he, along with the League of Prayer, opened the Bible Training College. He served the school as head teacher and principal. He had moved from being a spiritually confused artist to preacher, teacher, and head of a college.

Called into Egypt

Three years later, World War I erupted in Europe, a conflict that would last four years and take the lives of nearly ten million military personnel and wound another twenty-one million. Shortly after the battle started, Chambers felt called to serve in the war effort. He became a chaplain to British Commonwealth soldiers in Egypt.

Chambers had already been a world traveler, having ministered in the United States and Japan. He sailed to Zeitoun (Cairo), Egypt, in October of 1915, and as a YMCA chaplain ministered to Australian and New Zealand soldiers preparing for battle elsewhere in the world. Many of these soldiers would become one of the half million casualties in the Battle of Gallipoli in what is now Turkey. Some of the last spiritual encouragement those men received came from the lips of Oswald Chambers.

Chambers died in the city on November 15, 1917 from complications of appendicitis. He had suffered for three days, but delayed medical attention, not wanting to take a bed that might otherwise go to a soldier. He was just forty-three years old.

Biddy, Oswald Chambers' Secret Weapon

During a teaching trip to the United States, Chambers met Gertrude "Biddy" Hobbs. They married in 1910, and three years later Biddy gave birth to a baby girl named Kathleen. Kathleen was the only child the couple would have.

Biddy is a story in herself. It had been her goal to be an executive secretary, and she became a proficient stenographer capable of taking shorthand at 250 words a minute. Biddy traveled with her husband, taking down every sermon and lesson he taught. Thirty books bear the name of Oswald Chambers, but only one was penned by his hand. The others are drawn from his teachings as recorded by Biddy.

After Chambers' death, Biddy began to compile his messages for publication. Later, their daughter, Kathleen, would help in the process. One title became one of the best-known Christian books in the history of publishing: *My Utmost for His Highest*, a compilation of 366 one-page devotions. Today, thousands of Christians read material first delivered almost a century ago.

Oswald Chambers was not famous in his day, and had it not been for Biddy he might have remained lost in obscurity. Chambers' lasting ministry came about because Biddy took down every word by hand.

While Chambers covered many topics and hundreds of Scripture passages, it is easy to see a basic theme: the Christian's duty is to fully submit to Christ. Chambers' preaching often centered on a "less of me, more of him" theology. To Chambers, the Christian was at his or her best when fully absorbed by faith.

Chambers' lasting contribution to the shaping of the church was the fervent and consistent reminder that the faithful life is not about the Christian but about Jesus. To Chambers, everything orbited Christ.

My Utmost for His Highest is widely read in the twenty-first century, still changing hearts and educating minds, and will do so for untold decades to come. The artist turned preacher has touched more lives than he ever imagined he could, and helped shape the church in the process.

56

G. K. CHESTERTON

Giant Wit

(1874–1936)

The cross has become something more than a historical memory; it does convey, almost as by a mathematical diagram, the truth about the real point at issue; the idea of a conflict stretching outwards into eternity. It is true, and even tautological, to say that the cross is the crux of the whole matter.

G. K. Chesterton, *The Everlasting Man*

Gilbert Keith Chesterton cast a giant shadow: literarily and figuratively. He was a large man—six foot four and topping four hundred pounds—and a giant of literature. Although most of his eighty or so books, two hundred stories, four thousand essays, countless articles, and a few plays are largely forgotten in the twenty-first century, he influenced some of the greatest writers. C. S. Lewis credits Chesterton's *The Everlasting Man* in aiding his conversion from atheism to Christian faith. Mahatma Gandhi was also influenced by Chesterton. When he died, Chesterton was praised by T. S. Eliot and H. G. Wells (with whom Chesterton debated). His writing also influenced J. R. R. Tolkien, Franz Kafka, George

Bernard Shaw, Dorothy L. Sayers, Graham Green, Ernest Hemingway, Agatha Christie, Orson Welles, Philip Yancey, J. K. Rowling, and scores of others.

Sometimes the impact of a person's work is seen in the inspiration it provides others.

Humor as a Hammer

Great communicators have long known that people swallow more truth when it's served with humor. No matter how serious the topic, Chesterton could find a way to make an important aspect memorable. Consider the quote above. What could be more serious and weighty than the cross of Christ? The last clause, "to say that the cross is the crux of the whole matter," is a play on words. *Crux* is Latin for cross. "The cross is the cross of the matter." *Crux* came to mean "an important point in an issue."

Chesterton was a master of paradox, the twisting of the assumed into something new. He wrote, "I believe in getting into hot water; I think it keeps you clean."[1] That sentence carries more meaning than expected and demands additional thought.

Chesterton used this kind of communication to make his point stronger and make it linger in the memory. He used this device frequently and to great effect. He is one of the most quoted men in history. He can be found in almost any book of quotations.

The thing I hate about arguments is that it always interrupts a discussion.

If there were no God, there would be no Atheists.

Every man is important if he loses his life; and every man is funny if he loses his hat and has to run after it.

Art, like morality, consists of drawing the line somewhere.

He even found *himself* humorous. Once, while exiting a car, he became stuck in the door. Later he said, "I would have tried to exit sideways, but I have no sideways."

Leaving Canterbury

Although brought up in the Church of England, Chesterton became fascinated with Roman Catholicism. His famous series of mystery novels starring Father Brown came from a discussion he had with a Catholic priest. His defense of Christianity by word and by example remained profitable to Protestant and Catholic alike. In an age that more and more saw Christianity as a myth for the unenlightened, Chesterton fought back with unassailable reason and humility. Even anti-Christian writers like H. G. Wells and George Bernard Shaw (he of "I'm an atheist and I thank God for it" fame) remained friendly with Chesterton.

Whether Protestant or Catholic, Chesterton remained true to his conviction that Christianity was the truth needed by the world. "The Christian ideal has not been tried and found wanting; it has been found difficult and left untried."[2]

Some of the finest minds of history had decided atheism was the choice of thinking people, and only less enlightened folk clung to "old myths" like Christianity. Chesterton was proof to the contrary. He was every bit their match and then some. In his words, "Fallacies do not cease to be fallacies because they become fashion."[3] His books defending the faith (*Heretics*, 1905; *Orthodoxy*, 1908; *The Everlasting Man*, 1925) remain powerful and useful to those searching for a reason to believe.

Chesterton turned humor and wit into tools that won the admiration of the rationalists of his day even if he didn't win their souls. He died in June 1936 of congestive heart failure at the age of sixty-two.

57

T. S. ELIOT

More Than Just Cats

(1888–1965)

> The experiment [the trend toward a rational, non-Christian society]
> will fail but we must be very patient in awaiting its collapse; mean-
> while redeeming the time: so that the Faith may be preserved alive
> to the dark ages before us; to renew and rebuild civilization, and
> save the world from suicide.
>
> T. S. Eliot, *Thoughts After Lambeth*

In 1981, Andrew Lloyd Webber's *Cats* debuted in a London, West
End theater. A year later it opened on Broadway and became one
of the longest running musicals in history. It launched a hit song,
"Memory," and became a made-for-television film in 1998.

What many may not know is the musical is based on the work of
one of the literary world's brightest stars: Thomas Stearns Eliot,
better known as T. S. Eliot, poet and playwright. But while his 1939
Old Possum's Book of Practical Cats laid a good foundation for ac-
tors and actresses in cat suits, his other work—far more serious in
tone—is his greatest achievement.

The Writer

T. S. Eliot was born in St. Louis, but his family roots were in New England. His was a literary family that often gathered around Eliot's father to listen to readings from Charles Dickens. Eliot grew up a reader and remained in the business of words most of his life.

Harvard accepted him into its collegiate ranks, and Eliot finished his course of study in just three years. He would continue to study philosophy, literature, and other subjects at Harvard, Oxford, and schools in Germany and France. He settled in England and made it his home for the rest of his life. For a time, Eliot taught school and worked in a bank, then he landed a job with publishers Faber and Faber. He stayed with the firm until his death in 1965.

Eliot's first work of note was the poem, "The Love Song of J. Alfred Prufrock." Although written in 1911, it was not published until four years later. His poems are considered some of the first in the "modernist" movement. He took on difficult topics that he felt required complicated writing.

He also wrote plays, feeling the best way to reach the masses was through that popular medium. His plays are still performed today. For seventeen years, from 1922 to 1939, he also edited the influential literary magazine he founded, *Criterion*.

The excellence of Eliot's writing was recognized by his peers. In 1948, he received the Nobel Prize for Literature. The Nobel Prize biography of Eliot says:

> Eliot has been one of the most daring innovators of twentieth-century poetry. Never compromising either with the public or indeed with language itself, he has followed his belief that poetry should aim at a representation of the complexities of modern civilization in language and that such representation necessarily leads to difficult poetry. Despite this difficulty his influence on modern poetic diction has been immense. Eliot's poetry from *Prufrock* (1917) to the *Four Quartets* (1943) reflects the development of a Christian writer.[1]

The Christian

Eliot joined the Anglican church shortly after he became a British citizen and even served as churchwarden in his parish. Swimming against the tide of his times, Eliot let his faith permeate his work, especially in his plays such as *Murder in the Cathedral* (1935), about the martyrdom of Thomas Becket, and *The Family Reunion* (1939), and his poems, "Four Quartets" (1943) and the earlier "Waste Land" (1922), as well as others. At times he was criticized for this but he remained steadfast. He didn't believe literature could save society or replace the church, but it could open the doors of the mind. Eliot managed to provide entertainment, show great wit, and still deal with spiritual matters.

Eliot believed that the "experiment" to create a non-Christian society was doomed. It was just a matter of time.

Some have shaped the church through finely tuned theology; others through magnificent preaching. T. S. Eliot engaged society through the printed word, showing faith is for everyone, including intellectuals. Today there are many publishers printing Christian literature. They do a great service, as do the Christian writers who team with them. Some Christian writers, however, choose to work in the secular world, publishing in a way that reaches people on both sides of the fence.

T. S. Eliot was more than a literary giant; he was a man of spiritual depth and was unafraid to incorporate it in his work.

58

C. S. LEWIS

Sliding into Faith

(1898–1963)

> I believe in Christianity as I believe that the sun has risen. Not only because I see it, but because by it I see everything.
>
> C. S. Lewis, "Is Theology Poetry?"

Clive Staples Lewis may be one of the most quoted men in history (if not *the* most quoted). He was a teacher of medieval literature but is remembered for his children's fantasies and books defending Christianity. His mind was as sharp as any of his day or since, and his many books continue to find new readers even as those familiar with his work return to his pages frequently. He is so associated with Christianity that we cannot think of the one without the other. Yet he once was an atheist.

A Houseful of Books

C. S. Lewis—his friends called him Jack—was born on the cusp of the twentieth century, November 29, 1898, in Belfast, Ireland, to parents who loved reading. "There were books in the study, books in the dining room, books in the cloakroom, books (two deep) in the great bookcase on the landing, books in a bedroom, books piled as high as my shoulder in the cistern attic, books of all kinds."[1] Reading would be a lifelong habit.

Writing would become his other passion. As a child he wrote his own stories and illustrated them. Many children do this, but only a few do so throughout their lives. Since he had an endless source of books, he spent much of his time living in their pages.

It seems an idyllic life for a bookworm, but life has a way of turning cruel, even for those with giant intellects. A few months before Lewis turned ten, his mother died of cancer. In his book *Surprised by Joy*, Lewis relates events of the loss. Her decline had been noticeable even to the children, and she spent much of her time in a morphine-induced delirium. Doctors performed surgery in the home, as they did in those days. Lewis relates how he was in bed ill when his father walked in, tears in his eyes, to tell him she had died.

His mother's death made an already somewhat reclusive boy even more so. It also changed his view of God, whom he now saw as cruel—if God existed at all. He would go on to reject Christianity and any belief in God.

Oxford

Lewis began studies at Oxford University in 1917, and he would spend much of his life there, first as a student and then as an instructor. The school became home to him, a feeling he kept even when his teaching duties took him to Cambridge for nearly a decade.

It was while at Oxford that he published his first book of poetry, *Spirits in Bondage: A Cycle of Lyrics*, in 1919. It was written under the pseudonym Clive Hamilton. He would write another volume of poetry, *Dymer*, also under a pseudonym.

He began his teaching career in 1924, tutoring in philosophy, and soon became a Fellow of Magdalen College, one of the colleges in the Oxford University system. He taught English and literature.

Books and Friends and Books

Lewis read widely and was soon drawn to the works of George MacDonald and G. K. Chesterton. The work of both authors challenged Lewis' atheism and worldview. Of MacDonald's work he said, "What it actually did to me was to convert, even to baptize . . . my imagination."[2]

Friends also served as catalysts in Lewis' conversion. He had been surprised that brilliant men like Nevill Coghill and J. R. R. Tolkien were practicing Christians. As time passed, he could no longer reject God.

> You must picture me alone in that room in Magdalen, night after night, feeling, whenever my mind lifted even for a second from my work, the steady, unrelenting approach of Him whom I so earnestly desired not to meet. That which I greatly feared had at last come upon me. In the Trinity Term of 1929 I gave in, and admitted that God was God, and knelt and prayed: perhaps, that night, the most dejected and reluctant convert in all England.[3]

His conversion experience was one of motion, like a man on a journey. On separate occasion, a trip to the zoo, he became a believer in Jesus as the Son of God: "I was driven to Whipsnade one sunny morning. When we set out I did not believe that Jesus Christ is the Son of God, and when we reached the zoo I did. Yet I had not exactly spent the journey in thought. Nor in great emotion."[4]

Lewis changed in the light of his newfound personal faith, especially where it touched his writing. He moved from writing poetry and focused on Christian themes. He would continue to write academic works, but the bulk of his work fell into the Christian literature camp and it is those works that have lived after him. They still sell well.

He was a gifted writer capable of moving from academic treatments (*English Literature in the Sixteenth Century Excluding Drama*), to books defending the faith (*Mere Christianity*, *A Case for Christianity*, *The Problem of Pain*), to science fantasy (*Out of the Silent Planet*, *Perelandra*, *That Hideous Strength*), children's literature (The Chronicles of Narnia), and other categories. There are few writers who can work across genres and subjects with such skill as C. S. Lewis.

His work found an eager audience and the poor teacher was soon a well-to-do professor. Lewis' work sold well during his lifetime and still outsells many books published today. Lewis' work is filled with both heart and logic. He is one of the most quoted authors in history. Books of compiled quotations run six hundred pages.

During World War II, Lewis made a series of radio talks about Christianity to console a rattled British public. These radio addresses became the book *Mere Christianity* and made Lewis a household name.

He spoke of faith in a straightforward, logical manner. Apologetics is the study and practice of defending the faith against criticism and building a case for belief. Lewis was a skilled apologist. No atheist or agnostic who has read Lewis can say he was a superstitious, uneducated man. His logic is ironclad. People might disagree with his conclusion but they could not, and cannot, say he was unclear. This is true of both his fiction and nonfiction.

An Unchanged Changed Man

Lewis, now famous, remained in the lifestyle he had lived before. He continued to teach, continued to write academic work in his field, continued to read, and continued to live a simple life. He often used much of his income to help others, including poor students who couldn't afford school fees, underfunded seminarians, and others.

In most ways, he remained the sometimes rumpled professor.

At the age of fifty-nine his life took a dramatic turn. In 1952 Joy Davidman Gresham showed up on the writer's doorstep. She was an American in England and had come by to meet the man who, through two of his books—*The Screwtape Letters* and *The Great Divorce*—had brought her to faith. A friendship was born.

Joy's life became more difficult. Her husband abandoned her and her two adolescent sons. She moved to London and was soon in financial trouble. Lewis provided the help she needed. Friendship expanded into love and they married in 1956.

Joy, who was sixteen years younger than Lewis, was ill, something he knew when they wed. Their marriage would last only four years. Cancer once again took someone he loved. She was only forty-five.

His book *A Grief Observed* reveals his journey through the loss and the years that followed.

Friends?

C. S. Lewis had friends who often met at the *Eagle and Child*, a pub near the university. The group called themselves the Inklings. The gathering included author J. R. R. Tolkien and other intellectuals. There they would review writings of their members and others. "Member" is probably not the best term, since they were a simple gathering, not a club or a literary society.

Although supportive of each other, they could be critical, and one thing they criticized Lewis about was his Christian writing. It struck them as an unseemly thing for a scholar to do, but Lewis was unmoved. He continued the course he started after his conversion and the world is better for it. It is possible that Lewis' emphasis on Christian writing cost him a full professorship, something he only achieved when another college offered such a position.

Unheralded Passing

C. S. Lewis died in 1963 of renal failure. Few paid attention to his passing because he died the same day John F. Kennedy was assassinated in Dallas. New readers continue to discover him; readers familiar with his work return to it. Lewis has taken his readers to other planets and to mysterious lands on the other side of the wardrobe, has caused us to view our weaknesses uniquely and powerfully as discussed by a demon intent on tripping up a believer, has examined the purpose of pain and grief, and has caused us to think about the logic of faith. He is unrivaled in the church as writer, apologist, and thinker.

59

HENRY MORRIS

Soft-Spoken Warrior

(1918–2006)

> True science is never at enmity with God, and a true man of science
> can and should be also a true man of God.
>
> Henry M. Morris, *Men of Science—Men of God*

When Dr. Henry M. Morris died, news of it spread through the country, including articles in two major newspapers, the *New York Times* and the *Los Angeles Times*. Dr. Morris was a unique celebrity. A quiet, unassuming man with a gentlemanly air, he was one of the most controversial men of the century. With his balding head, glasses, and reserved smile, he looked like everyone's favorite uncle. But behind the appearance was a soft-spoken warrior, a man convinced of a truth he would not abandon, a man dedicated to a cause that consumed much of his life. He went to his grave a crusader for the cause of "creation science," a term he coined. He left behind sixty books, a vibrant organization, and a college. He also left behind a new kind of convert: the young-earth creationist.

He was loved by many Christians and reviled by many scientists and teachers. Loved or reviled, he spent his life in promoting what he believed to be one of the most important doctrines of Christianity: creationism.

Background

Born in Dallas on October 6, 1918, Henry Madison Morris turned his interest to science and engineering. He earned a civil engineering degree from Rice University in 1939, then a master's degree and PhD in hydraulic engineering from the University of Minnesota. For several years he worked as a civil engineer and taught at the college level.

In 1951, he became the chair of civil engineering at the University of Louisiana, Lafayette, and then held the same position at Virginia Polytechnic Institute and State University.

Along the way, he became convinced that the Bible was the inspired Word of God and was therefore infallible. He adopted the literal model of biblical interpretation, holding that the Bible accurately revealed events in the past, including the seven days of creation and Noah's flood as revealed in Genesis.

His first book, *That You Might Believe*, was published in 1946.

Books and ICR

Dr. Morris was a hydraulic engineer, a specialist in water flow, and combined his knowledge of the topic with the biblical record. Teaming with Dr. John C. Whitcomb, he wrote *The Genesis Flood* in 1961. Morris provided the science; Whitcomb, a theologian, provided the theology. The book defended the global flood idea and the concept that the apparent age of earth is due to the catastrophe brought on by Noah's flood.

Most of his many books deal with creationism or controversial aspects of biblical interpretation. Books like *The Genesis Record* and others also dealt with matters other than creationism. He demonstrated a skilled eye for interpretation.

Scientific Creationism (1974) put the creationist movement on the map. The book, meant to be a textbook for creation science, continues to sell today, as do most of his books. Morris wrote with clarity and conviction. Many disagreed with him, including those in the church, but none could say he wasn't clear in his convictions. "Evolutionist teaching," he wrote in the book's first foreword, "is not only harmful sociologically, but it is false scientifically and historically."[1] He was not one to mince words.

Morris and other scientists decided to take a more proactive approach in challenging evolution. He and nine other scientific creationists formed the Creation Research Society. In 1969, he left his post at Virginia Tech and founded the Institute for Creation Research (ICR) in San Diego, assembling a research group associated with what was then called the Christian Heritage College (now San Diego Christian College).

The organization was dedicated to creationism research and education. It drew scholars from the fields of astronomy, microbiology, and other disciplines. It would later grant master's degrees in science education and became a separate entity from the college. It has since relocated to Dallas.

Morris served as president of the organization. He traveled widely, speaking at conferences around the world. He, along with other associated scientists and theologians, participated in over a hundred debates. ICR continues to do the same work under the leadership of Dr. Morris' sons, Dr. Henry Morris III and Dr. John D. Morris.

Creation

Morris is considered the father of "scientific creationism." His approach was to do more than deny evolution by elevating the level of evidence for the accuracy of the biblical account of creation. He rejected other views of creationism such as the gap theory (that there are eon-long gaps between the days of creation listed in Genesis) and old-age creationism (that the earth and the universe are as old as they appear but are still the result of a set of creative acts by God).

Creation, to Morris, meant the universe was young, maybe ten thousand years old, and that the apparent older age of the planet was the result of Noah's catastrophic flood. His belief in a six twenty-four-hour-day creative week put him at odds not only with geologists, astronomers, and evolutionists but with old-age earth proponents

301

like astronomer and Christian minister Dr. Hugh Ross of Reasons to Believe. Other Christian apologists argued for a limited flood.

Dr. Morris stayed the course he had charted decades before. While usually mild and gentlemanly in conversation and debate, he was clear and pointed in his writing.

His life was spent enduring heated ridicule of his opinions and his teaching. Evolutionary scientists dismissed him first as a crackpot religious fanatic, then later as a danger to the education of children.

Those who knew him respected him. Even some of his opponents admired his tenacious beliefs and untiring effort.

Death

The father of modern scientific creationism died on February 25, 2006 in Santee, California. He suffered from a series of strokes, but continued working until his health no longer permitted it. He spent his final days in a convalescent hospital.

Dr. Henry Morris shaped the church by bringing the idea of biblical creationism to the forefront and gave Christians an intellectual basis for dismissing evolution. Agree with him or not, he was influential.

60

BILLY GRAHAM

The Face and Voice of Modern Evangelism

(1918–)

My one purpose in life is to help people find a personal relationship
with God, which, I believe, comes through knowing Christ.

Billy Graham, biography, Billy Graham Evangelistic Association

Tall, with deep-set eyes, a strong chin, and a straight spine, Billy Graham has a smooth, powerful, baritone voice that seems to reach from the ear to the soul. Even as an elderly man in his nineties, he leaves a lasting impression.

More than 215 million people in 185 countries have heard him speak; hundreds of millions more have heard him over radio, television, film, and the internet. For over seventy years he has proven to be a man of singular purpose, displaying a dedication to evangelism seldom seen.

He is the face and voice of modern evangelism, not only in the United States but throughout the world.

Baseball Field to Pulpit

Born in 1918 near Charlotte, North Carolina, Graham grew up like many boys with his penetrating gaze set on a career in baseball. It was a dream he would never have opportunity to pursue. Growing up during the Depression, he spent his childhood and teenage years working on his family's dairy farm, spending his off-time reading.

At the age of fifteen, in the fall of 1934, he attended a revival preached by Mordecai Ham, a traveling preacher. Soon after he felt a call to ministry and attended several colleges: Bob Jones University, which he found too strict; Florida Bible Institute, where he began preaching; and then Wheaton College in Illinois. It was at Wheaton where he met a young woman who would become his wife: Ruth Bell, the daughter of a missionary surgeon.

After college he became the pastor of First Baptist Church in Western Springs, Illinois. His time as pastor was short, and that church would be his only local ministry.

Youth for Christ International was a new organization founded in the mid-1940s. It focused on reaching young people through mass rallies. Billy Graham left his church to become the organization's first full-time employee. He preached throughout the United States and overseas. Graham would forever be associated with evangelistic crusades.

The Canvas Cathedral

In 1949 Billy Graham set up a tent at the corner of Washington Boulevard and Hill Street in Los Angeles. The tent was nicknamed the "Canvas Cathedral." A three-week crusade was planned, but the crowds kept coming. The effort stretched to eight weeks.

Graham was just thirty years old. In one afternoon over six thousand people attended the services, and hundreds of others had to be turned away. They walked the aisle by the score. It was a pivotal moment in the evangelist's career.

Some have seen a connection between the success of the 1949 Los Angeles event with newspaper publisher William Randolph Hearst, who sent a telegram to his editors: "Puff Graham." Whether this was a factor to the effort's success or not is impossible to ascertain.

In 1950 Graham founded the Billy Graham Evangelistic Association (BGEA) and established headquarters in Minneapolis. Years later, it would be moved to Charlotte, North Carolina, near where

Graham lived. The organization enabled Graham to more efficiently and effectively take the message to the world.

The BGEA proved to be a progressive group, using whatever medium it could to promote the message. *The Hour of Decision* was a BGEA radio program that broadcast around the world for over fifty years. The organization also arranged to have Graham's sermons shown on US and Canadian television. Millions tuned in for every show. BGEA's Worldwide Pictures has produced well over one hundred movies and documentaries with Christian themes.

My Answer is a syndicated newspaper column distributed by Tribune Media Services that has run for over thirty years. Another print medium is the well-known magazine *Christianity Today* and its family of periodicals. Started by BGEA in 1956, with Carl F. H. Henry as editor, the magazine continues to bring in-depth and topical material to its readers.

Billy Graham is the author of thirty books, many of them bestsellers. *Peace with God* (1953) was well-received and reflected Graham's message in a clear, straightforward manner, much like his preaching.

Graham, who started as a small church preacher, has used every possible means to take the gospel to the world. The BGEA's annual report reads like that of a major corporation. It is one of the busiest ministry enterprises in history.

Preaching

Age and illness have kept Dr. Graham from preaching duties in recent years. That work has shifted to his son Franklin Graham, but the elder Graham will always be remembered for his pulpit skills. Billy Graham's style has changed over the years. During the 1949 Los Angeles crusade, he spoke like a machine gun, with carefully enunciated words, and sounded every bit like the "sawdust trail" evangelists of the previous generation. Such preaching was effective. His earnest appeal, rapid delivery, serious enthusiasm, and pulpit craft made it impossible not to listen.

Over the decades his cadence and style changed somewhat, but never his message. He always delivered a sermon anyone could understand. White-collar professionals and blue-collar laborers alike found themselves riveted to Graham, hanging on every phrase. The power of his preaching was not diminished when delivered over radio, television, or the big screen. Many consider him one of the greatest communicators to have ever lived.

He was also fond of using current illustrations, anecdotes drawn from his life or some current event. Often these were told with humor, something that allowed his audience to relax. He could, in the same message, sound like a friendly next-door neighbor and a moment later like an Old Testament prophet. The news of the day provided material for his sermons. He had no reluctance in quoting a story from a magazine or newspaper.

His message was directed at the heart of the listener, and the goal was always the same: salvation for each person.

Celebrities

Graham was comfortable around celebrities, many of whom were drawn to him, fascinated by the preacher. In 1969, he made a guest appearance on an interview show with Woody Allen. Allen was an agnostic Jew and Billy Graham a Southern Baptist preacher. Graham looked relaxed and the two shared a conversation. In the end, Graham made sure to invite the comedian to the crusade he was leading. Graham also made an appearance on the television game show *What's My Line?* in 1960. Again, his natural charm was unmistakable, and again, he made a point of his mission to take the gospel to the world.

Politicians found him a source of encouragement, although some may simply have wanted to be seen with a man of Graham's stature and one who had the ear of millions. He became an acquaintance and sometimes counselor to US presidents from Eisenhower to Clinton, although he pulled back some after Watergate, fearful that close political ties could damage his work. Richard Nixon instructed one of his advisors to maintain contact with Graham every few weeks. On December 30, 1969, Nixon wrote a memo to his chief of staff Robert Haldeman: "On the political side, I would like you to follow up with Billy Graham in his work with Negro ministers across the country. He feels this is our best chance to make inroads into the Negro community. I am inclined to agree with him."[1]

Such associations brought criticism, which is to be expected. Politics divides more people than it unites. While Graham was supportive of the civil rights movement, he seldom lobbied for any other cause.

Other problems arose from his dealing with US presidents. Harry S. Truman, a Baptist, later claimed to distrust Graham and said, "he was never a friend of mine when I was president."[2] The Nixon tapes contain a section where Graham appears to agree with Nixon's anti-Semitic views. Graham's life and writing show that he had no such feelings, but he nonetheless apologized for any offense caused.

Criticism

One criticism haunted Graham, whose approach to evangelism was to ignore denominationalism. At times he would be supported by liberal Christian groups. Graham's critics were quick to bring that to light, but Graham refused to be bullied. His goal was to take the message everywhere he could, and he didn't care who made it possible as long as he was free to preach as he saw fit. As he told the National Association of Evangelicals, "I intend to go anywhere, sponsored by anybody, to preach the gospel of Christ, if there are no strings attached to my message."[3]

Success always brings out the critic, but Graham persevered, proving his approach was correct, godly, and honorable. He would focus on the gospel, not the complainers.

America's Pastor

On September 14, 2001, while the world was still reeling from the September 11 attacks on the World Trade Center towers, Dr. Graham, in response to an invitation, led a memorial service at the Washington National Cathedral. He had done something similar for the families of those lost in the Oklahoma City bombing of 1995.

Billy Graham has been, and remains, America's pastor.

Age and illness have taken their toll. At this writing, Dr. Graham is in his early nineties and plagued with medical issues. For over fifteen years he has battled Parkinson's disease, a degenerative disorder of the central nervous system. He's also been hospitalized for severe ailments including pneumonia, bronchitis, and other issues. The media reports each time he's hospitalized, proof that he remains in the hearts of the American people—and the world.

NOTES

Introduction

1. Bruce L. Shelley, *Church History in Plain Language* (Waco: Word, 1982), 9.

Chapter 1 Peter

1. Eusebius, *Ecclesiastical History*, 3.1.2.
2. Clement of Alexandria, *Stromateis*, 7.11.

Chapter 2 Paul

1. Shelley, *Church History in Plain Language*, 32.
2. See Acts 14:19.
3. Henry Van Dyke, *The Works of Henry Van Dyke: Counsels by the Way*, vol. XV (New York: Charles Scribner's Sons, 1921), 87.
4. John Adams, letter to Benjamin Waterhouse, May 21, 1821. As quoted in Eugene Ehrlich, Marshall De Bruhl, eds, *The International Thesaurus of Quotations*, rev. ed. (New York: HarperCollins, 1996), 253.
5. Clifton J. Allen, gen. ed., *The Broadman Bible Commentary*, vol. 10 (Nashville: Broadman, 1970), 124. See Acts 21:15–26.

Chapter 3 Josephus

1. Flavius Josephus, *Jewish War*, 3.9.
2. Josephus, *Antiquities of the Jews*, 17.5.2, from *The Works of Josephus*, trans. William Whiston (Lynn, MA: Hendrickson Publishers, 1980), 382.
3. Ibid., 18.3.3, 379.
4. Ibid., 20.9.1, 423.

Chapter 4 Polycarp

1. "World Stadiums," accessed October 1, 2013, http://www.worldstadiums.com/.
2. Eusebius, *Ecclesiastical History*, 4.15.1 ff.

Chapter 5 Justin Martyr

1. Justin Martyr, *Dialogue with Trypho*, 8.
2. Justin Martyr, *First Apology*, 67.
3. Alexander Roberts et al, *The Ante-Nicene Fathers, Justin Martyr. Irenaeus* (New York: C. Scribner's Sons, 1885), 306.

Chapter 6 Clement of Alexandria

1. Edwin Markham, "Outwitted!" *The Shore of Happiness and Other Poems* (New York: Doubleday, 1915), 1.
2. Shelley, *Church History in Plain Language*, 96.
3. Clement of Alexandria, *Miscellanies*, 1.5.
4. Clement of Alexandria, *Exhortation*, 6.
5. Clement, *Miscellanies*, 6.8.
6. Ibid.

Chapter 7 Origen

1. Origen, *Against Celsus*, 8.73.

Chapter 8 Diocletian

1. Tertullian, *Apologeticus*, 50.

Chapter 9 Eusebius of Caesarea

1. Martin Luther King Jr., *Strength to Love* (Philadelphia: Fortress Press, 1977), 23.
2. Eusebius, *The History of the Church*, 1.1.4.
3. Paraphrase of Epiphanius of Salamis, *The Panarion*, 5.8.

Chapter 10 Constantine

1. Eusebius, *The Life of Constantine*, 24.

Chapter 11 Athanasius

1. Athanasius, *Thirty-Ninth Festal Epistle*, 6.

Chapter 12 Ambrose of Milan

1. William Shakespeare, *Twelfth Night*, act 2, scene 5, lines 156–59.
2. Theodosius, *The Theodosian Code* (February 28, 380), 16.1.2.
3. Ambrose, *Epistle XX*, 8.
4. Ambrose, *Letter LI*, from Phillip Schaff, *Nicene and Post-Nicene Fathers*, vol. XI (New York: Cosimo, 2007), 451.
5. Theodoret, *Ecclesiastical History*, 18.
6. Augustine, *Confessions*, 9.7.

Chapter 13 Jerome

1. Jerome, *To Eustochium*, 22, 7.
2. Jerome, *Address to Pope Damasus* (383).

Chapter 14 John Chrysostom

1. Socrates and Sozomenus, *Ecclesiastical Histories*, 2.1.
2. John Chrysostom, *Homilies Concerning the Statues to the People of Antioch*, 2.2, trans. J. B. Morris (Oxford: James Parker and Co., 1877), 564.
3. Ibid, 582.

Chapter 15 Augustine of Hippo

1. Augustine, *Confessions*, 8.7.
2. Ibid., 13.12.
3. Ibid., 9.12.

Chapter 16 Pope Leo I

1. Shelly, *Church History in Plain Language*, 149.
2. Adapted from Jordanes, *The Origins and Deeds of the Goths*, trans. Charles Christopher Mierow (Princeton: Princeton University Press, 1908), chap. 56.
3. Friedrich Gontard, *The Chair of Peter* (New York: Holt, Rinehart and Winston, 1964), 142–43.

Chapter 17 The Venerable Bede

1. J. A. Giles, ed., *The Venerable Bede's Ecclesiastical History of England* (London: George Bell & Sons, 1887), 24.
2. Ibid., xx.
3. Ibid.

Chapter 18 Anselm

1. Anselm, *Cur Deus Homo*, in Henry Bettenson, ed., *Documents of the Christian Church*, 2nd ed. (New York: Oxford University Press, 1963), 137–38.

Chapter 19 Francis of Assisi

1. Adapted from Murray Bodo, OFM, *Tales of St. Francis: Ancient Stories for Contemporary Living* (New York: Bantam Doubleday Dell, 1988), 24–25.
2. Philip Schaff and David Schley Schaff, *History of the Christian Church*, vol. 5 (Grand Rapids: Eerdmans, 1960), 402.
3. Philip Schaff, *History of the Christian Church*, vol. 4 (Grand Rapids: Eerdmans, 1960), 70.
4. Francis of Assisi, *The Canticle of Brother Sun*, in Regis J. Armstrong and Ignatius Brady, eds., *Francis and Clare: The Complete Works* (Mahwah, NJ: Paulist Press, 1982), 38.

Chapter 20 Thomas Aquinas

1. D. Kennedy, "St. Thomas Aquinas," *The Catholic Encyclopedia*, vol. 14 (New York: Robert Appleton Company, 1912), accessed October 1, 2013, www.newadvent.org/cathen/14663b.htm.
2. Ibid.

3. J. James Dixon Douglas, Philip Wesley Comfort, and Donald R. Mitchell, *Who's Who in Christian History* (Wheaton: Tyndale, 1992), 34.

Chapter 21 John Wycliffe

1. Gotthard Victor Lechler, *John Wiclif [sic] and His English Precursors*, vol. 1 (London: C. Kegan Paul & Co., 1878), 256.
2. Thomas Murray, *The Life of John Wycliffe* (Edinburgh: John Boyd, 1829), 113.
3. Bruce Shelly, *Church History in Plain Language,* 3rd ed. (Nashville: Thomas Nelson, 2008), 229.
4. Ibid.

Chapter 22 Nicolaus Copernicus

1. Nicolaus Copernicus, "Preface and Dedication to Pope Paul III," *On the Revolutions of the Celestial Spheres*, trans. Charles Glen Wallis, ed. Stephen Hawking (Philadelphia: Running Press Books, 2002), 2.
2. Ibid., 4.

Chapter 23 Martin Luther

1. Shelly, *Church History in Plain Language*, 239.
2. Ibid., 241.
3. Douglas, Comfort, and Mitchell, *Who's Who in Christian History*, 434.
4. Shelly, *Church History in Plain Language*, 263.

Chapter 24 Ulrich Zwingli

1. Ulrich Zwingli, *Sixty-Seven Articles*, article 1.

Chapter 25 King Henry VIII

1. Charles Dickens, *A Child's History of England* (Boston: Estes and Lauriat, 1880), 237.

Chapter 27 William Tyndale

1. John Foxe, *Foxe's Book of Martyrs*, ed. William Byron Forbush (Grand Rapids: Zondervan, 1978), 184.
2. Erasmus, "Preface," *Novum Instrumentum Omne*, in Douglas, Comfort, and Mitchell, *Who's Who in Christian History*, 239.

Chapter 28 Menno Simons

1. Menno Simons, "Renunciation of the Church of Rome," *The Complete Works of Menno Simons* (Amazon Digital Services, 2011), loc. 182.
2. Ibid., loc. 215.
3. Ibid., loc. 194.
4. Ibid., loc. 182.
5. Ibid., loc. 231.
6. Menno Simons, *The Complete Works of Menno Simons*, ed. J. C. Wenger, trans. Leonard Verduin (Scottdale, PA: Herald Press, 1974), 670–71.
7. Simons, "Renunciation of the Church of Rome," loc. 319.

Chapter 29 John Calvin

1. Roderick Graham, *John Knox, Man of Action* (Edinburg: Saint Andrew Press, 2001), 104.
2. John Calvin, personal letter to William Farel, August 20, 1553.

Chapter 31 Jacob Arminius

1. Carl Bangs, *Arminius: A Study in the Dutch Reformation* (Eugene, OR: Wipf & Stock Publishers, 1998), 42.
2. Ibid.

Chapter 32 Francis Bacon

1. Francis Bacon, *The Advancement of Learning.*
2. Francis Bacon, *Of Atheism.*

Chapter 33 Galileo Galilei

1. Galileo, *Letter to Grand Duchess Christiana*, 1615.
2. Galileo, *Letter to Benedetto Castelli*, 1613.
3. Galileo, *Letter to Grand Duchess Christiana.*

Chapter 34 Brother Lawrence

1. Brother Lawrence, *The Practice of the Presence of God* (Grand Rapids: Revell, 1958), 30–31.
2. Ibid., 97.
3. Ibid., 31.
4. Ibid.
5. Ibid., 47.
6. Ibid., 39.

Chapter 35 Blaise Pascal

1. Blaise Pascal, *The Mind on Fire*, ed. James M. Houston (Portland, OR: Multnomah, 1989), 41.
2. Ibid., 129–34.

Chapter 36 John Bunyan

1. John Bunyan, *The Pilgrim's Progress and Grace Abounding to the Chief of Sinners* (New York: Random House/Vintage Spiritual Classics, 2004), 284.
2. John Brown, *John Bunyan: This Life Times and Work* (New York: Houghton, Mifflin and Company, 1888), 240.
3. Ibid., 64.
4. Bunyan, *The Pilgrim's Progress and Grace Abounding to the Chief of Sinners*, 284.

Chapter 38 George Frideric Handel

1. Patrick Kavanaugh, *Spiritual Lives of the Great Composers* (Grand Rapids: Zondervan, 1996), 27.

Chapter 39 Jonathan Edwards

1. Jonathan Edwards and Henry Rogers, *The Works of Jonathan Edwards*, vol. 1 (London: William Ball, 1839), lxii.
2. Jonathan Edwards, *A Faithful Narrative of the Surprising Work of God*, section 1.

Chapter 40 John Wesley

1. John Wesley, *The Journal of the Reverend John Wesley*, June 6, 1742.
2. Ibid., January 24, 1738.
3. Ibid., May 19, 1738.
4. Ibid., March 29, 1739.
5. Ibid., June 28, 1774.

Chapter 41 Charles Wesley

1. Charles Wesley, journal entry, May 17, 1738.

Chapter 42 George Whitefield

1. George Whitefield, "A Short Account of God's Dealings with George Whitefield," *George Whitefield's Journals* (repr., Mulberry, IN: Sovereign Grace Publishers, 2000), 17.
2. Ibid., 26.
3. Ibid., 132.
4. Benjamin Franklin, *The Autobiography of Benjamin Franklin*, ed. Leonard Woods Labaree (New Haven, CT: Yale University Press, 1964), 175.
5. Ibid., 91.
6. Ibid., 90.
7. Ibid., 148.

Chapter 43 John Newton

1. John Newton, *Thoughts on the Slave Trade* (London: J. Buckland, 1788), 2.
2. Richard Cecil, *Works of the Rev. John Newton* (New York: Robert Carter, 1844), 53.

Chapter 44 William Wilberforce

1. William Wilberforce, *On the Question of the Slave Trade* (London: J. Walter, 1789), 18.
2. John Hippisley, *Essays* (London: T. Lowdes, 1764), 17–18.
3. Stephen Tomkins, *William Wilberforce: A Biography* (Grand Rapids: Eerdmans, 2007), 95.

Chapter 45 William Carey

1. Eustace Carey and Francis Wayland, *Memoir of William Carey, D.D.* (London: Jackson and Walford, 1836), 623.

Chapter 46 Charles Finney

1. *The City-Road Magazine*, October 5, 1876 (Oxford: Oxford University), 256.
2. Charles Grandison Finney, *Memoirs of Rev. Charles G. Finney* (New York: A. S. Barnes & Co., 1876), 15.

Chapter 47 William Gladstone

1. William Gladstone, *The Impregnable Rock of Holy Scripture* (Philadelphia: John D. Wattles & Co., 1896), 7.
2. H. C. G. Matthew, *Gladstone 1809–1898* (Oxford: Oxford University Press, 1997), 336.
3. William Gladstone, personal letter to Sir A. Panizzi, February 8, 1874.
4. Roy Jenkins, *Gladstone* (New York: Random House, 1997), xvii.

Chapter 48 Fanny Crosby

1. Fanny Crosby, *Fanny Crosby's Life-Story* (New York: Every Where Publishing Co., 1903), 13.
2. Ibid., 126.
3. Ibid., 52.
4. Ibid., 127.

Chapter 51 Hudson Taylor

1. David Howard Adeney, *China, the Church's Long March* (Ventura, CA: Regal Books, 1985), 39.
2. Howard Taylor, *Hudson Taylor's Spiritual Secret* (Chicago: Moody, 1989), 114.

Chapter 52 Charles Spurgeon

1. Charles H. Spurgeon et al., *Autobiography of Charles H. Spurgeon*, vol. 1 (Chicago: Fleming H. Revell, 1898), 105.
2. Ibid., 106.
3. *Ipswich Express*, February 27, 1855.
4. C. H. Spurgeon, letter to the editor, *The Chelmsford Chronicle*, April 24, 1855.

Chapter 53 Dwight L. Moody

1. William R. Moody, *The Life of Dwight L. Moody* (Chicago: Fleming H. Revell, 1900), 149.
2. Ibid., 523.
3. Dwight Lyman Moody, *Day by Day with D. L. Moody* (Chicago: Moody, 1977), 133.
4. Ibid., 554.

Chapter 54 Billy Sunday

1. William Thomas Ellis and Billy Sunday, *Billy Sunday, the Man and His Message* (Madison, WI: J. C. Winston Co., 1917), 41.

Chapter 55 Oswald Chambers

1. As quoted in Wesley L. Duewel, *Ablaze for God* (Grand Rapids: Zondervan, 1989), 304.

Chapter 56 G. K. Chesterton

1. G. K. Chesterton in the *Illustrated London News*, March 10, 1906.
2. G. K. Chesterton, *What's Wrong with the World* (New York: Dodd, Mead & Co., 1910), 48.
3. G. K. Chesterton in the *Illustrated London News*, April 19, 1930.

Chapter 57 T. S. Eliot

1. "T. S. Eliot—Biography," Nobelprize.org., April 26, 2013, http://www.nobelprize.org/nobel_prizes/literature/laureates/1948/eliot-bio.html.

Chapter 58 C. S. Lewis

1. C. S. Lewis, *Surprised by Joy: The Shape of My Early Life* (Orlando: Houghton Mifflin Harcourt, 1995), 8.
2. C. S. Lewis, *George MacDonald: An Anthology* (New York: HarperCollins, 1946, repr. 1973), xxxviii.
3. Lewis, *Surprised by Joy*, 228.
4. Ibid., 237.

Chapter 59 Henry Morris

1. Henry M. Morris, *Scientific Creationism* (Green Forest, AR: Master Books, 1974), iii.

Chapter 60 Billy Graham

1. Richard Nixon, "Memorandum for Bob Haldeman," December 30, 1969 (Nixon Library).
2. Merle Miller, *Plain Speaking: An Oral Biography of Harry S. Truman* (New York: Putnam, 1974), 63.
3. Billy Graham, "Item 9," *Why We Must Go to New York* (Minneapolis: BGEA, 1957).

Alton Gansky is the author of twenty-four novels and eight nonfiction books. He is a Carol Award winner and an Angel Award winner, and has been a Christy Award finalist. He holds a BA and an MA in biblical studies and has been awarded a doctor of literature degree. Director of the Blue Ridge Mountains Christian Writers Conference, Gansky also serves as an editor and collaborative writer for top tier authors. He lives in California.

Connect with

Sign up for announcements about
new and upcoming titles at

www.bakerbooks.com/signup

 ReadBakerBooks

 ReadBakerBooks